THE JOB

30 years a Cop

THE JOB

30 Years a Cop

Paul Heslop

Froswick Press

British Library Cataloguing-in-publication data
A catalogue record for this book is available from the British Library.

Copyright © 2000 by Paul Heslop

Published by Froswick Press, P.O. Box 7, Keswick, Cumbria. CA12 5GD

ISBN 0-9538066-0-X

Printed by Antony Rowe Limited, Chippenham, Wiltshire, SN14 6LH

Foreword

by

Arthur McKenzie

Paul Heslop is one of those unusual human beings – a rare and endangered species: "A THINKING MAN'S POLICEMAN".

An elegant and eloquent writer, his portrayal of life on the tough streets of the North-East as a copper in the swinging sixties, to Hertfordshire in the nineties, spans a unique generation of policing.

Not only is this a lively read, studded with precious gems, but it is written with authority and integrity and mirrors his approach to the job exactly. He gives a unique insight into the humour and pain of the job, breathing fresh air into this closed world.

This highly personal account makes "The Job – 30 years a Cop" an important social document and a must to read.

Arthur McKenzie is an established author, playwright, television scriptwriter, radio pundit and journalist. His stageplays include *The Boilerhunters,* which also featured on BBC Radio Four's 'Saturday Night Theatre', *Man in a Bottle, Standing in the Stalls*, and *My Son's in the Force*, which appeared in the North-East, London and abroad.

His television credits include *The Bill, Harry, Casualty, Spender, Wycliffe* as well as many documentaries.

ACKOWLEDGEMENTS

The author wishes to acknowledge the below-named, for their kind permission in the use of quotations herein, as follows –

Spike Milligan

Norma Farnes, on behalf of Spike Milligan Productions Limited

Flann O'Brien

Copyright © The Estate of the Late Brian O'Nolan, reproduced by permission of A. M. Heath & Company Ltd on behalf of the Estate

Sir Arthur Conan Doyle

Copyright © 1996 The Sir Arthur Conan Doyle Copyright Holders. Reprinted by kind permission of Jonathan Clowes Ltd., London, on behalf of Andrea Plunket, Administrator of the Sir Arthur Conan Doyle Copyrights

Marlene Dietrich

Stephen Chapeck, on behalf of Global Icons, Los Angeles, California, USA

Vidal Sassoon

Harriet Andrews, on behalf of Vidal Sassoon Salons, London

The author wishes to thank the following for their help and support in the production of this book –

Arthur McKenzie, for writing the foreword; Alan Oliver, for his Quotation; Percy Mather, for his considered advice; and all former colleagues, north and south, who helped over thirty years and gave their valuable support.

Cover design: Ray Liberty

Interior artwork: Charles Petrie

The author wishes to make it clear that throughout his service he served in two police forces: Newcastle upon Tyne City Police (later, after amalgamation, Northumberland Constabulary, then Northumbria Police), and Hertfordshire Constabulary.

There is no suggestion, express or implied, that procedures outlined herein, are or were ever in place, in any other police forces; or that they are in place today anywhere.

Where appropriate, some names of the persons herein have been changed.

The truth is untouched.

To my former colleagues

…most of them, anyway

The sergeant looked at my 9½ stone frame, my P. J. Proby haircut.

'You have to be five-ten...'

He shook his head. Fair enough. I'd try the army. Yet the army didn't appeal: I wanted to help people, not kill them. Or I could look for work locally. After all, I'd completed the apprenticeship. I was now a qualified electrician.

'If you sort of stretched...'

I secretly lifted my heels a fraction.

'That's it!' he declared. 'Five-ten!'

It was 1965 and I'd joined "The Job". But the haircut would have to go.

What kind of Men?

We were very smart. Our mothers had said so. Blue serge uniforms, smart, white gloves, new boots that squeaked when you walked. Mine did, anyway. Some wore helmets, with badges bearing fancy coats of arms. Others wore caps. Our Newcastle City one was different, with a blue and white striped band – 'the only one in the country' we were told, meaning we should wear it with pride. So we stuck a piece of wood inside the front to make us look like the Gestapo. *Seig Heil!*

Smart was not the word booming over the manicured lawns of Newby Wiske when our drill sergeant emerged to meet his consignment of new recruits. He was ex-Guards, boots bulled so much you could see the reflections of passing clouds. We were a rabble. We knew we were because he was saying so from a range of thirty yards. Thank goodness I'd had the P. J. Proby chopped.

'I'm Sergeant Hall from Middlesbrough', he declared, identifying forces by headwear. His voice dropped to a whispered threat. 'I can't stand anyone from North Yorkshire.' He saw Les, the only policeman in Britain lighter than me and now identified by Sgt Hall as coming from North Yorkshire. I think he ended up working in a bank.

He lined us up on parade, glared menacingly from the dark recess beneath the peak of his guardsman's cap, said something about being sorry we never knew our dads. Then we marched to the refrain of an army band as it drifted across the square from an old 78. He marched alongside, carrying one of those baton things: 'Left, right, left. Left, right, left.' Someone muttered something. He heard. 'Report to me at eight o' clock tonight.' In other words, just when it was time for a well-earned pint. He was right: we were a rabble. A rabble without a cause, you might say. But thirteen weeks later we could march in line, about turn, right-dress, open-order march. Not as good as your professional army boys, but we'd achieved. So had he; he was brilliant.

We learnt first aid and firefighting. In the former how to apply a sling to a patient with a broken arm, only to be told we wouldn't actually have one on the beat, so call an ambulance. Firefighting meant learning how to use a stirrup pump, but we wouldn't actually have one of those either, so call the fire brigade. Best of all was the instruction on what to do after nuclear attack. We were even provided with a manual. I never got round to reading it. Thank God the Russians never dropped the Bomb.

We learnt how to deal with traffic accidents, including which animals a motorist had to stop for if he ran one over: cattle, horses, asses, mules, pigs, sheep, dogs and goats. You can flatten a cat and just keep right on driving, no problem. There were practical tests, too, including one with a fibre-glass pig which was forever being run over at the corner of Classroom Square. We marked its position with yellow chalk, carefully noted the car 'driver's' details. In thirty years' service I never came across a pig which had been run over, but I would have known what to do if I had.

Then there were the definitions. A firearm:

"Any lethal barrelled weapon of any description from which any shot, bullet or missile may be discharged..."

We learnt it parrot-fashion; it was in the book. The Definitions book, that is, along with another ninety or so. Larceny:

"A person steals, who, without the consent of the owner, fraudulently, and without a claim of right made in good faith..."

Dave was top in everything. When the instructor sought an answer, Dave could be relied on to provide it. Then we had to give 'evidence' in a mock courtroom, witness box and all, and answer questions from a 'solicitor', in this case one of the instructors, whilst other students stood in as magistrates, the press and so on. In the witness box, Dave seized up, went into beetroot mode. He was a nervous wreck. How he fared in the real world I do not know. They probably posted him to headquarters where he wouldn't have to worry about witness boxes and things.

Tom, on the other hand, was always bottom of the class. It was a formality. The rest of us vied for second top (after Dave) and second bottom (above Tom). Years later I met up with Tom on an operation somewhere. He was still a constable, but he'd made detective status: arresting criminals, interviewing criminals, recovering stolen property, giving evidence in a *real* court. In short, Tom was a good copper. So, while Dave had the makings to go all the way, Tom did the job. This was a pattern to be repeated throughout my career, at all ranks.

'Constable' to us meant a male constable. "The police service is always on the lookout for men of the right type" it said in the recruiting booklet, *Your Career - Life in the Police*, and there were photographs to prove it: a policeman on point duty, a policeman arresting a drunk, a policeman giving directions to a motorist, a policeman supervising sheep dipping in the Highlands (most useful for someone about to be unleashed on to the streets of Newcastle). A police *woman* appeared in just one picture, chatting to a woman passer-by outside a delicatessen, notebook and pencil poised.

'She's writin' t'bloody shoppin' list,' said a Yorkshire voice, disparagingly.

Policewomen went to their own training centre at Liverpool or somewhere. So it was just the lads: ex-army, ex-navy, ex-air force, ex-police cadets, ex-electricians. But I was okay. I had Sergeant Hall to guide me. And when I was released into the big, wide world, my uniform would protect me. Sergeant Hall said it would, so it must. And if that wasn't enough, I could always blow my whistle.

1

"Policemen are numbered in case they get lost"

Spike Milligan

He was barely visible, a darting, shadowy figure whose stooping form barred the progress of two young women as they hurried home from the office. They pressed unseen coins into his outstretched hand, glad to be on their way as he moved on to the queue of weary commuters who ignored him, mutually checking watches, tut-tutting at the non-appearance of their bus.

I stepped forward, grabbed a skinny arm.

'You're under arrest.'

He looked at me with pleading eyes. 'Don't take me in, *please.*'

If I couldn't feel pity at that moment I had no business being in the police force. But the job was the job. He was a beggar, well-known to officers on 6-beat. 'A cinch', I'd been told, meaning I could make an arrest, and arrests were something probationer constables needed to prove they could do the job.

'Just gimme a good hiding,' he pleaded.

When someone won't come it's not easy.

'I'm arresting you for begging. You are not obliged to say anything unless you wish to do so...'

'Please,' he implored, 'just take me round that corner...'

'...but what you say may be put into writing... '

'...an' gimme...'

Clearly, the last of his worries was what I might put into writing. All he wanted was a smack round the chops and to visit the Salvation Army for his tea.

'...a good hiding.'

He slumped to the pavement, preparing himself for the good hiding he so craved. Instead, I dragged him to the *Tardis* at Eldon Square. He struggled to break free; I struggled to hang on to him and my hat. Our hats always got in the way. Policemen's hats should be glued to their heads. At the box I pulled my whistle chain from my breast pocket. There was a Yale key attached. Whoever installed locks in police boxes never allowed for someone wanting to get in holding a prisoner. The lock was nearly six feet from the ground, much higher than the chain would stretch to anyway. Somehow I got the door open, pushed him into the corner and picked up the telephone.

'257, George,' I said to PC George McNally. 'Can you send the van?'

George was one of the old brigade, privileged to be an operator. In other words, off the streets. He asked if I needed assistance. In my best heroic voice I said I was OK.

'Who've you nicked?' he asked, in obvious admiration.

'William Hutchinson Stewart.'

I could almost see George choking into his tea. I knew what he'd be thinking. Just give him a clip round the ear and kick his arse.

'Why don't you just give him a clip round the ear and kick his arse?' asked George. Then, after a pause: 'Okay. Van's comin'.'

Suddenly, Stewart made a bid for freedom. Probably knew when I was a kid I couldn't reach the sandpit from the springboard in the long-jump. A weak, unfit frame isn't much use in a fight, and he wasn't much better. As we struggled in the confines of the police box, the rope holding his trousers up became undone, and we found ourselves on the floor in a *69* position, with his trousers around his ankles. He hadn't washed for weeks, so this was a new experience for me. Finally, I dragged him to his feet, forced him over the wooden stool, and jammed myself against his bare backside to keep him from moving. We were still in situ when the door opened.

'What the hell's goin' on?' asked my van-driving saviour.

Resigned to defeat, Stewart pulled his trousers up, and reluctantly climbed into the van. There was no escape now.

The Station Sergeant was Jack. Arms like Popeye (after the spinach) and no neck. One grasp of Jack's hand on a prisoner's neck ended all hostilities.

'Why have you arrested this man?'

Stewart held the British, European and World records for being arrested for begging, but he still had to ask. I laid out sundry coins on the desk.

'What have you to say for yourself?' asked Jack.

'Just gimme a good hiding.'

Whether Jack granted his wish I cannot say, for I was ordered back into the night, told to fill out my report at 5 a.m. Coppers weren't allowed to hang about the nick in those days.

Alas, my first arrest did not end up at Court. Stewart evaded trial by jumping off the Tyne bridge. I don't think it was to spite me. Lots of people jumped from the bridge, and not just tramps either. I recall a bank manager doing the very same thing.

*

Why the police anyway? My dad was a coal miner, my brother worked in the shipyards. The only experience I'd had with the police was when our local bobby stopped me on my bike when I was a kid. 'Somebody's stealing apples from those private gardens,' I was told by the voice of authority. It wasn't me, honest. (I was stealing them from the orchard behind the *Runnymede* pub). He looked in my saddlebag. Just a few spanners

3

and a crumpled edition of *Health and Efficiency*. 'Might have to tell your father,' he said grimly, clearly doubting my protests of innocence. This filled me with horror. Innocent or no, I'd be for it if a copper knocked at the door. Yet the experience served me well; I never forgot the feeling of being wrongly suspected or accused.

My skills as a tradesman were limited. I'd worked as an electrician, installing lighting and power points in schools, shops, factories. The problem was, every time one job was finished you were liable to be paid off, and you had to search for employment elsewhere. Finally I got a maintenance job in a factory, where hundreds of young women sat at machines. The motors kept burning out, and it was my job to repair them. I spent hours on the floor in a forest of shapely legs which, in the days of short skirts, was all too much for a lad of twenty.

I didn't want to be an electrician forever. Fred, a colleague aged sixty, was crawling about lofts in workingmen's clubs. There had to be something better (lofts in workingmen's clubs are inches deep in coal dust). Dad suggested the pit, where he worked for 49 years down a black hole with nothing to show for it except gnarled hands and an ability to remain in a crouched position for hours on end. No thanks, I told him. No factories, no lofts, no coal mines.

Somewhere along the line the police force and the army came to mind. In the former, in those pre-amalgamation days, there were two forces for me to consider: Northumberland County or Newcastle City. The first meant I could be posted as far away as the Scottish border, which wouldn't have suited me; the second seemed the better option, but the City force had a minimum height requirement of 5' 10" and I barely measured up.

Strangely, my main problem was my weight. One of my mates could put his hands around my waist and touch his fingers and thumbs together (the only reason he did that, incidentally, was to prove how skinny I was). What if I got into a fight, as surely I must if I worked in Newcastle. The army was for fighting, too, but they gave you a rifle. The police force it was, and I went off to training school to learn about the law and unarmed combat. I

4

played a man with a gun who was thrown over a policeman's shoulder. I was knocked cold.

When I was posted to Newcastle Central division I asked my sergeant about self defence holds and how to deal with violent prisoners.

'What do you mean?' he asked.

I told him self-defence hadn't been given much priority at training school. He just shrugged.

'Do what I've always done,' he said.

'What's that?' I asked.

'Kick 'em in the goolies.'

*

It was 2.15 p.m., only 7¾ hours till the end of my shift, my very first day on the beat. Alone, that is, after spending a fortnight accompanied by experienced officers.

You *rang in* then. There was no such thing as personal radios, no contact with the nick once you'd left the telephone. There were no 'panda' cars, unit beat cars, call them what you will. Just the 'GP' car (I think the initials stood for General Purpose, not that anyone ever said so). It stood by at the police station where it could be called to an incident or take the superintendent home for his tea. The odd traffic motor might pass, its driver relieved that it was you who was out in the pissing rain. Still, as they say, a good copper never gets wet.

You started at a designated street corner, and at so many minutes past the hour you rang in to the operator who gave you a *chalk*. Ringing in followed at hourly intervals until you ended up on another street corner to finish. Each day's ringing-in time varied, the idea being criminals wouldn't know when you'd be around. This ritual was used by the operators to establish their authority over patrol officers, even though they held the same rank: they told you when you could take your *bait*, gave you permission (or otherwise) to attend the station, and dished out special duty at St James's Park, the one and only way to earn overtime in those days as well as watch Newcastle United free of charge.

I well recall my first taste of the operators' power. Say the ringing-in time was twenty minutes past. I ambled up to the pillar, looked at my watch. *Nearly* twenty past. I picked up the telephone.

'257, George.'

You were known by your number, not your name; only operators had names.

There was a pause, as though George had never heard of me.

'What's up?'

I checked my watch. Had George got mixed up with the day, the time of the ring?

'It's 257.'

'Yes, but why are you ringing?'

'My chalk, George.'

'It's twenty past on Tuesdays.'

'This *is* Tuesday...'

'Then ring at twenty past,' and down went the phone. Ringing at *nineteen* past was too early. Similarly, if I rang at twenty-*one* minutes past:

'Where've you been?'

'What do you mean?'

'You're late. We've been worried sick about you...'

You couldn't afford to upset those operators, not if you had young mouths to feed and you needed that special duty.

On some beats, you ate your bait in the police box or section station, and did your paperwork there too. You got 45 minutes. No more. I remember one night shift when the north-east was under blizzards as only the north-east can be. The duty sergeant telephoned to say that in view of circumstances we could have a *full hour* for our bait. So, I needn't set off with the huskies to check the shops until 2 a.m.

You had to check your property. On nightshift, anyway. Once before bait, once after. You tried the doors, checked the windows. Then you went round the back and did the same. If you found any insecure or any damage you'd report it and await the keyholder. Failure to find a break-in meant a local officer knocking on your door when you were tucked up in bed after a long night, with a requirement to attend the station at once to tell the superintendent why a second floor window measuring a foot square at the back of Jones the Butchers was broken and you hadn't found it. To ensure you tried the doors on your beat the sergeant just might call before you and place a ha'penny on the latch. If it was still there at the end of your shift...

But I was talking about my first day on the beat.

Jesmond is a sort of Victorian suburb, inhabited by the well-to-do, university students and, in the sixties, the odd druggie when druggies were in their development phase. It was hardly the Bronx, but walking up Osborne Road that afternoon was a traumatic experience for a 21 year-old. Every police officer has this moment, the first time alone. My purpose in life was to look for motorists double parking, or perhaps witness a flasher in action when the schools turned out. Or, if I was lucky, see my first dead body if someone decided to jump from Armstrong Bridge, which was in vogue at the time (and may still be). The only incident I was sent to was a report of kids running over the electrified railway. Since I wasn't sent there for over half an hour after the report it came as no surprise that they had long departed, presumably with their lives. I didn't discover any incinerated corpses anyway.

This was 4-beat, a big patch. Strictly, I should have taken a pedal cycle, but we regarded bikes as naff, so we'd say the bike had a puncture or give some other excuse for not using it. If we were dispatched to an incident, we could always flag down a passing motorist. We did, too. Thought nothing of it. Just like in the old films, when policemen jumped on to the running boards of passing Rileys and demanded the driver to 'follow that car.'

The first two or three days drew a blank as far as catching out motorists were concerned. I had noticed the odd car causing an obstruction, but took no action due to its driver being (a) an old lady, (b) a young lady, or (c) the driver never appeared. Okay, I was nervous about approaching someone and exercising the full might of the law. But when my sergeant passed comment about 'nothing from 257 yet', it was time for action. And there it was: a

7

car parked on the crest of a hump-backed bridge in Sandyford Road. I could see myself in the witness box at the magistrates' court:

"I was proceeding along Sandyford Road, your worships, when I saw the aforementioned Ford Consul parked in such a manner so as to cause an obstruction".

I kept observations, noting that the view of approaching motorists was impeded, and on at least two occasions persons crossing the road were endangered. There'd be no let-offs this time, no matter what. I waited. Even missed my chalk. I had my reward; a middle-aged gent in a suit appeared and opened the driver's door. I pounced just as he was getting into the car. It was time to recall my training at Classroom Square (an injured pig would have made it perfect).

'Are you the driver of this vehicle?'

His look of disdain said it all.

'This vehicle is causing an obstruction,' I declared, and told him I required his name and address, and to see his documents. Out came the notebook.

As he spoke, my hand shook so much I could hardly write down the words. He saw, I know, but provided the information I required. I issued him with a slip requiring him to produced driving licence and insurance at a police station in Yorkshire or somewhere.

I cautioned him, told him 'the facts would be reported', meaning he'd be summonsed to Court. He shrugged. Okay. No problem. Thank you, officer. And goodbye. Off he went, my first capture. And my first cockup. When things checked out there was no trace of the address he gave me, nor even the registration number of the car. What's worse, George had been on the point of organising a search party as I'd missed my chalk. Lesson learned: never let appearances deceive.

Few of us owned cars, so using public transport was common. Being a police officer in uniform meant a free ride. This led to an embarrassing moment the first time I caught the bus to work as a boy in blue. The bus was full – people used public transport in those days – and the conductor, ignoring me, asked the person next to me for his fare. But I spoke up.

'Single to town please.'

He brushed my hand aside, took the fare of the other guy. I tried again. This time he hesitated; people were looking, had seen the policeman wanted to pay.

'Single to town,' I repeated.

I only had a ten-bob note. He took it, gave me my change, moved on.

'Scuse me,' I called after him – now the whole bus was looking – 'you didn't give me a ticket.'

'Didn't I?' he asked. We were seated on one of those side seats near the front, and I could see even the driver was looking. I held open my palm, showing the change but no ticket. Reluctantly, he thumbed his machine, tore off a ticket, handed it over. 'Thank you, I said, satisfied justice had been done. But when I came to get off the driver had a word.

'He didn't give you a ticket,' he said, 'cos he didn't charge you.'

He could see I was bemused.

'If you check your change…' he said, meaning I still had my ten bob.

You couldn't pay if you tried.

*

Denys spoke in barely more than a polite whisper.

'Move on.'

But they wouldn't move on. Instead, they watched, grinning, an inference that four on to two – or, possibly one and a half – meant they held the upper hand. Denys spoke again: slowly, and *ever* so politely.

'Move on.'

It was done with such authority I almost moved on myself.

They moved on. Denys wouldn't dream of actually *arresting* anyone. What, all that paperwork, going to court and all? 'Move on' was the command, and they did. I never saw anyone who didn't.

Denys was a former para who'd served in Palestine after the war, then joined the police. There were no fancy entrance examinations in those days, when police forces were struggling to enlist manpower. All you had to be was tall enough with good eyesight and common sense, and the ability to deal on the street, on your own, without recourse to assistance. Working with Denys and others like him meant a rapid learning curve for recruits who joined up in the mid-sixties. They were excellent coppers. Did the job without fuss. They were *characters*, a breed unto themselves. Denys once gave me a piece of advice. Noting my fragile frame, he pointed out that many lightweights can get the better of heavyweights.

'It's all about bottle,' he explained. 'A good little 'un can beat an ordinary big 'un.'

Very encouraging. Thanks, Den.

'But,' he added, 'a good big 'un will always beat a good little 'un.'

So, the bigger they were, the harder I'd fall.

There were lots of characters. Take Stan. He took me for a pint one Sunday morning on Newcastle's Quayside where, as now, there is an open market, attended from far and wide. I went there with dread for, as I had been warned: 'If you have to jump into the river to save someone you'll be taken to hospital.' Meaning you'd be liable to catch malaria or something. The Tyne was an open sewer; you could see it all pouring in. Anyway, Stan and I walked the length of the Quay to show the flag, then at high noon presented ourselves in the pub where we joined the natives.

'Two pints,' ordered Stan, not bothering to ask if I wanted Newcastle Exhibition or sarsaparilla. I sipped my beer slowly, on a very empty stomach. 'Your round,' said Stan, plonking a quickly-emptied glass on the bar counter. I got them in.

It was all too much for my constitution on a Sunday morning. I remember a woman handing me a bunch of keys she'd found. In an alcoholic haze, I recorded details in my pocket book. What she must have thought of the dashing young policeman who reeked of

10

booze God only knows. I never drank on duty again, in uniform anyway.

Then there was Old Johnny. He'd manned Grey's Monument traffic point in the days when my mum took me shopping as a kid in short trousers. He was still there when I joined the police. Now and again, beat bobbies would relieve him so he could go for a cuppa. Point duty gave you your first taste of power. With just a wave of your hand you could stop the traffic! Or let that blonde in the E-type through. Worth a smile at least.

I'll never forget the first time I stood in the middle of the road for Johnny. As I waved a van past, the early edition of the *Evening Chronicle* appeared in my hand. Five minutes later I was the proud owner of a Mars Bar. After fifteen minutes I could have done with a carrier. These were Johnny's perks, and when he reappeared he asked if I had his newspaper and of course I handed it over. But I always kept the chocolate. Sorry, Johnny, but there it is.

Tommy had been around for years, too. He was so frail, rumour had it old ladies had to help *him* across the road. He came in for bait one night and told us he'd just said 'Good evening' to a bloke who did no more than try and throw him into the Tyne. We wondered how he'd failed; the faintest zephyr would have done the trick. Conscientious, was Tommy. Proof that long in service is no excuse for lying back and taking it easy. Tommy always crossed his t's and dotted his i's. I learned a lot from him.

Another character was Sleepy, so-named because his drooping eyelids made it appear as though he would fall asleep at any moment. Which, quite often, he did. In fact, he was liable to nod off mid-sentence. One night Sleepy failed to ring off at 6 a.m. This was a serious situation, where the call from the pillar was the only contact. We were sent forth to find him, expecting the worst. It didn't take long. Fed up with his all-night patrol on foot, he'd gone to his car to sleep, setting his alarm clock for 5.30, in time to get up and make his last call. He admitted he'd done it for weeks. Unfortunately for him on this occasion his alarm had failed to operate and he'd overslept. That was the end of Sleepy as far as the police force was concerned.

Then there was John, who spent his time focusing on one thing: arresting thieves. Not after being assigned to incidents where the prisoner was already detained. John is a predator. He starts duty at 2 p.m. Some of his time is spent 'showing the flag'. Come evening, he's off to a darkened doorway where he can keep an eye on a parade of offices or shops, a car park maybe. He stays there for hours, leaving only for the hourly ring. Sooner or later, his chance comes: the loitering thief, the burglar, usually two-up or more. It doesn't matter. He takes his prisoners. His *chalk*, as we called it (not to be confused with the ringing in *chalk*).

I was proud to become a John myself. It was on nights, on 9-beat. Some burglars were 'active' on my patch. I made my way to an alley at the back of some offices and waited, leaving only to make the hourly rings. Did it several nights on the trot. Then, just after midnight on the fourth or fifth night, two men emerged from a window, and climbed down to a flat roof. They'd broken in when I'd been ringing in and now they were leaving with the spoils: a typewriter, and some petty cash. I had to make a decision: return to the pillar and ring for assistance, or tackle them on my own. The pillar was a no-no. By the time I got there they'd be gone, probably in a car parked up somewhere. There was nothing for it but to go it alone. I waited until they reached the ground, and as they were lowering the stolen property I ran from the shadows. They split. It was as well they did, or I would have faced them in a dark alley without recourse to assistance. In the event I chased the one who'd run off to my left, shouting *'Stop!'* As if!

Would you believe it, he ran straight into the GP, which happened to be cruising along in our direction. There were three of us now, including the inspector (they patrolled in those days too) and between us we grabbed my man. He told me later over a cup of tea (prisoners and arresting officers often ended up over a cup of tea) that he'd thought there were lots of policemen, not just one. The inspector was pleased. 'Good chalk, good chalk,' he kept saying. This developed into 'deserves a commendation.' But when he kept glancing at his watch, I realised, alas, he hadn't the time to fill in the forms. What the hell. Anyway, we arrested chummy's companion too, and recovered the stolen property. But you can never win: the owner complained that the typewriter was damaged, and why can't the police be more careful!

I mention this incident, not because it was unusual, but because it was the first time I arrested someone for crime as a result of my own endeavours. It's the way the job was done – on foot, alone, learning from experienced officers and from our sergeants.

I also learned about *tenacity*.

One night an alarm went off. Police officers have a thing about alarms, meaning they know when one goes off it's nearly always a false call. But you never know when it might be for real, so you always get there as quickly as possible. On this occasion someone rang in to say they'd seen someone on the roof of an office block. This was the signal for all-out response, officers searching every nook and cranny. Even the fire brigade turned out, their searchlights scanning the roof. The entire block was detached, so there could have been no escape to another building. Yet no-one was found, no trace of entry discovered. Everyone resumed patrol. Everyone, that is, except an experienced hack, also called John. He wasn't satisfied, even though it was by now after ten and we should have been going off duty. 'I reckon there *was* someone on the roof,' he said, 'and they've got down into the building.'

Fair enough. But where were they? Police, and dogs, had searched everywhere. It was an old building, with a maze of corridors and lots of staircases. We went up to the top floor, where a long corridor led to nowhere except locked doors. Then John spotted scuff-marks on a wall directly beneath a hatch which led into a loft. Lofts are always searched in houses, but in a huge office complex no-one had thought of it. We'd spotted stepladders earlier so I went and got them. They were old and very unsteady. John held them and sent the recruit up.

I was used to climbing into lofts. Learned all about it from my electrician days. As a matter of fact, this was to stand me in good stead throughout my career. Years later, as a sergeant and inspector, I was still the first to go into the loft. Anyway, I pushed the hatch cover up and stuck my head up through the hatch opening. Typically, my torch had batteries so run down the beam scarcely penetrated the darkness.

'Anything?' called John from below.

The silence was deafening.

'Nothing,' I had to admit, switching off the torch, preparing to come down. 'Gerrup and 'ave a closer look then,' called John.

I did what I was told, gave my eyes a moment to accustom themselves to the darkness, and switched on the torch again. Slowly, I panned it round. In the darkness, the faint shaft of light picked out a human hand. 'There's someone here,' I called out.

With John fighting a losing battle with the rickety stepladders, I moved forward towards the hand. Even when next to the man who lay so still in that loft, still he did not move. When I touched his shoulder I swear he almost jumped out of his skin. So did I. You wouldn't have known who was the more nervous! There were two of them, and I am happy to relate they came quietly, as they say. It was just as well. Back at the hatch, John had barely managed to get halfway up the ladders. Later, he admitted he didn't like heights!

Another arrest for crime was bizarre. I was on duty in the Bigg Market, a busy spot in the city centre, renowned for its bustling market by day and busy pub life at night. Just before ten, all was quiet as I strolled over to the box for my chalk. When I put the telephone down I turned to find myself facing three men. Two of them were burly, and wore suits. The third, a small chap holding the handlebars of a moped, was very drunk. One of the burly guys spoke.

'He's just coughed nicking this from outside the *Blackie Boy*,' he said (a nearby pub). The series of events that followed took about thirty seconds: one of the men opened the door to the police box, pushed the little guy inside and sort of helped me in behind him.

'RCS,' he said. *'We'll leave you to it.'*

Then they were gone, leaving me with a drunken bloke and a moped.

RCS, I knew, meant Regional Crime Squad, a new crime department I'd heard of. All I could do was ask the prisoner – for the little man *was* a prisoner – what had happened. All he could do was tell me he'd found the moped and taken it. He was so drunk he was incapable of further explanation. The station sergeant was Nick Carter.

'Why have you arrested this man?' asked Nick.

'I'm not sure,' I replied.

Nick looked. 'What do you mean, you're *not sure*?'

I recounted events, such as they were.

Nick realised they'd dumped the prisoner on me because they didn't want to piddle about with someone who'd nicked a moped. So, we had a prisoner, and a moped that wasn't reported stolen. Come morning, we hoped he could throw some light on events and, to be fair, he tried. But he'd been so drunk he couldn't. In the end, when the owner of the moped reported it stolen, we charged the hapless prisoner with taking it without consent. When he appeared at court he pleaded guilty and got a conditional discharge. I can't imagine what I would have said in evidence if it had been otherwise.

Returning to the subject of characters, Arthur had a great impact on me, both as a policeman and an individual. He was an international discus-thrower and weightlifter. This powerhouse of a man was an inspiration to a rookie cop: he led by example, with lots of arrests for crime, and stood no nonsense from drunks and louts on the street. I wanted to be like him, but I lacked his raw, physical strength. Still, I could at least get fit, and as I fancied myself as a runner over 3 miles (accepting I'd never make it in the long jump), we decided to help each other out by training together at the City Stadium: he would time me as I ran laps around the track, I would help him with the discus. Sounds grand, except the City Stadium was no more than an ash-track next to British Paints, and the fumes from the factory meant as you ran for fitness you were liable to die from lung disease. Incidentally, in case you're wondering how one person can help another with the discus, the answer is simple. Arthur threw it, I went and fetched it. I forgot to mention he was something of a con. He also took me to a derelict school where we trained with prehistoric weights. This was a con too. Arthur didn't have the key, and said it would take someone *very* thin to slip in through a window to unlock the door from the inside.

His power with the weights was unbelievable: what Arthur could lift had to be seen to be believed, what I couldn't lift, the same. But where Arthur went on to win the National Police Championships, I went on to win a new belief in myself. Still under ten stones, I patrolled my beat, confident I could take on anyone, even though, in reality, I was no different – physically – from the man who had worried about unarmed combat. By the time I'd completed a Charles Atlas course I was ready for anything.

This new-found confidence was put into practice one Saturday afternoon outside St James's Park, home of Newcastle United. With most of the crowd in the ground, I felt a tug at my sleeve. It was the licensee of the Strawberry Arms, a diminutive woman who looked as though she couldn't knock the skin off a rice pudding. 'There's a man in the bar,' she said. 'He's got a small boy with him. Would you tell him to leave? He won't take any notice of me.'

You were supposed to summon assistance when entering licensed premises, and there was plenty (around 90 police officers at the ground), but it seemed straightforward enough. Just a matter of asking the man to go.

A larger version of Giant Haystacks stood at the bar holding a full pint. I knew he wouldn't want to go; he was drinking Exhibition. Everyone was looking. All that was missing was a honky-tonk piano and John Wayne appearing through imaginary batwing doors.

'He's too young,' I said politely. 'Would you leave please?'

He took a sip of beer. Never moved.

'Come on,' I said. 'You know the law.'

'I'll go when I'm ready,' he said.

'You'll go now,' I said, threateningly.

'I've paid for this pint and I'm drinkin' it,' he declared.

Enough was enough.

'Out!' I ordered.

'Or what?' he asked.

'Or *I'll put you out*,' I said, remembering Arthur's weights (even though I could hardly lift them). I still had the option of summoning assistance, but this was my party now. So I sent out a hand and grasped the front of his shirt.

'Out!' I repeated, tugging at his shirt.

He didn't budge, and when I pulled again the only thing that seemed likely was that I'd tear his shirt. Then he calmly placed his glass on to the bar and took hold of my wrist with both hands. I should have mentioned my wrists are so thin I have to have extra holes punched into watch-straps.

'Let go or I'll break your wrist.'

As I tugged at his shirt, his face turned to a mean Jack Palance, lips curled, eyes narrowed to mere slits. 'Let go,' he hissed, hatred replacing his look of disdain, fingers tightening their grip. I was bracing myself for the inevitable when, giving one more tug on his shirt, out he came, submitting to the authority of the uniform. The little lad followed, together with a round of applause from the blokes in the bar. Ten minutes later, my entire body started shaking. It was an incident I never forgot.

There's a sequel. Weeks later, Newcastle were playing an evening match. We used to patrol around the perimeter of the pitch then, and towards the end of the game, in a rare period of silence, I heard a voice calling from the depths of the crowd.

'That's him,' called the voice. 'That's the bastard.'

I peered across a sea of faces, finally identifying Giant Haystacks by his big arms and moon face. He was telling people about what happened, it was obvious. But no-one was listening. I think Newcastle must have scored or something.

*

Most point duty was as relief for the regular officers. Great for smiling at the office girls on their lunch-breaks! Looking back, every point seemed to have something to remember it by. Grey's Monument merits recall because it was *awkward*: a whopping great monument stuck in the middle of a major road junction. I don't know who decided to stick it there, but it was a nuisance, especially for trolley buses which, if they didn't get the angle of approach right, would suddenly conk out in the middle of the road when they became disconnected from the overhead electricity cables. You had to wait patiently until the driver removed a long, bamboo pole from underneath the bus and fiddle about reconnecting it to the wires.

Then there was Barras Bridge, at rush hour. Whenever a car with the number DAN 1 passed by, its driver gave a polite little wave at the policeman, a salute almost. Who *is* that guy, I wondered, before discovering his identity to be T. Dan Smith, leader of the city council, 'Mr Newcastle', as he was known. He worked hard for the city, said he wanted Newcastle to be an outstanding regional capital. So it became, but the 'morning officer' and 'evening officer' came to an end with Smith's conviction for corruption in the Poulson case, when he was sent to prison.

Everyone *hated* Dean Street point.

Dean Street leads straight up from the river. It's excessively steep, and when lorries and buses groaned up the hill towards the point the exhaust fumes were unbearable. You needed a gas mask on Dean Street point. The traffic in all directions was continually heavy. No-one would relieve you if you were rostered for a full day, not even for ten minutes.

You started at eight, finished at six, a long time to be waving your hands in a state of near-asphyxiation and liable at any moment to be run over by a truck. It did my head in, I don't mind admitting. I remember once waving a motorist up Dean Street and at the same time waving another across his bows. Fortunately, both drivers braked and avoided collision. They glared at me in my white coat and white gloves and white face. I raised a hand to each in apology and they nodded in acknowledgement. I think they understood. Probably drove off muttering 'poor bastard', or words to that effect. I had nightmares about lorries and buses and cars and motorcycles turning left, turning right, going straight on, looping the loop. It was more than I could bear. I can now divulge that once, after a two consecutive days on the point, I went sick rather than face up to the third. It was the only time I bottled out of anything, and I always felt shame because it meant some other poor sod would have to do it in my place. Whoever it was, I'm sorry. But it was either that or turn into a zombie.

From time to time naval warships paid courtesy visits to the Tyne, mooring alongside the quay. Any crew arrested for drunkenness were taken to HMS something or other for punishment. I had a wrestling match once with a drunken sailor on the cobbles by the gents' toilets in the Bigg Market. I tried to get him to calm down and go, anything but take him to the ship. He'd had a good time, just he'd had about ten too many. In the end I had to arrest him. As I handed him over to the duty officer aboard ship, he uttered a four-letter expletive, which I took to mean he didn't really appreciate what I'd done. Anyway, around four in the morning I was told there was a message from the ship: during the course of his arrest, chummy had lost his contact lenses.

5 a.m. I commence a fingertip search of the cobblestones in the Bigg Market. Sadly, in vain. I wanted to return to the ship and hand over the contact lenses, and to tell the lad there was no hard feelings. Later I wondered if the message had been a hoax, that maybe the Royal Navy had had the last laugh on old bill.

A Russian frigate was moored alongside the quay once. This was at the height of the cold war. As I ambled by on nights, looking at the ship, I noticed a rating looking at me. He nodded, and grunted something. Might have meant hello or up yours, who can say? He *seemed* friendly enough. Then one or two other crew appeared, looking at the English policeman in the funny hat. I decided to scarper before they could get down the gangplank and take me back to Minsk for questioning. At least the search party found Sleepy that time. They'd never have made it to Minsk.

This was 16-beat, the domain of the aforementioned Denys. Young policemen would only be assigned to it if Denys was day off or on leave. The area covered was right by the Tyne, beneath the famous bridges. There were no shops to dive into for cups of tea, just huge office precincts and, in those days, ships unloading grain, etc., alongside the quay. (You won't find any ships now, except one, which is a nightclub). Here I saw what six weeks floating in the Tyne can do to human beings; bodies swollen grotesquely, with huge chunks of flesh gnawed away by the river rats. At the time I'd still not got used to seeing dead bodies, let alone an 18-year old man with no flesh left on his head. He'd had a few pints, wandered behind some building next to the river for a pee and was never seen again. Until, that is, he ended up high and not very dry on the wooden supports of an old jetty. The Tyne is tidal, and if you're in the water and you're dead you drift up and down river for weeks on end, until you end up like our friend. We identified him by his dental records. (Stories of police officers in Newcastle pushing bodies towards the Gateshead side – a separate force area then – were never verified).

Bodies from the river were put into a small mortuary, conveniently situated close by. Inside was a slab, enough for the pathologist to have a quick look. The bodies stank so much you could tell from the pavement if there was a stiff inside the mortuary. Sometimes older officers would take rookies to the mortuary on nights without telling them what they'd find, one way of introducing someone to the real world, I suppose.

As for the rats, Denys must have been on first-name terms. They were harmless, except they'd half eaten that 18-year old I mentioned. But he was dead anyway. Sometimes you'd see them beside the lapping waters of the river. We'd chase them, a sort of pied piper in reverse. They always got away. The only time a rat turned my blood cold was once when I found an abandoned car on the Quayside. As I lifted the bonnet a rat leaped from the engine and darted off, ignoring the opportunity to take a bite out of me. Probably not enough flesh to make it worth its while.

A low point on 16-beat came on my first Christmas as a policeman. Christmas Day, actually. It was deserted. Even the rats seemed scarce. It was a joy to ring in and speak to George. When I did I could hear laughter in the background. They were obviously enjoying their day in the nick. Whenever I see pictures of those bridges – in *Spender* and other tv programmes – I always think of that day. Now the Quayside is vibrant, a place of commerce and nightlife, with the bridges illuminated and new luxury flats overlooking the river. Presumably the rats have moved on.

Death is part of a police officer's routine. I remember my first; it was on a night of heavy rain. There was a huge marquee in

Newcastle's Exhibition Park, where different companies held displays, a sort of Earl's Court under canvas. The army had a display too, part of their recruitment drive, as I recall. Their vehicles were outside, parked up for the night. As I wandered through the marquee, checking security, I was called outside where a young soldier lay on the grass in the pouring rain. His skin felt warm, yet he did not move to my touch. He was dead. I felt so helpless. Just moments before he had been going about his duty, just like me. As the rain spattered into his lifeless face, it occurred to me he could even be thinking: why don't they make me breathe again?

What caused his death?

He'd come into contact with an electrical generator, whose motor was still running. Near his body, on the sodden grass, lay a heavy-duty cable, a loose end lying unconnected next to an earth-pin, which was firmly driven into the ground. The heavy rain had probably shorted the current, and as the cable was not earthed the soldier had been electrocuted. Maybe he'd been careless; maybe it was someone else's fault. I was reminded that tragedy can strike anytime, and when it does it's so impersonal. When I looked in his wallet for identification purposes, there were photographs of his parents and an attractive young woman, probably his wife or girlfriend. They were all smiling for the camera. The thought that they wouldn't be smiling when they heard the grim news of his death flashed though my mind, and stayed with me for ages after-wards. This was a tragic, but accidental death, and there'd be plenty more in a career of over thirty years. But it was the first, and you remember the first of anything.

Another death seemed less tragic, although I am, perhaps, unkind. A big, drunken bloke had assaulted a bus conductor. There'd been lots of assaults on bus crews at the time, and this was one of the worst. The conductor was a small chap, and his appearance was enough to bring tears to even the hardest coppers. His face was swollen almost out of recognition due to being repeatedly punched. He'd had a pasting.

His assailant was incarcerated in the cells. He would have been charged with grievous bodily harm, but through the night when

21

the gaoler made his routine check he found him dead on his bunk. He'd been sick and drowned in his own vomit. A few of us were called in to cart him away to the mortuary. I don't mind admitting those of us who'd seen the bus conductor's face were hardly filled with grief. Next evening, when he came in to make his statement, I told him there'd be no prosecution. When he demanded to know why, I told him the man who had beaten him up was dead. He was delighted!

Today, you hear of criticism of the police when prisoners are found dead in their cells. This makes me angry. Once, prisoners were searched and had all property removed. This included belts and ties, anything they might use to injure themselves. But in later years they were permitted to retain personal items – including their belts and ties. Yet, when they hang themselves, blame is levelled against the police. To the authorities I say: you can't have it both ways. Either dangerous items are removed and prisoners' safety is assured; or they keep their belts and ties and don't blame the police if they hang themselves.

Another aspect of death is the duty of the police to pass on tragic news to relatives of the deceased. One night the Haymarket box light was flashing. Pre-personal radios, this was a way of drawing attention to a call from the station. The main electric light inside the police box would flash, lighting up the windows. If the *Tardis* was supposed to be a police box, it was given further credibility when the light flashed. There'd be a right moan from George if you didn't respond quickly.

'Been flashing you for half an hour. Where the hell have you been?'

'I didn't pass that way, George.'

That meant nothing to George.

'You should keep your eyes peeled, you never know when you might be wanted.'

On this occasion it was three in the morning, hardly a common time for the box to flash. Anyway, George's message (or whoever's – it wasn't always George) concerned an old lady who had died in Edinburgh. She was 85, so presumably it was old age. Edinburgh police wanted her granddaughter informed.

'It's 3 a.m.,' I said. 'Can't the early turn do it?'

'Do it now,' said George.

Not wanting to lose the chance of special duty, I told George that of course I would carry out his instructions and sorry for not responding to his flash earlier.

Five minutes later I was knocking on the door of a bedsit. We had no special training on passing on bad news, but I decided it should be straightforward enough. I'd seen how it was done at the pictures. You asked the person if he or she was so-and-so, and when they said yes you took off your hat and said there was bad news and is there anyone who can make a cup of tea? Then you passed the message and after making sure the recipient of the news was suitably distraught left quietly, job done.

There was no answer to my knock. Surprise, surprise, the occupants were asleep. I knocked again. Nothing. Another, louder effort, woke the neighbours who opened their windows and demanded to know what was going on and did I know what time of night it was? Finally, a barking dog did the trick. The door opened and I found myself looking at a young bloke who was stark naked. He spoke in a rich, Scots tongue.

'What the fuck d'ye want at this time o' neet?' he asked.

I asked him if Miss so-and-so lived here.

'She's done nowt,' he replied defensively.

Just then the Miss so-and-so in question appeared in her nightie.

'What the fuck d'ye want at this time o' neet?' she asked.

'I've been asked to inform you your grandmother has died.'

They looked at one another, then at me.

'Is that all?' she said, turning for her bed.

Her man looked.

'Couldn't it have waited until the mornin'?' he asked.

I had to admit it could, but before I could explain about George and the special duty he slammed the door in my face.

*

We arrested people for being drunk and disorderly with monotonous regularity. You were on the beat, on foot, and if

23

someone was drunk and causing a disturbance you told them to be quiet and move on. Your uniform commanded respect; told to move on they usually did. Sometimes slowly and wanting the last word. If they didn't move on they'd get arrested. There was little of the dreaded paperwork, just a form to fill in with the *circumstances*, which were virtually identical:

At such and such a time I was on patrol in so and so street when I saw the defendant shouting and swearing in the presence of passers-by. I told him to be quiet and move on. He continued to cause a disturbance, and I noticed the smell of alcohol on his breath, that his speech was slurred and he was drunk. I arrested him for being drunk and disorderly. When formally cautioned and charged he replied: "I'm sorry officer, it won't happen again".

All you needed to fill in were name and address, date of birth, and time, date and location of the arrest. We became blasé about it. One Monday, at Court, a man arrested for drunk and disorderly entered the dock. I got into the witness box and gave the usual evidence. He was found guilty and fined £10. As I left the court a colleague spoke to me.

'What the hell d'you think you're doing?' he asked.

'What do you mean?' I said.

'That drunk was *my* prisoner, not yours.'

When I looked, I saw my prisoner was still waiting to go into the dock! So I had to give my evidence again.

Another time I entered the witness box to give evidence on a drunk who pleaded not guilty. To my astonishment, one of the magistrates lived in the same street as my parents. I knew magistrates were lay-persons from all walks of life, but not from my humble origins. I thought I should say something, but decided that was his prerogative, not mine. So I gave my evidence to nods of approval, and when the defendant had given his I watched my parents' neighbour in serious consultation on the bench. The verdict, after about 1½ minutes' deliberation, was 'guilty'.

There was once a man who *wanted* to be arrested. It was two o'clock in the morning, a quiet night. A chap in his fifties appeared through the revolving door of the nick. He was a Scot.

'Could ye put me up for the neet?' he asked.

'We're not an hotel,' he was told.

'They'd put me up in Edinburgh.'

'Then go to Edinburgh.'

'Just say I'm drunk.'

'But you aren't,'

'Och, ye must have an empty cell.'

'We only put criminals in cells.'

He shrugged and left. Two minutes later the crash of breaking glass from the antique shop across the street. We ran outside to find our man returning to the station.

'Am I a criminal the noo?' he said, passing once again through the revolving door. He got his cell.

Of all the drunks I arrested, just one case was dismissed by the magistrates. It started as a nothing incident, a group of young lads out of their skins, shouting and swearing. I told them to shut up. All did, bar one, who disappeared into a nearby fast-food shop with one of his mates. After a few minutes they reappeared, each eating an enormous piece of chicken. The shouting started again and they kicked a few doors. I went over and told them to scarper. One did – after the usual mutterings about fascism – but the other just stood there, shouting and swearing. I told him to move on, but it was no good, so I arrested him. When you arrest someone you take hold of your prisoner, and when I did his arm came off.

He'd a false arm, which had become detached and now hung limp inside his coat sleeve. He was still a prisoner, so I summonsed the van. The chicken, which had fallen to the ground in the struggle, I kindly presented to a tramp who regularly slept in one of the shop doorways nearby. He had a great, matted beard, and I'll never forget his face, beaming at the sight and smell of an unexpected supper.

My one-armed prisoner pleaded not guilty at court, when I noticed his false arm was not inside his coat sleeve, which was rolled up. So, it looked as if that nasty policeman had picked on a helpless man with one arm. I made sure the magistrates knew I had no means of knowing but it did no good. They took sympathy and found him not guilty. I was just about to leave the court when I heard him speak from the dock.

'I want to make a complaint,' he said.

The clerk looked up from the bench.

'When I was arrested', said the prisoner, ' I had just bought some chicken.'

A deathly hush.

'And that policeman ate it.'

I was hauled to the front of the court.

'Did you eat his chicken?' asked the Chairman of the Bench.

'No, your worship,' I replied, truthfully.

'Well, was there any chicken?' he asked.

'Um...' I replied, trying to look as though I was trying to remember what might have become of it. Then the clerk intervened. 'If you have a complaint,' he said to the prisoner, 'you must pursue it through the appropriate channels.'

That was that. We could all go and let the court get on with its business. I found myself walking down the stairs with my prisoner. 'No hard feelings,' he said, offering his one hand. When I looked he was almost in tears. There he was, a young fellow without his arm. God knows how he lost it but life had not been kind to him. So I shook his hand, decided the not guilty verdict was okay, that justice had been done – especially as the old tramp had had a good supper!

Looking back, I often wonder how I never sustained any serious injury coming to grips with drunks. One case almost proved an exception...

He was powerfully-built, but in the police box he quietened as I awaited the *Black Maria*. He had to be taken in. You couldn't arrest someone then release them afterwards; only the magistrates could deal with him now. (The only exception was a man I once arrested and released as soon as I put him into the box. As he'd emptied his bowels into his trousers, I told him I would caution him on this occasion, pointed him in the direction of Gateshead and made sure I never saw him again).

In the van, a partition separated the driver from the arresting officer and the prisoner. PC Derek Smith locked us in and commenced the drive to the station. All I could hear was the sound of the engine and Derek's monotonous whistle as he drove. It seemed it would be a quiet journey, for my prisoner by now was almost asleep – or so I thought. Then, without warning, I suddenly found myself on the floor, my prisoner's hands around my throat, his thumbs pressing forcefully into my windpipe. He had awaited the opportunity, and now, in the darkness, I could see the whites of his eyes as I fought for breath, with Derek whistling *The Happy Wanderer*, oblivious to events in the rear.

Somehow, I managed to push him backwards. It's amazing where you can find strength when you have to. As we grappled in the darkness to Derek's rendering of *The Bonnie Banks of Loch Lomond*, he again got a grip of my throat, and again I pushed him back. He was much too strong for me, so when he lunged again I kicked him in the face. It didn't half hurt. My ankle tweaked for weeks afterwards.

Reasonable force. That's what you apply. And kicking prisoners in the face is not the accepted method to assert control. But I was desperate. I feared for my life at the hands – literally – of this guy, and when Derek pulled into Pilgrim Street police station yard to the strain of *Tulips from Amsterdam*, chummy and I were still at it in the rear of the van. By now my prisoner and I were drenched in blood, oozing from a mighty wound on his forehead; I was uninjured, though my shirt had been torn almost from inside my tunic.

'Was this really necessary?' asked the station sergeant.

I told him what had happened, but it did no good. He seemed convinced I had launched an unprovoked assault on a bloke twice my size. He said I'd be for it at court. I said I didn't think so, not when the magistrates heard the truth. At court next morning, my prisoner's wound, now stitched, looked dreadful. After I gave evidence, the clerk asked him if he wished to say anything. He pointed to the wound on his forehead, now swollen, as though he'd been hit by a tank. The chairman of the bench was looking directly at me; the court wanted an explanation.

'It's where I kicked him, your worship,' I explained, producing my torn shirt and skinny body as evidence.

'You were fortunate not to be charged with assault,' the chairman said – to my horror, before I realised he was talking to the prisoner. Then he fined him, and told him to pay for a new shirt. To me this incident proved that if you're honest and do your job to the best of your ability you should always be safe, no matter how spurious the complaint. The day honesty doesn't pay will be a sad one indeed.

Not long afterwards I was on patrol on Christmas Eve. As I was graciously accepting a few kisses from the office lasses, I spied my assailant, not twenty paces away. He gave me a look of hate, then took a step towards me. 'Oh no', I thought, 'not again'. Then he checked, and with a snarl uttered just three festive words.

'Happy fuckin' Christmas.'

2

"A thing of duty is a boy forever"

Flann O'Brien

'257 to Alpha Control. How do you read? Over.'
'Alpha Control to 257. Loud and clear. Over.'
The Battle of Britain had nothing on this.

I was standing in Market Street with the police force's latest piece of equipment, the Personal Radio, or PR as it would become known, one of the first in Newcastle upon Tyne. It was small and light, with a cute little aerial that sprung out when you pressed a button. Amazing, how such a dinky little gadget worked.

Well, it worked in Market Street. As this was about fifty yards from the nick it wasn't really a fair test. So I gave it a go in Leazes Terrace at the back of the football ground. Zilch. I didn't know if Alpha Control could hear me or why I couldn't hear them. The advice was straightforward. 'The close proximity of high buildings affects the signal,' I was told. 'Use it on the main streets instead.'

'Right, so next time I catch somebody stealing a car in Leazes Terrace I'll point out my radio doesn't work and would they kindly steal one somewhere else?'

These were only teething problems. The PR's were fine, and their introduction would be the first of two major changes to policing in the years 1967-69.

Before PR's, we carried whistles. The idea was to blow for assistance, just like in the old films where London bobbies clattered along dark alleys in the smog. One night, a colleague remarked he'd never used his whistle and had I ever used mine? No, I hadn't. In fact, neither of is could think of a single incident when anyone had. What would happen if we blew the damn things? It was around four in the morning, dead as a stone. We stood outside the nick, took out our whistles and *blew*. Nothing. We tried again. The same. We went back inside where George and the sergeant sat in silence.

'Hear anything just now?' I asked casually.

They looked at one another, then at me.

'I thought I heard somebody whistling,' said George. 'Otherwise... no. Why, what's up?'

No wonder they never caught Jack the Ripper.

The PR enabled us to communicate, but officers still conformed to the old, established practices. For instance, if you were on 10-beat, you stayed on 10-beat; you didn't encroach onto 11-beat. If you did you had to have good reason. I once crossed Westgate Road to give directions to a lorry driver, a manoeuvre which took me across the border, as it were. By chance, the PC on that beat happened along.

'What's goin' on?' he asked, even though it was obvious. He was just reminding me I was on his patch. We were like cats, if you think about it. This is my territory, that's yours. Of course, it was different if we needed assistance, or if we were officially dispatched to another beat by He Who Must Be Obeyed – George.

The sergeant made sure we patrolled our beats diligently.

'See you in the Haymarket in ten minutes,' he'd say. So you stood in the Haymarket and waited. He'd sign your pocket book, join you on patrol. Any problems on your patch he'd help you out.

In other words, led by example. I mention this because in later years I didn't see this happening; young constables were left to their own devices.

Those sergeants were characters too. One, who shall be nameless, was always up for a laugh. ' 'Ave you 'eard this one, then?' he'd ask, meaning his latest joke. I suppose we laughed most when his wife, who evidently hadn't seen him for a while, came to the police station enquiring of his whereabouts. The amazed constable broke the news. 'He's retired, love,' he told her, and could only shrug his shoulders when asked where on earth her husband was.

Sergeant Duncan was a bit of a joker too. One morning, at six, I found myself at my finishing point, after eight hours on foot. I'd made my final call from the pillar, and I was standing at the roadside, as the city was awakening to its first signs of life: a milk float here, a Royal Mail van there. It was cold and wet. All I wanted was my bed. Then, unexpectedly, a car pulled up. When I looked, there was Duncan, wearing a wide grin.

'Got no home to go to?' he asked, before speeding off to his.

Next day, I wondered if I should just bugger off, miss the finishing point. Old Duncan wouldn't make two consecutive appearances, surely. I decided against it, stood there dutifully instead. It was as well that I did. He showed up, on foot this time, preaching the gospel: stick by the rules, show the flag, do your duty. He signed my book, bade me a brisk 'good morning' and was off. You had to be on the ball. He was.

Getting back to those PR's, my first experience with the wonders of the wireless came just before Christmas, 1966, when they issued four of us with army radios. It was somebody's brilliant idea to assist with what was known as *Christmas Traffic Patrol*. In the days before the out-of-town superstore, everyone shopped in Newcastle. At Christmas, the place heaved, so a team of constables was assigned to man traffic points to keep things moving. It was an impossible task: a policeman on Point A would have no idea what was happening on Point B. Consequently, traffic might be sent to an already cluttered junction; or, conversely, where one junction was relatively free, the policeman on another wouldn't know. It was mayhem. If only we could communicate.

The sergeant decided they would be issued to the PCs on the most important points. As I had the busy crossroads outside St Nicholas' Cathedral, where traffic entered the city from Gateshead, I was one of those selected. From here, with knowledge of what was happening elsewhere, I could divert traffic left or right, or send it straight on. Or even back into Gateshead.

Each radio was housed in a backpack, with the aerial sticking up three feet above your head. They were fitted with a hand-held telephone. We looked like Yanks in those old war films. Anyone today would feel a right plonker. Not us, not then. We were out on the street in record time, aerials and all. When a double-decker bus passed by, packed with Christmas shoppers, I could see the passengers staring, mums telling their kids about the policeman with the wireless, and wasn't that a treat before they went off to see Santa? Smugly, I reached for the handset, feeling important as I sent a message to someone about the traffic.

Well, actually, I didn't send a message. I didn't receive any messages either. None of us did, and for a very good reason: the bloody things didn't work. Unless *hrhrhrhrhrhr* means something. How we won the war I'll never know. The odd expletive filtered through, mouthed from angry officers whose self esteem, heightened by being chosen to use the radios, now plummeted through their inability to get the damn things to function. It hardly contributed to our efforts to cope with the traffic. And to think, Marconi was relaying signals across the Atlantic in 1901. (Got Crippen arrested, if I'm not mistaken).

One incident that highlighted the value of radio communication – when there wasn't any – was when a herd of cattle escaped from a pound near the river. They were last seen making their way along the railway at the end of the King Edward railway bridge, which carries the main London-Edinburgh line, a disaster begging to happen. Alone, and with no means of communication, I hastened to the bridge. No sign of any cattle. It seemed to me they had either proceeded into the Central railway station, or (hopefully) crossed the Tyne into Gateshead. I had to find a telephone before a train ran into them. The only one was in the station. By the time I got there I was knackered. There was no sign of any cattle, so I presumed they had made their way across the river. I rang in and said so.

'Oh no,' I was told, all matter-of-fact, 'they've turned up in their pen again.'

Where they'd been God only knows. But the point was even if I'd found them a major disaster could have occurred, as I had no means of communicating with anyone. Obviously, a radio would have made all the difference.

The introduction of the PR meant there was no longer a need to ring in every hour, so the old police pillars were defunct. The boxes stayed, as they were still handy for incarcerating prisoners and keeping warm on nights. But in time they went too. Now we could communicate, George could get us any time he wanted (provided we weren't in Leazes Terrace). What today's police officers take for granted were miracles of science to us. As well as communicating with the nick, we could communicate with each other: an urgent call to an incident – contact by PR; a message for so and so – contact by PR; police officer in trouble – call for assistance by PR. The benefits were endless. Even Cliff Richard got in on the act.

It came about at the City Hall, popular venue for concerts. We'd hang around the stage door to prevent any trouble. Sometimes, out of the kindness of my heart, I'd slip inside to the dressing rooms and get autographs for the teenage girls patiently waiting outside. I met lots of famous stars: Engelbert Humperdinck, Cat Stevens, the Hollies, Walker Brothers to name a few. They all signed up for the girls. Cliff was especially accommodating. After signing he noticed my PR. I could see he was interested, and allowed him a peep.

'You're lucky,' I told him, 'not everyone's allowed to see it.'

He wanted to know how it worked, and to cut a long story sideways he ended up transmitting a personal message to all the nice policemen in Newcastle Central division. Later, I asked the boys if they'd heard Cliff, and were they impressed? 'It was you arsing about,' they said. They never did believe me, but it was true. Honest.

Once we had radios, it was hard to imagine how we'd ever managed without them. Proof of this came almost as soon as they were issued, when I arrested a man for being drunk in charge of a horse and cart. A woman passer-by complained about the drunken man on the cart. 'He went thataway,' she said. It was an easy trail, thanks to the horse. He was so drunk he was almost asleep at the reigns. He was a *ragman*, with rags and old junk on the cart. I arrested him and got on to the radio.

'I've arrested a man for drunk in charge,' I said, 'can you send assistance?'

When Norman turned up I pointed out the problem.

'It's the horse.'

'What about it?'

'We can hardly leave it here.'

Norman smiled. It wasn't often a budding detective arrested someone with a horse. 'How can I help?' he asked. He soon found out, and never forgave me for the task of leading the horse and cart, in full uniform, all the way to the station.

Another time Norman and I had just started 2-10. From nowhere a man appeared and punched me in the chest. We could easily have taken him in, but he was clearly short of a full dozen. 'Oh, leave him,' I said. 'He doesn't know what he's doing.' We carried on, and I thought nothing more of the incident. A couple of hours later I entered the chargeroom to see a traffic warden nursing a black eye. On the other side of the room sat my friend, a smile on his face. I realised, of course, that if I had acted promptly in the first place the traffic warden would not now be the victim of his next assault. I confessed to the station sergeant.

'Never mind,' I was told, 'it couldn't have happened to a nicer chap.'

The second major change was the panda car. It made sense: if criminals were mobile, the police should be. Ours were Hillman Imps, light and nippy, ideal for nipping around congested city streets. They were also ideal for the yobs to turn upside down if they found one unattended.

Naturally, every eager young bobby wanted a panda: dead flash and kept you dry in the rain. Yet I held fire. Instead, I chose to keep to my beat, where there were lots of places for good chalks and tea-spots. I knew the people and what was more important they knew me. It was community policing before the term had officially been invented. I wanted to catch criminals without being sent to somewhere where somebody else had caught them and all that I had to do was take them in. I must have been successful, for I was twice commended during my probation.

The first was by the magistrates for arresting a woman for receiving stolen property. I saw her sneak into a dark alley opposite the railway station and watched from the shadows as she handed stolen packets of cigarettes to a bloke with a beard. Once he'd stuffed his pockets full, I pounced. It turned out there'd been lots of thefts of cigarettes from the railway station, and the woman was only too pleased to name her supplier whom I also arrested. The woman's name was Kathy. She had form, and we were amused when we saw the 'tattoos' section on her Descriptive Form. It read: *Roses on private parts.* Was it true? The entire station staff and the arresting officer were dying to know. She smiled, lifted her skirt. It was.

The second commendation was awarded after Sergeant Bill Cuthbertson submitted a report to the Chief Constable. It was for a 'high number of arrests on foot patrol'. He never even told me he was doing it, and it meant more to me than any of the others over the years. They talk today of management versus supervision. It should be management *and* supervision. Bill proved it. Not that commendations, when awarded, are always merited. There were times I thought I deserved a commendation and didn't get one, other times when I didn't and one was given. Most operational police officers would agree with this assessment.

But I was talking about pandas. Their introduction changed the way we worked more than anything. Where before we had to make our way on foot or bicycle, or commandeer that passing Riley, now we could be anywhere in minutes – traffic permitting. Yet, for me, deterioration in police-public relations came with the introduction of the panda. Where before officers mingled with the public, stopped and chatted to the public, had cups of tea with the public, once they were put in cars, they drove past the public. They became the faceless ones who, if they had to speak to the public, did so with the window down, as though it was an inconvenience.

In later years, as a supervisory officer, I tried to encourage patrolling officers with cars to stop and park up, at a parade of shops, say, or near a school, and actually get out of the vehicle. It was difficult to get the message across, to destroy the culture of having to be *inside* the car. 'What if there's a shout?' they'd ask, wanting to be first there if there was. Contact first hand with the public never seemed to occur to them, nor did the notion that they might instigate an arrest of their own volition rather than just being sent to incidents, fire brigade style.

I cannot over-emphasise the difference between the help the public gave to the police thirty years ago to today. There would always be a good chance someone would help you if you were in difficulties – arresting a drunk, say, or chasing a felon. Now it's so unusual Divisional Commanders write letters of thanks. I believe the police in the main can blame themselves for this.

A classic case of being helped by the public occurred one evening when I saw two hoodlums pick up a young woman and swing her through the air. Most un-chivalrous, I thought, so I gave them a pull. Far from showing remorse, they quickly sized up the situation and suggested it might be a good idea to swing me through the air too. As we struggled, I heard a gruff, Geordie voice calling from the direction of the Black Swan, directly across the street. 'It's a copper,' it cried, and my heart sank when a large group emerged from the pub. But the crowd hadn't come to help the hoodlums, they'd come to help me. They seized my would-be assailants, held on to them until help arrived, returning to the pub when the job was done. I never seemed to see that sort of thing in later years. Of course, the panda – or unit beat – cars had to come. But, like any tool, they have to be used properly. Sitting on your backside for eight hours, driving around aimlessly, is not the way to do it. To today's young police officers I say: get out of your cars, even if you remain with the vehicle. Say good morning to people, tell them it's a nice day, see and be seen. Get to know them and, most important, get them to know you.

It was around this time the breathalyser was introduced. Before, if someone was driving under the influence of alcohol it was very much at the discretion and judgement of the police officer whether they were arrested. Like the lorry driver who knocked a pedestrian down in Northumberland Street. It was obvious he'd been drinking. I didn't consider him in a fit state to drive. There was no way I was going to let him back into his cab. I decided to arrest him, the only way I could prevent him driving. I couldn't say: 'Look, you've had too much to drink. Leave the lorry here and come back for it in a few hours.'

'I'm not pissed,' he insisted, trying to climb into his cab.

I pointed out he was just as much a danger to himself as anyone.

'Prove it,' he said, defiantly.

There was a long, continuous white line on the road.

'Walk along it without stepping off,' I said.

He failed miserably, so I arrested him for being drunk in charge. He pleaded not guilty and appeared at the Quarter Sessions. Came the moment in my evidence when I'd asked him to walk the line. The defence barrister gripped the lapels of his black gown and leaned back – as they do.

'Qualified to do this sort of thing, are you?'

'Well, not exactly.'

'Quite,' said the barrister. Smirks from smug little clerks, a frown from the judge, who then intervened.

'Well, did he walk along the line or didn't he?'

'No, your honour,' I replied.

The judge looked at the barrister.

'The officer has made his point, I believe.'

The judge then instructed the jury to return a verdict of not guilty. The court was perplexed. But as the beak explained: 'The officer acted in good faith, but as a new breath-testing device is soon to be introduced I feel a conviction would be unsafe.' Well, why didn't he say so in the first place!

That's the thing about courts and judges. If, in the opinion of the judge, there might be some doubt about something, no matter how trivial, they are liable to throw the entire thing out. I've seen some travesties in my time. Guilt must be proved *beyond reasonable doubt*. Fair enough. But because a defendant is found not guilty, it doesn't necessarily mean he never did it; it means there wasn't enough proof to secure a guilty verdict, if you see what I mean.

*

As the recruitment booklet said: *the police service is always on the lookout for men of the right type...*

You wouldn't normally find women officers on patrol in the sixties, except during office hours when they might patrol in pairs. What few there were remained indoors where they could be called upon to search female prisoners, deal with women or juvenile shoplifters or make the tea for the station staff. The Policewomen's Department wasn't part of any shift, and not, as I recall, on equal pay. It never occurred to us that it could be otherwise. They were *there*, that's all, one of the three P's I was told could be trouble: pocket books, property and policewomen (not necessarily in that order).

So when, nearing the end of my two-year probationary period, I attended a course at Dishforth training centre, it came as a surprise to find women present, billeted in their own block which, we were told, was out of bounds to us males. Only the knowledge that being caught inside would result in immediate expulsion from the course, together with a report to our chief constable – a sacking offence – kept us at bay. We conformed, but it wasn't easy, especially after a couple of pints in the bar when male bravado took over. We couldn't enter their quarters, but we could look inside. So there we were at 11 o'clock, staring into brightly-lit dorms at *les girls*, who in turn (presumably) were enjoying the experience. Yet back in division, women remained virtually non-operational. If you wanted one, you could find one on the policewomen's extension. Then came the news: women would join us on foot patrol.

To a man we thought the entire notion crazy. What if you called for assistance with a violent man and a woman turned up? A senior (male) officer went on tv, told the nation it would never work. 'Course it wouldn't. When I was told to take a WPC on patrol one Saturday evening from 10 o'clock until midnight, I was horrified. What if *something happened*?

We walked down Grainger Street, back up Grainger Street, then I escorted her back to the nick. Yes, *escorted* her: if I'd been with a bloke I'd have just said cheerio and he'd have walked back on his own. But I couldn't leave a woman alone on the streets. It wasn't till she'd gone I got to thinking about the main problem we (the men) had with policewomen. They were no good in a scrap. That's why we didn't want 'em along. If women were creatures of great physical strength that would have been okay. Then the penny dropped. Nine stone-odd and couldn't reach the sand from the springboard in the long jump, remember? How many times had I turned out to assist a colleague who needed assistance, and what had they thought when they saw it was me? In other words, what was the difference – a nine-stone man or a nine-stone woman? Apart from the obvious, none that I could see. Refusal to accept women officers as equals after that was without merit in my opinion. They *are* equal, and in some circumstances more than equal. Physical strength isn't the only solution to the world's problems. In fact, it's usually no solution at all.

The release of police *women* into the big, wide world meant they worked alongside their male peers. To wives or girlfriends who worry about loved ones tucked up in patrol cars on nights with officers of the opposite sex, let me reassure them: they have every right to be. What can you expect, when young people are put together in confined spaces? It amazes me to read of the surprise at the sexual shenanigans of men and women in the Navy. They coop them up in warships and send them out for weeks at a time into the Atlantic or wherever, then react with pained surprise when they get at it. Frankly, I'd be surprised to read that they didn't. Everything from elephants to stick insects are banging away, why should police officers – or sailors – be any different?

Temptation came my way, I don't mind admitting. Recently posted from training school, Sarah caught my eye in her uniform and fancy hat. And no wonder. I was Potent Paul, a guy in his twenties, a drooling, dribbling slave to her charms. Naturally, being pure as the driven slush, I could look but not permit the call of the flesh to interfere with my professional duties. But the more I saw of her, the more she drove me crackers. Even her name haunted me (her real name, that is).

By chance (honest), around five o'clock one summer's morn, I found myself on patrol with Sarah, pushing doors at the back of the shops in Clayton Street. Every time I turned, she was there, an alluring temptress, her presence too much – almost – for a young red-blooded male to resist. Turned on? I'll say! I resisted, not out of some professional code. I was scared she'd blab, that's all. Then again, she might've fancied me. Mum did say I looked nice in my uniform.

Talking of Clayton Street – and women – I learned a hard lesson one day in my quest to apprehend a milk thief.

Someone was nicking a pint of milk every morning from shop doorways in Clayton Street. The milkman was delivering the milk around 5.30 a.m., and it was being stolen shortly afterwards, probably by someone on their way to work. Trouble was, the doorways were set back several yards into shop premises, where the lighting was poor, especially on dark, winter's mornings. In other words, getting sight of someone actually picking up a bottle of milk was almost impossible.

A few of us took it upon ourselves to try and catch the culprit. On early turn, we wore civvy coats on top of our uniforms, and took up our positions in various doorways. It was a dark, dank winter's morning, the sort where you turn your collar up and your feet quickly become numb with cold.

I waited, as workmen, office cleaners and whoever hurried past. None spared me so much as a glance. Then, just as it seemed the combined efforts of our shift had been in vain, I spied a woman, forty-ish, on the opposite footpath. She looked as though she might be a cleaner. (It was too early for your office staff and professional sorts). One moment she was hurrying up the street, like everyone else, the next she turned swiftly into a darkened doorway of a furniture store. I knew from checking earlier there were several pints of milk in there, so I made a beeline for the dark recess opposite.

As I reached the entrance, she appeared in the darkness before me. Instinctively, I grabbed her arm and stopped her in her tracks. Her scream of terror, amplified in the confines of that doorway, will remain with me until my dying day.

Milk thief or not, the last thing in the woman's mind was that I might be a police officer. Instead, she would have thought she was being attacked by a crazed madman or sex fiend, and did what any woman would have done – screamed the house down. She also tried to break free, and I wouldn't let her.

My mission to apprehend what I took to be a thief now took second place to trying to placate the poor woman, as well as defend myself against possible imminent attack by some workmen who were passing at the time. Fortunately, my colleagues, close at hand, turned up and the situation was sorted – and no, she'd not nicked any milk, although why she entered that doorway remains a mystery.

The lesson, although it seems obvious, was that no matter how sincere a police officer's endeavours to catch a criminal, unless your identity is obvious the public won't know who you are. The woman I grabbed that dark morning was okay, once she realised who I was and she wasn't going to be murdered. But there's always a fine line between doing the job to the best of one's ability, and doing the job right, if you see what I mean.

*

Police officers in those days did not receive payment for overtime. There was no such thing and we didn't expect it. Arresting someone for crime was our payment, and we worked over the eight hours to ensure the job was done properly. You wouldn't hand your prisoner over to anyone else. There *was* that payment for special duty at St James's Park: for a First Division match, about 90 officers; a reserve game (which could attract a crowd of around 6,000) required four constables and a sergeant.

For a Saturday afternoon fixture, you'd finish night shift at 6 a.m. and report at the ground for 11. You were back at ten for night shift again. A Wednesday night match was covered from early turn. For this you were paid the princely sum of around £3.

I once got a rollicking at a reserve game. Newcastle were playing Leeds, when the ball rolled out of play near the corner flag. Instinctively, I teed it up and centred it to the Leeds keeper, getting a cheer for the accuracy of my cross. The sergeant didn't appreciate my football skills. 'You're here as a policeman,' I was told. 'Concentrate on your duty.'

He was right, I suppose. Concentrating on our duty was what we were there for. When Newcastle scored we had to face the crowd, not easy for young policemen who were fans themselves.

St James's park, like all grounds then, was standing on the terraces, with seating for just a few. The ground held around 62,000 at the time. We loved patrolling the perimeter of the pitch, seeing the game close up. The one dreaded position was the Office, where cash from the turnstiles was taken. You saw nothing of the game, although you could hear it. Still, there was the satisfaction of being in the best position to deal with any armed robbers who might have a go at stealing the takings. Of ninety bobbies at the ground you'd be on your own if someone turned up with a sawn-off. I had a spell at the Office once. It was for a match against arch-rivals Sunderland, and I was really grieved about missing out. As Newcastle lost 3-0, it wasn't so bad after all.

The atmosphere in the ground – for all matches – was unbelievable, with the chant *United, United* urging on the team. The crowd sang many songs, my favourite being (to the tune of *Clementine*) -

> Who's your father
> Who's your father
> Who's your father, referee?
> Go on admit it
> You haven't got one,
> You're a bastard, referee.

Happy days!

Sadly, a section of the crowd in the Leazes end persisted for a time with chanting the name of Harry Roberts, who murdered three police officers in London. The stand would be packed, with spectators shoulder to shoulder, so there was little you could do. Some of us got wound up about it. Then again, they were just young blokes. Today most, if not all, if they were asked whether there was any malice about their odious chanting, would probably shake their heads. There was no question of alcohol playing a part, incidentally. These were the days before the tragedies of Hillsborough and Hersel.

Not that Newcastle were ever in with a shout for the championship, and, in the sixties at least, they were utterly dismal in the FA Cup. Yet, in 1969, they qualified for a European competition, the Inter-Cities Fairs Cup (now the UEFA Cup). Even that was by default. The rules at the time were that no two clubs from one city could enter at the same time. Liverpool and Everton qualified, so Everton had to drop out, leaving Newcastle to make their debut in Europe.

United were drawn against Feyenoord, first leg at home. For this and the ties that followed, special duty was performed twice: once for the allocation of tickets, when thousands queued all weekend, and again on the night of the game. Newcastle won 4-0. As usual, every time they scored there was a pitch invasion. We were supposed to stop it, but were helpless against thousands of delirious Geordies. I didn't care. I ran onto the pitch, ostensibly to remove the fans, but secretly pleased to be alongside the likes of Wyn Davies and Pop Robson. Surprisingly, United kept winning until they reached the semi-final against Glasgow Rangers.

What police, club and media had always regarded as trouble paled into insignificance the night of the Rangers match. It started before noon, when coachloads of Scots supporters arrived from Glasgow. They'd been drinking on the road, so were already tanked up when they arrived in Newcastle. The atmosphere was carnival-like at first, the invading Scots parading around the city streets. But then they got into the pubs and were blattered by kick-off. Most didn't have tickets. It was obvious there'd be problems at the game.

The Rangers fans – those with tickets – filed in to the Gallowgate end. Almost every one seemed to be drinking from a bottle of *Newky Broon*. Those without tickets were turned away, but nearing kick-off many climbed the outside wall of the ground in the belief they were getting in to see the game, only to find themselves in the players' and directors' car park. This made them angry, and what with the thousands of Newcastle fans queuing in the car park too the scene was ripe for a major catastrophe. Yet kick-off came and went without any significant incident. But real trouble was to come.

My position was a flat roof alongside the main stand, facing the Rangers fans at the Gallowgate end. From here, you had a good view of the crowd – and the game – and could summon help by PR if necessary. You never left the roof once the game started, as your position was important. Anyway, when Newcastle scored a second goal around 2,000 Scots invaded the pitch.

Battle ensued between drunken Scots and police and officials, whilst bottles flew from the crowd. Many police and ground staff were struck, as were St John's Ambulance teams and stewards, and even some of the invading Scots by their own countrymen. Things got so bad the referee took the teams off. Then police formed a thin blue line right across the pitch, and slowly order was restored and the match restarted. I witnessed the entire scene from my rooftop position. You hear of bravery awards, yet to the best of my knowledge none was awarded that night. There should have been, to police, stewards, St John's Ambulance, all who braved that crowd.

Newcastle won and played the Hungarians, Ujpest Dosza, in the final. What a great night it was when Newcastle beat them at St James's. This time there was a carnival atmosphere, without any problems whatsoever. Then again, you wouldn't expect many fans from Hungary. United won the return leg, too, so won the Fairs Cup at the first attempt. That was in 1969, and despite all the millions they've spent they haven't won a single major trophy since.

It was after a match in those early days of my career that I came close to death, on a traffic point on the old A1. It was a crossroads, manned only when the hordes were turning out from St James's. In the distance I spied a flat-backed lorry bearing down the A1. I could see it carried a load of planks, or battens, the sort you see on scaffolding. They were resting on top of the driver's cab, pointing into the air like missiles from a rocket-launcher. I signalled the driver to stop, and waved football traffic across the junction. I didn't realise the driver of the lorry was asleep, possibly dreaming about Newcastle's last win. What he wasn't doing was looking where he was going, hadn't seen me in the middle of the road. I *had* to get him to stop, as drivers of cars leaving the match had seen my signal and were committed to proceeding. Still the lorry roared on, the driver in a world of his own. (Okay, remembering the last time Newcastle won wouldn't be easy).

When the driver saw me, the look on his face said it all as he hit the brakes. The wheels locked and the lorry skidded to a halt. The lorry stopped, its load didn't. As the last of the traffic cleared the junction, the planks were launched in my direction, soaring through the air, narrowly missing my head and rattling onto the ground all about my tender being. *Zulu* had nothing on this. If one had hit me I was a dead duck. When they finally came to rest I looked at the driver, now sitting motionless in his cab, ashen-faced, wondering what retribution he would now have to face having almost wiped out one of Her Majesty's Constabulary.

'Just pick them up,' I said. And he did. One by one, saying sorry over and over. I should have knocked him off for an insecure load, but I didn't. He looked so wretched, I let him off. I didn't feel there was anything to gain by booking him. He was in such a state I decided he'd been punished enough. I reckoned he'd never daydream at the wheel again. I hope I was right.

Pay was poor in those days, so to make ends meet I was obliged to return to my skills as an electrician, installing lighting and power points in peoples' houses. It was strictly against regulations, but with a wife, five kids and a Dalmatian to support I had no choice. Hardly a rest day came and went without me working somewhere or other – a ring main here, a cooker point there. As you never worked on your rest days and there was no means of making extra cash (apart from the football) I could not see the harm.

One day a police car arrived at my door. PC Wanless had a message.

'Super wants to see you.'

'I'm rest day.'

'Super wants to see you – *now*.'

Superintendent Wade came straight to the point.

'I've an anonymous letter here which says you've been moonlighting.'

Before my trembling jaws could get a word in he spoke again.

'You haven't been moonlighting, 257, have you?'

I was lost for words. It doesn't often happen, but there it is.

'Thought not,' he said dismissively. Then he looked up.

'Well, bugger off.'

I packed it in then, struggled by on the police pay. Later, things got really bad in the service as far as pay was concerned. Experienced officers left in droves, took up jobs in security, as van drivers, anywhere where the money was better, which was just about everywhere. Inevitably, there was talk of strikes. By law, police officers cannot be members of a trade union and cannot strike. So the Police Federation balloted its members, asking them if they wished to have the right to withhold their labour.

I do not believe police officers should strike, no matter what. To me, anyone in the police force who wants to strike shouldn't be in the job. Have they stopped to think what would happen if they did? What about all those children they protect every day? What about the elderly victims of burglary, the woman who walks alone? Presumably they have their welfare at heart every day they report for duty. It's not their fault if the police get lousy pay; it's no good withdrawing protection because of politicians. As the recruitment booklet had said: *there's more to the job than the money you get out of it.* Coppers don't just work for the money, surely. I voted 'no' in the ballot.

Earlier, I mentioned having a cup of tea with prisoners. A classic case of 'no hard feelings' came when I arrested a young fellow I'd caught trying to break into the cash box of a public telephone. I was in plain clothes, driving an unmarked car, when I saw two fellows obviously up to good in the kiosk. I got out of the car and arrested one – the other ran off – for possession of a chisel he was using to prise open the cash box. I pushed him into the front passenger seat of the car, and radioed for assistance. As I was leaning into the car, I was grabbed around the neck from behind by the other man, now trying to rescue his buddy. There were many passers-by, but in plain clothes and with an unmarked car, they probably thought it was a fight between some men – they couldn't tell I was a police officer.

As I struggled to prise the man's arms from my neck, my prisoner was trying to kick me where it hurt. The threat of imminent strangulation and permanent injury to my nether regions I considered valid for deployment of whatever method I could use to hang on to my prisoner in the restricted confines of the open doorway of a Hillman Imp. So I seized my prisoner's nose between my teeth, and held on to it, a situation which prevailed until, suddenly, my neck was freed when the second man was seized by other officers who had responded to my call. I released my prisoner's nose, and both men were taken into custody.

They were charged with attempted theft and possession of an implement. By this time my man's nose was now a brighter shade of crimson, and at least twice its normal size. I had explained to the station sergeant what had happened, that I'd had no alternative to do what I did. In fact, there was the question of them assaulting a police officer. But we never charged prisoners with assaulting the police unless it was serious, and I wasn't injured. In the end there was no charge of assaulting me, and he didn't wish to pursue the injury to his nose. Instead, he and his mate accompanied me to an all-night restaurant for breakfast. They said they were sorry for what they had done. I said I was sorry about his nose.

My first experience of someone wishing to complain against the police came after an incident one afternoon in the Haymarket. It was nothing really. A few youths kicking litter bins, shouting abuse. I told them to be quiet, and they complied, slinking off with silly smirks. A couple gave 'V' signs and called out something about me being related to Hitler. No big deal. I hustled them on their way. That was that, or so I thought. Half an hour later I was in the police station when a young man with an accent he might have acquired at Eton came to the enquiry counter. I asked him how I could help.

'It's about your conduct in the Haymarket,' he said.

I turned to Brian Hardie, one of the Operators. Brian was ex-navy, with war service behind him. It was rumoured when his ship was sunk during the war he and a few survivors had drifted for days on the Atlantic until one died and the others, in desperation, had eaten him. Or part of him anyway. Brian asked about the incident. I told him it had been nothing, that there had been no arrests, that I had sorted it out. Brian then faced the man at the counter.

'What is it you want – *exactly*?' asked Brian.

'I want to make a complaint,' said the man.

There was nothing to complain about. Brian knew it, I knew it, and chummy from Eton knew it. So Brian placed him in one of the quarters of the revolving door and gave it a push until our friend found himself standing in the street. Brian said not a word, but just went back to typing up the Occurrence Sheets. So, we could all get on with our work.

Today, a sergeant or inspector would be summoned to interview the man, record his complaint, and then either send for the officer concerned – take him or her from patrol – or forward the papers to Headquarters, where the Complaints Department would assign a senior officer to deal, a process likely to take weeks. They might spend hours on end tracing the youths to ask their accounts. For what? Is this what the public want? I do not think so. They want the police to get on with patrolling the streets, dealing with trouble or potential trouble. It was about this time, incidentally, that notices about *How to Complain Against the Police* appeared in police stations, a real morale-booster.

Complaints against police officers are actively encouraged nowadays, not least by solicitors seeking 'out of court' settlements on behalf of their clients, with a nice legal aid fee. Of course, genuine complaints should always be pursued. And as far as bent coppers are concerned, those who are straight – the overwhelming majority – are the first to want rid of them.

*

Promotion one day was my aim, and though I couldn't expect it for a few years I could at least pass the exams. There are two examinations: to sergeant, then inspector. In those days you could take them both, even though you still held the rank of constable. I decided to get them out of the way pronto, and embarked on a correspondence course, studying the literature, doing fake exam questions. It wasn't easy with a young family and working shifts. It seemed the harder you worked, the more often you were at court, sometimes on your day off. It left less and less time for studies. Then Arthur and I came up with the Great Plan. Each of us would tell the other to read up on a given subject. Then we'd read up on it ourselves, and set an examination paper for the other. After our 'exam', we'd hand the papers in to each other for marking, discussing any points afterwards in the pub, usually after a spell on the weights. It's a great idea, and I would recommend it to anyone. You couldn't skive off, as you'd be letting the other down. When the sergeant's exam came round we buried it. But we still weren't qualified; there was still the *education* exam.

This was a test in maths, English and geography. Many a good officer had failed to gain promotion because he didn't know the square root of 625 or the capital of Mongolia. Quite what this had to do with police work you might well ask. Anyway, for the geography paper, they told you in advance which part of the world the questions would be on, in my case Australia: its rivers, its mountains, its cities, its industry. I studied hard; you name it, I learned it. Everything from the Great Australian Bight to Skippy the Kangaroo. Then, just before the date of the exam, they scrapped it! I've been a leading authority on Australia ever since, for what good its been.

The sixties were a time of another great change in the police service: amalgamations. Up and down the country they were at it. City and Borough forces joined with the counties: my own, Newcastle City, joined with Tynemouth Borough (less than 100

49

officers, as I recall) and Northumberland County to make a new force, Northumberland Constabulary. On 1st April, 1969, we had to forsake our unique blue and white striped cap band for a chequered one.

The powers that be were keen on integration: an officer from the sticks was posted to Newcastle, an officer from the city to the county somewhere. We city lads didn't accept this, saying that where we dealt with real criminals, our colleagues in the sticks did nothing more than ride around on bikes looking into kids' saddlebags for stolen apples, and check the local Co-op door on nights. We called our county colleagues sheep-shaggers; no doubt they had equally suitable names for us. I formed my own opinion when I was told by a county bloke how, alone, he patrolled Ashington and Bedlington, coal mining towns where there was plenty to do, especially at weekends when the workingmen's clubs were turning out. In the compact area of a city centre, assistance for us was always near at hand; in the county it could be half an hour away.

City blokes talked of resigning, although I can't think of anyone who did. Some made their feelings known by inscribing 'TJF' everywhere: on notice boards, in toilets, even on the wall in the lift. They stood for 'The Job's Finished', or similar. It wasn't, of course. The job's always there, no matter what.

Some city officers didn't realise Berwick-upon-Tweed is in Northumberland, now their own force area. 'But they play in the Scottish league,' they protested, proving that the extent of their knowledge of their native land (like my own) was based on a town having a football team 'in the league'. In the end, an atlas provided the proof: Berwick is in England!

One of my city colleagues, Tom, was posted to a tiny Northumbrian village right on the Scottish border. A year or so later I bumped into him. How was it going, I asked? His face beamed as he recounted how his life had been transformed from the rough and tumble of Newcastle to fishing for salmon in the Tweed. There'd been just one problem early on. He'd arrested a drunk on the English side of the Tweed and taken him to Berwick, twelve miles away. When he got there he got a rollicking from the station sergeant who identified the prisoner as a man who lived in Coldstream, just across the river. 'He's always pissed', he was told, 'y'should've just kicked his arse across the bridge' – i.e. into Scotland.

Years later, the bridge was the scene of a tragic abduction of a schoolgirl who was later found murdered hundreds of miles away. Proof that you can never tell what might happen, and where.

Amalgamation with the County force brought one benefit to former city officers. It concerned special duty. For years Newcastle United had provided officers on special duty with a cardboard cup of tea and a meat pie. You'd normally go in for this treat about ten minutes after kick off. Once we joined up with the County, we had to cover Newcastle Races too, at Gosforth Park (in the former County area). Naturally, when I was told it was time for 'refreshment', I looked forward, as always, to tea and a pie. Instead I found myself in the restaurant for a three-course dinner! Another plus was the news that a steward on a certain turnstile was a must for a tip.

'Don't all go at once,' we were told, 'just filter past, one at a time.'

The steward glanced furtively over his shoulder. 'Horty Bill in the 3.30,' he whispered from the corner of his mouth, in such a way it was top secret info and don't let on where it came from. One by one we placed our money, in some cases the entire amount we'd earn for the day's special duty. I managed to get myself into a good position to watch the race – good enough to see Horty Bill somersault over the third fence from home, anyway.

Back on the beat…

I mentioned avoiding injuries. One event where it looked as though I might get a hiding stands out, yet I came out smiling thanks to an earlier incident where, I like to think, my good fortune was of my own making. A barmaid in Pink Lane asked me to order a group of Irishmen to leave her pub. It was closing time and they were still at it, each with a full pint. They were building the Tyne Tunnel at the time, and I think they were off the site.

'Drink up lads,' I said, 'the lady wants to go to bed.'

Adding 'the lady' was the key. If I'd just said 'drink up' they wouldn't have taken kindly to it; but as it was for the lady that was different. They all drank up, bar one. (There's always one). He was a powerful individual – 'brick outhouse' comes to mind – clearly capable of sorting me out, thank you very much. His mates plonked their glasses on to the bar and awaited events.

'Come on,' I said, 'it's closing time.'

He gave me an 'I'm-not-going-and-what-you-gonna-do-about-it' look.

'Drink up,' I said again, this time taking hold of the top of the glass with a gloved hand. He glared defiantly.

Some sort of compromise was needed.

'Tell you what,' I said in my best compromising voice, 'if you can drink that in one, fair enough. If not, put it down and get out.' Meaning if he was man enough he'd drink it straight down. Then his mates and I watched in silence as he steadied himself, then poured a full pint straight down his throat. A look of triumph and laughs all round, and they left without further ado. 'They're nice chaps really,' said the barmaid.

A few nights later I was on Neville Street around eight o'clock when a crowd of Geordie youths surrounded me. Just yards from the police box, they knew I couldn't reach it. Someone shoved me from behind. Bad language followed, with a suggestion about what to do with my truncheon.

'Move along,' I ordered.

'Or what?' said one. 'There's six of us.'

'And six of us,' said a familiar Irish voice.

It was my friend from the pub, and his mates. The lads didn't fancy their chances, and slunk off in silence.

'Thanks,' I said to my knight in shining armour. He just smiled.

*

Life for a young constable in Newcastle Central division was a busy one, with ample opportunities for arrests, especially for crime. I dealt with burglars – shop and office premises mainly –

car thieves, drunks breaking shop windows, drunks breaking peoples' heads, endless shoplifters. I never arrested anyone for stealing apples. I realised my ambition lay with CID, although you had to have around five years' service before you could even think about that. First I had to get through two years' probation, which meant, apart from those arrests, a steady flow of process – everything from arresting drunks (which didn't count for crime) to knocking off motorists. And if I got desperate there were always the barrow boys.

They sold fruit and veg from handcarts, much to the chagrin of shopkeepers who had to pay rates. Was that a matter for the police? Superintendent Martin said it was: 'I've had a delegation in here complainin', so knock a few off.' The offence was obstruction of the highway. If they moved on my approach I let them be. If they didn't, they were 'done'. It was a sort of ritual. A lookout signals the approach of the *pollis*, and right in the middle of weighing a pound of bananas they wheel their barrows off.

'Shite!' says Frankie, leaving a bemused customer still holding her ten bob note.

If the lookout fails I call out the immortal words: 'I'm putting you in, Frankie' (not forgetting to caution him, of course!). It costs him £2. Serves him right for employing a lookout who fails to clock a bloke wearing a uniform with a silver chain dangling from the breast pocket.

Beggars were sitting ducks. Like the one who sat on the ground outside St Thomas' church with a sign: 'No legs'. I hadn't the heart to report him – at first. I changed my mind when I saw him get up and wander into the nearest pub. There was a 'blind' guy who did the same. Both suffered the due process of the law after that as far as I was concerned.

I had five great years as a uniformed copper, but you have to move on. My ambition lay in catching criminals: thieves, burglars, murderers. A case of the latter hit the headlines at the time, when two schoolgirls were arrested for murder. One of them, Mary Bell, eleven years old, was convicted of manslaughter. It had such an impact on me, the facts are worth recounting.

A 4-year old boy had been found dead on waste-land in Newcastle's west end. Shortly after, teachers at a nearby nursery school discovered one of the classrooms broken into and four notes in a child's handwriting left at the scene. One of the notes mentioned the death of the boy. Two months later another boy was found strangled, also on waste-land, in the same locality. His body was marked with a series of small cuts. Police questioned over 1,000 local children, including Mary and another girl, each of whom accused the other of 'squeezing' one boy's throat. Mary said the other girl had cut his body with a razor blade. Both admitted writing the notes found at the nursery school two months before, one of which, drawn by Mary, showed a picture of the body of a child. Both girls were charged with murder, and appeared at the Assizes. Mary was described as being 'calm, self-possessed, demonstrating guile and understanding beyond her years', the other girl 'bewildered and child-like'. Mary was sentenced to life detention (not really life, of course). The other girl was acquitted.

Another case, even closer to 'home', taught me police should always keep an open mind when dealing with the public, and that what seems obvious doesn't necessarily turn out to be the case. One Saturday afternoon a man and woman reported 'losing' their 5-year old son in a department store in Newcastle. It happens almost every week in any large town. A description was taken, and they were asked to wait until details were circulated. It would only be a matter of time before child and parents were reunited. But something about the couple just didn't seem right, and when questioned the father told detectives they'd been walking in a remote wood somewhere in Northumberland when somehow they'd lost their son. He accompanied detectives on a protracted but unsuccessful search for the wood. Police weren't satisfied, and the man was kept in custody. (Could they do this today?)

The following day they resumed their search, finally spotting an item of the boy's clothing hanging from a tree. A search led to the body of the boy, who was discovered pressed into the soft earth. His father then admitted striking him with a wooden arm of a settee at home, that the boy had died and he'd buried him where he now lay. I never forgot this case, always kept it in mind in later years when I had to deal with reports of missing persons. The chance to play detective came when I was posted to CID at Newcastle Central for six months as an aide. I was determined to succeed.

3

"Detection is an exact science"

Sir Arthur Conan Doyle

We stand in line, silently enduring the familiar smell of the weekend's urine and vomit, not yet swilled away from the tiled floor of the cell-block, the only sounds the distant clank of the cleaner's bucket, punctuated now and then by an irritating, tuneless whistle. Then a cultured Geordie voice briefly breaks the silence.

'Why doesn't that twat get his arse down here before we do?'

The first prisoner appears, stands in his stockinged feet, nervously examines his fingernails. Finally, he gets the bottle to look up, his gaze flickering at the line of impassive detectives, then at Sid, the duty detective sergeant. Slight of build, sharp featured, dapper, he could be a bank manager.

'What's *your* story, bonny lad?'

This was the form. Around 8 a.m. prisoners arrested for crime were brought one at a time to the end of the cell block corridor to face the CID. There was no doubt the sight of all those detectives was daunting, especially for the inexperienced. It didn't work so well on the hard cases. But this guy was out of his depth.

Sid, all matter-of-fact.

'Pissed were yer?'

He nodded.

'Guilty as charged. Right?'

Another nod. Somebody had a question.

'Didn't I pull you in the Bigg Market once?'

The man couldn't remember. Just studied his big toes, which peeped out of his socks. Sid turned to me.

'Yours. Okay?'

He meant he wanted a full admission about the offence and as many others he would admit. Have them taken into consideration – t.i.c., as we said.

One by one, the prisoners faced the line, virtually interviewed then and there, preparatory to the real thing in an hour or so. No caution, no solicitor, no quarter given. Today, officers familiar with the Police and Criminal Evidence Act (PACE) would be astonished, lawyers and judges mortified. That first prisoner Sid told me to interview wouldn't admit any other offences. I duly returned to the CID office to find Sid at his desk.

'Well?' said Sid.

'Wouldn't have anything,' I told him.

'I meant "Well, what are you doing back here so soon?" said Sid. 'Go back and try again.'

I went back and opened the steel door of matey's cell. 'You'll have to have something,' I told him, 'the sergeant says so.' He understood.

'Any chance of a fag first?' he asked.

Prisoners were either your own, or had been arrested by uniformed patrol officers on nights and left for CID next morning, although the latter were loth to hand their prisoners over unless it was absolutely necessary: the seriousness of the offence, for example, or because the case was too involved for a patrol officer to take on. Those two guys I arrested in that office block: you'll recall I was a uniformed PC at the time, and when told to 'hand them over' to CID I almost went to war over it. The duty detective sergeant sent for me.

'That's a great chalk, but you must hand the prisoners over to CID.'

'They're mine,' I told him, pointing out that other officers, including CID, had given up on the search. It didn't matter. 'These men are burglars. We have to interview them, search their houses. Your place is on patrol.' He was right, of course. But I make the point to mark the contrast with the way things were 25 years later, with arresting officers obliged to unload because they won't get paid for working past the eight hours. I'm not blaming them. It's the way things turned out once police officers were paid for working overtime (1975).

Different police areas generate different types of arrests for crime. In a city centre, most day-to-day arrests are for burglary, robbery, stealing cars, stealing from cars, stealing bikes, deception, assault, including sexual assault, damage and shoplifting (which is just about everything except sheep rustling and badger baiting). And all arrests generate the inevitable paperwork.

Paperwork for detectives included crime reports, reams of 'em. Every one was sent to CID. We sat for hours 'investigating' undetected crimes. In other words, most crimes. The detective inspector had to keep the detection rate up, that is to say as high a percentage as possible. Thirty percent? Too low, get it up. Seventy-five percent? Too high, you're cooking the books. It's all nonsense. Detection rates distort the truth. Take four crimes: three shopliftings and a murder. The shopliftings are all detected, the murder isn't. 75% detection rate. Fair? The family of the murder victim wouldn't think so. I remember a man who was arrested for stealing a bottle of milk from somebody's doorstep. He admitted stealing a hundred bottles. A hundred detections! (It would be one now). Years later, as DI, I paid little attention to detection rates. The Home Office were forever ringing up about them. I didn't care. My focus was on the criminals and the crimes they committed, not statistics.

As CID Aide I had my fair share of crime reports. In theory, I was supposed to investigate every one, and the back of the report had lots of little square boxes which you ticked to prove you had. A handbag stolen from a parked car in Morden Street car park: I had to show I'd searched the place on my hands and knees looking for clues. 'Enquires made with a negative result', we wrote on the form. It was a paper exercise, a waste of time. Nowadays, crimes where you haven't a hope are recorded and that's it. You can focus instead on those you might detect. Or, better still, focus on those you suspect of committing crime in the first place.

It was strange, that first morning. Wearing a suit, I mean. Where before I identified with my uniform colleagues, now, it seemed, I was, a new bloke just arrived at the nick. I'd no special training, in fact only the day before I was one of them, but now PC so-and-so was seeking my advice on what to do about such-and-such a prisoner, or how to investigate such-and-such a burglary. CID were held in high esteem, the CID general office door remained closed, and anyone seeking to enter had to knock – uniformed constables *and* sergeants.

My first visit as an 'expert' to a scene of crime was to accompany an experienced hack, Bernie, to a shop. Someone had tried to force the shutters through the night, though failed to gain entry. 'Where would you start?' asked Bernie.

Difficult. I could have considered searching for fingerprints, but I knew they would be too busy to bother with just an attempt, where nothing had been stolen. No point in making enquiries nearby; no residences overlooked the scene.

'Dunno,' I admitted.

'Me neither,' said Bernie. 'Let's go for a coffee.'

So off we went, to a snug coffee bar. Different from the regimentation of uniformed duties, where a cuppa was taken covertly, where you were still liable to be called on your PR. Here we could take our time, read the paper, liaise with store detectives (who happened to be women). Then proceed to the next scene of crime. Find a clue somewhere and we were off, working all the hours God sent for a result. This is the life, I thought, so I opened an account at Hepworths the tailors. (I couldn't afford to pay cash for a new suit).

This freedom of movement extended to disappearing acts, mainly on lates. Some would slink off for a quiet pint, or simply disappear. Fred, a DC, would vanish around seven, and re-emerge again at 8.30. As he was tall, dark and handsome we assumed there was a woman somewhere. Many a theory was offered about who it might be. Fred offered no explanation, but then he wouldn't, would he? This mystery continued for over a year, before I happened to be the one to uncover it by chance. See later for the result!

The minute a newcomer like me came along someone like Sid – the detective sergeant I mentioned – wanted to sound you out. The ritual was well known. You'd be crouched over your desk around eight in the evening ticking off the boxes on a mountain of crime reports saying you'd searched the scene of every crime when Sid would appear.

'Put your coat on bonny lad.'

You put your coat on.

'Time to visit a few hostelries,' said Sid. It was right we visited the pubs; there should be no public place out of bounds to the police. Sid led me to Pub No. 1.

'What's your poison?' he asked.

'Half of shandy, thanks Sarge.'

'Two pints of bitter please,' said Sid to the barmaid. Then he spoke to me *sotto voce*.

'No rank in here lad. First names only.'

Calling a sergeant by his first name was like calling the Duke of Edinburgh Phil. I forced myself.

'Righto… Sid.'

A full pint of bitter. I took a sip.

'Ready?'

I looked to see Sid wiping froth from his mouth, his glass empty.

'C'mon,' he was saying, 'Got to do the round.'

I gulped it down. Next pub, my round. Another two pints, Sid at express speed. Four pints later I was back in the office. Pissed, and still not nine o' clock.

'Right,' Sid was saying. 'I'm off. Make sure you hand over to the night shift at ten.'

'Right Sid.'

Right *sergeant*,' said Sid.

He knew everyone, did Sid, meaning all the criminals who frequented the city centre. They knew him, too. Everywhere you went with Sid, villains nodded and spoke. Stopped and chatted even.

'Why are they all so friendly to Sid,' I asked a colleague once.

'You know he's called the Gurkha?'

I did, and asked why.

'He takes no prisoners,' came the reply.

No wonder they liked him.

Jack was a detective sergeant too, one of the most laid-back human beings I have ever met. He would hang around the office all day. You might ask how he made the rank. Let me make something clear: ability isn't always a factor in an officer getting promoted, and this goes right up the scale. Some would make excellent senior officers but don't pass the qualifying promotion examinations; some are promoted because they have a degree in agriculture or something equally useful in the fight against crime. And there's the freemasons, those stalwarts whose 'achievements' are won through ritual and favoured contact. But more of that later.

One small incident summed Jack up perfectly. I was up to the eyes in paperwork, answering telephones, ticking off crime reports, dealing with an urgent case due to be heard before the magistrates, searching for a brush to stick up my backside and sweep the floor at the same time. I told Jack I had to shoot out to take a statement. Jack, laid-back so far he was almost falling over, took a drag on his ciggy.

'Mmm... Pop into the market on your way back and get me a cabbage, there's a good chap.'

The DI was God. To an aide, even higher. He was a typical wheeler-dealer, with a keen eye on the detection rate. If you spoke to him it had to be important. What you *never* did was call him at home, especially in the middle of the night. The only possible reason for ringing would be a murder, or the abduction of the Queen. Ring him for anything less and there'd be hell to pay. Today, too many ring the DI instead of engaging their own brains first, making decisions for themselves.

A high standard of court files was required, meaning no spelling mistakes and no bad grammar. A file would be returned by the sergeant if it wasn't up to scratch. When you got your file past the sergeant there was still the DI, who read every one. That was a lot in Newcastle Central. One day, the DI breezed into the office and tossed one of my files on to my desk.

'Use words in the English language, clever dick' he declared.

I looked to find a red circle around 'juxtaposition'. I had the audacity to return it, with a note: *Juxtaposition: closeness, contact, propinquity (Oxford dictionary)*. It came back with a note, written in bold, red handwriting: *Funny hat, woolly suit, nightshift*. I got the message.

I worked hard throughout my aideship, and was successful, not surprising for someone working in the centre of a city like Newcastle where you'd fall over prisoners if you were blindfold. There were some interesting and unusual cases, not least to do with shoplifting. Shoplifting, incidentally, is another reason to scorn the so-called detection rate. How many shopliftings are there in a city in the course of a day? No-one knows. Almost all which come to light are 'detected', those that don't – the vast majority – aren't. So, they aren't recorded. Anyway, one Christmas I became aware of someone who was regularly at it. I'll call him Maurice. Someone pointed him out to me, so I knew who to look out for. And there he was, in Fenwicks.

As I watched, Maurice picked up the *Beano Annual*, stuffed it up his jumper and left the store with paying for it. I stopped him in Northumberland Street.

'Have you taken any property from Fenwick's?'

He looked me straight in the eye.

'No.'

'Are you carrying a book anywhere on your person?'

'No.'

I slipped the *Beano* from beneath his jumper.

'I don't know how it got there,' said Maurice, straight-faced.

I arrested him and searched his flat. There were over a hundred books belonging to the Central and University Libraries, countless religious books from various bookstores, and a hundred or so *Playboy* and *Men Only* mags. All nicked. Maurice was a paid-up member of the Kleptomania Club (Books Division), obviously. 'I like books but I can't afford them,' he explained. Then he opened one of the books, a hardback on poetry. 'They printed one of mine,' he said proudly, turning to the relevant page. So they had.

I returned the books to their owners. Not one knew of any loss. Then Maurice handed me a hard-backed dictionary which, he assured me, he'd bought. As he'd readily admitted stealing the others it seemed unlikely he'd lie over one book. Inside the front cover he'd written: 'To Paul, with best wishes.' My look must have said *why?*

'You treated me right,' he said. I knew what he meant.

Maurice is black and, as he explained, he'd always lived in the belief that police were racist, that he'd been surprised at the fair treatment he'd been given after his arrest – by uniform station staff and CID. He was amazed when I went into the witness box and told magistrates he'd made 'full and frank' admissions, that every book he'd stolen had been returned to its owner, factors which the magistrates must have taken into account when putting him on probation. I've never understood how one person can be prejudiced against another because of the colour of his or her skin. They might as well be prejudiced against people who happen to be left handed, for what sense it makes.

In a sense, Maurice was a one-off, meaning shoplifters are usually arrested by store detectives, not police. But on another occasion, by chance, I happened along – it was Fenwicks again – just as a schoolboy was helping himself at the stationery display. It was obvious he wasn't going to pay. I watched as he slipped pens and pencils up his sleeve, a rubber or two into a pocket, a pencil sharpener here, a ruler there. I interrupted him, told him who I was and what I'd seen. He turned ashen.

Busy detectives know the feeling: you're up to your arse in alligators, and the last, the very last thing you need is a juvenile who's just nicked a shopping list of nothing. My duty was to arrest him, of course, and to call staff to take formal statements. But I hesitated.

'Either put 'em back or I'm taking you to the police station.'

It was his turn to hesitate. He still needed convincing I knew for sure what he'd done. I tugged his sleeve. Pens and pencils clattered to the floor. It was time for tears.

I looked at him, felt pity. I knew lots of kids were at it, partly to make a few bob, but mainly out of bravado – like the time I once pinched a jam roly-poly from our local Co-op (I was only seven). Anyway, I made him put all the property back on to the shelf and let him go. In later years I wondered if he ever looked back, thought the copper who gave him another chance was okay. Or was he at it again ten minutes later? I'll never know.

I didn't dare tell the DI. All those lost detections…

Then there was the man who stole clothes. He was 70, and when we turned his house over we found over thirty suits, 90 pairs of shoes, countless ties, handkerchiefs, underpants, shirts, socks. He could have opened a tailor's. He'd also nicked over five hundred paperbacks from shops everywhere, as well as after-shave, shampoo, razors, stationery, etc. It took three Transit loads to recover it all to the nick. 'And I've been telling him off for wasting money,' said his wife, shaking her head.

He needed help, not punishment. Not because of age, let it be said, but because anyone who steals that much property and sticks it in the wardrobe isn't stealing for profit. They're stealing because there's something the matter with them. They put him on probation too. Like Maurice, he offered me a book, but as it was one of those he nicked, I had to decline. The author was Mickey Spillane, so I wasn't racked with disappointment.

Another shoplifter was a young woman of nineteen who'd been caught stealing nail varnish. She'd put up a fight in the store, so I was surprised to find she was training for a position with the church. Few were cautioned in those days, so she had to go to court. Because of her position, I was obliged to notify the church authorities she'd been convicted of a criminal offence. This rule applies to several professions: medical, law, teaching and so on. I told her the news and she was beside herself. Obviously, the disclosure of her conviction could end her career.

'Please don't tell them,' she begged on the pavement outside the Court.

'It's my duty,' I said.

'Please…'

She looked me in the eye, then moved closer, the sweet smell of her perfume wafting into my nostrils.

'I'll do *anything.*'

As though a young thing of 19 could possibly influence me…

I told her not to worry, never reported her to the authorities. Should have, I suppose, but I hadn't the heart. I just hope the church weren't let down by my dereliction of duty.

It was during my aideship that I helped deal with my first suicide. Someone had gone to the gents toilets in the Central railway station, and opened the cubicle door to find a chap sitting on the loo. As you might expect, his trousers were around his ankles. As you might not expect, his jumper was pulled up over his head, a polythene bag was pulled over that, and he was dead. In such cases, police must suspect foul play. Eddie, a detective sergeant, and I went to the post-mortem, my first. There was a certain clinical atmosphere about it all, as the top of chummy's head was removed with a sort of circular saw, and his brains placed on to a table. Then they peeled back the skin across his chest and cracked his ribs with a pair of giant bolt-croppers, which they removed to permit access to vital organs. All very neat and professional. The pathologist showed us the contents of his stomach, which contained the partly-digested baked beans he'd had for breakfast. Then he methodically sliced up the organs: liver, kidneys, heart, and so on.

The purpose, of course, is to determine cause of death, which in this case was closure of the windpipe. Chummy had gone to the gents, pulled his pullover and polythene bag over his head and probably masturbated. It's a known fact that a degree of suffocation stimulates an erection (I read it somewhere). Unfortunately for him he suffocated completely. Still, he probably died happy.

As far as employing real detective ability was concerned, I was pleased at the outcome of a case of theft and deception. Someone was stealing unused cheques from the nurses' lockers in the Physiotherapy Department at the Royal Victoria Infirmary. One-off cheques were being taken from the middle of cheque books, so the owner wouldn't notice anything until weeks later when a bank statement would show a strange transaction. Seventy nurses had access, so there were seventy suspects. The cheques were being used to obtain cash and goods. Whoever it was left no fingerprints.

I went to security and asked to see samples of handwriting. I'm no expert, but even so it was possible to eliminate around three-quarters of the 'suspects' by careful examination of their handwriting, which I did methodically with a magnifying glass, much to the amusement of colleagues who began dubbing me Sherlock. Then I checked the dates when nurses were on duty or off duty, or away on leave, until, in the end, only a dozen possibles remained. I visited the banks and shops where the cheques had been passed, trying to obtain a description of the suspect. This proved difficult; the transactions were always weeks before, and staff couldn't remember faces, understandably.

One by one, I managed to eliminate all bar one. I decided she was the culprit and sent for her. She flatly denied it but I arrested her and took her in. When it came to formal interview the look on her face said it all. It's a look I'd see a lot more of over the years. It says 'guilty', and detectives everywhere will know what I mean. It's not admissible in evidence, of course, and more is the pity. She'd stolen the cheques, she said, because her father, who was a doctor, refused to send her enough money. Dad repaid all the money to her victims and she was put on probation. (Today she would be provided with a solicitor, who'd tell her to say nothing, in which event I would probably have failed to secure the truth).

All good things come to an end, and when it did Malcolm, another aide, and I had to return to uniform duties. There were two places awaiting us: one as a panda driver, the other on the dreaded 16-beat (Denys had moved on). I was eager now to have a crack at a panda car, but so was Mal. The sergeant told us to sort it out ourselves, but we couldn't.

'Right,' said the sergeant. 'There's nothing for it but to toss a coin.'

I called.

'Tails.'

It was heads.

Only those who have experienced it can know how it feels to revert to uniform duties after a spell in CID. I mean no disrespect. It's just you succeeded in doing what you wanted and now you're back where you started. In my case it was worse, for I was banished to 16-beat. But I was a man with experience. I'd be wasted on 16-beat. I went to see Chief Inspector Coan.

'I want a panda,' I demanded.

He frowned, meaning a young whippersnapper like me shouldn't 'want' anything, never mind I used to take him to his home for lunch in the GP. I gave my reasons anyway, put forward a compelling case. He heard me out, waited a moment, as though carefully considering the position, then slowly leaned forward, placing his elbows firmly on his desk.

'You've been put on 16-beat for a reason,' he said.

I waited for the earth-shattering proclamation that must be coming.

'The fact is, we want an experienced man down there. The sergeant and I deliberated long and hard to find someone.' He sat back in his chair, pointed a finger.

'That man is *you*!'

It must have been a double-headed coin.

*

It was just over a year before I returned to CID, this time as Temporary Detective Constable (TDC). When I did it was the mixture as before...

Someone was stealing money from handbags in an office. There was no obvious suspect. Liz, a voluptuous blonde of twenty, always had a smile, might have been the last person you'd think would steal her colleagues' money. For reasons I cannot define, I fancied her (for the thefts), which were pretty mean, actually.

The thefts were inconsistent, and liable to occur at any time, then not for ages afterwards. New-fangled at the time was the process of treating money with an invisible flourescent powder, and placing it into a purse. When the thief took the money, her hands would make contact with the powder which, unknown to her, would be smeared all over her clothing, hair, everywhere. She would then be exposed under the glow of an infra-red lamp.

Trap sprung, I went to the scene. It was just a matter of wheeling everyone in, one by one, and switching on the infra-red.

I asked Liz if she was responsible. She would never do such a thing, she declared. In that case she would have no objection to the infra-red light being shone on to her person. Of course not, she said. She was so confident I decided it couldn't be her, but switched on the light anyway. There was no mistake as she glowed brightly under the infra-red. It looked as though she'd had a going-over with a highlighter pen. When she realised the game was up, she admitted all the thefts and said she was sorry, explaining she found it hard to make ends meet – paying for her clothes and flashy lifestyle. I told her she should be saying sorry to her workmates, not me.

Months later, I happened to bump into Liz on the street. She was wearing smart clothes and a lovely smile.

'Hello,' she said, as though we'd once met socially somewhere.

'How's things?' I asked (as you do).

'Great,' she replied, adding that she was making lots of money now. 'I pose nude at a gallery in Jesmond,' she explained. I quite believed it.

'It's art, you see.'

I saw.

'D'you want the address?' she asked, enticingly. I had to admit I wouldn't mind, and said so. But I was on the wrong tack.

'So you can pose too.'

'What, me? Who'd want to look at me nude?'

'You'd be surprised,' she said with an air of conviction. So would Superintendent Wade. He might turn a blind eye to fixing washing machines and installing ring mains, but I doubted if he'd appreciate one of his DC's posing starkers, even in the cause of art. Anyway, I declined her kind offer.

C was at it on a daily basis in three specific locations: the polytechnic, the university and the Royal Victoria Infirmary. His MO was to wander at large, purporting to be a student or workman; when I saw him one day in the infirmary he was passing off as a doctor wearing a white coat! He'd steal anything he could get his hands on, usually women's purses or coats from temporarily unoccupied offices. He was a real gent. Well, if he was persistent, so was I. The more times he stole the more times I arrested him. It was just a matter of keeping my eyes peeled and giving him a pull. In the end he complained of harassment. How can it be harassment when every time you're stopped you've got stolen property in your pocket or you're wearing it? One day I caught him with two coats he'd stolen from the poly. As we had got to know one another quite well by this time I asked him why he did it.

'Eighty percent of the wealth is owned by twenty percent of the population,' he replied. He was right. That's what they teach you in sociology. (If he'd a degree he could join the job and get rapid promotion).

'Did you learn that at the poly or the university?' I asked, knowing he visited both.

'It's alright for you,' he sneered. 'You've got a job.'

'What about the students?' I asked. 'Or the nursing staff at the hospital? They work hard for a living and you steal their property.'

'They've got jobs too,' he explained.

So, if you earned a living you were a suitable target.

At court his solicitor put forward his theory about the imbalance of wealth.

'My client is one of the have-nots,' the court was told. The magistrates fined him anyway. So now he had even less. Another reason to steal, I suppose.

Another case concerned a man who was forever sneaking into ladies' toilets to peer over the top of a cubicle when someone was spending a penny. One night, in a city-centre restaurant, a woman saw him and told her boyfriend. Responding to the call of a disturbance, I came to his rescue just as a group of blokes were about to murder him. When the inevitable reports came in you knew it was him because, strangely, no-one else seemed to be doing it. They always sent for me to deal, as he got to know me and always admitted it. (The DI regarded it as a waste of a detective's time because it didn't count for crime statistics). When I asked him why he kept on doing it he said it gave him lots of sexual gratification. I said he should get help. He said he'd had help.

'They made me look at men's magazines,' he explained, 'then they put electrode things on my bollocks.'

'And?'

'They switched the current on.'

'Did it hurt?' I asked. Okay, it was a stupid question.

'The idea was to put me off sex,' he explained. It didn't do any good, obviously.

Not all my efforts turned to gold. Take the case of the handbag thefts at the *Haymarket* cinema. Somebody was creeping up in the dark in the stalls and nicking handbags belonging to young women who, at the relevant time, were distracted, either by events on the screen or by the attention they were getting from their boyfriends. The handbags were always found in an alley outside, minus cash and anything of value, of course. What was needed was a cunning plan. I was just the man.

I checked the crime reports, and saw that all thefts occurred Mondays to Thursdays. Not Fridays and over the weekend, when it was busy.

I went to the Policewomen's Department. Could I 'borrow' a woman officer for obbos in the *Haymarket*? She'd have to wear a civilian coat over her uniform, I added. There were no shortage of volunteers (from the three available). Must be my charisma, I thought, without realising the film showing that week was *Magnum Force* with Clint Eastwood. Anyway, on a quiet Monday evening I went to the pictures with a pretty young thing and her handbag.

We plonked ourselves in the middle somewhere and settled down to watch the film. I realised if I kept looking round for the suspect I'd soon show out, so focused on the film like everyone else. My worry was the thief would steal the handbag without either of us realising it. That would be a disaster, both in terms of failure to catch him, and explaining it to my colleagues afterwards. So I told her to stick one of her ankles through the looped handle of her bag, and if anyone tried to slide it from the floor from the row behind she was to whisper *now* into my earhole, at which point I would leap bravely over the seat and arrest the villain.

We sat through the entire length of the film. Apart from enjoying the sight of Clint bumping off a load of bent cops, the whole venture was a waste of time. Still, as my woman colleague explained, it was a change for her and I did buy her an ice cream.

I was at it again the following evening, this time with a different WPC. Unfortunately, her bag didn't have a looped strap, so we had to tie it round her ankle with string. Clint was his usual, brilliant self, but that's all. Nothing untoward again. I tried again. Nothing. I was getting strange looks from the WPC's, so I showed them the crime reports to prove my good intentions. Thursday I was landed with a shoplifter and couldn't make it. And guess what: the thief struck.

He stole three handbags. My colleagues, by this time of the view that I was either an ardent Clint Eastwood fan or simply on to a good thing – taking attractive young women to the pictures and getting paid for it – had a good laugh at my expense. I said it was rotten luck I missed out. One said I must be showing out as old bill. 'You should act natural,' he said, meaning I should do what any other male would be doing at the pictures: kiss my girlfriend.

Monday, the following week: another young WPC to the *Haymarket*. Sadly, Clint had moved on, and we were stuck with Reg Varney in *Holiday on the Buses*. Needless to say, there wasn't quite the same attraction but, as I explained, it was as much her duty as mine to catch the thief. Actually, the Policewomen's

Department to a woman were pleased that someone was putting in so much time and effort to catch the toad who was stealing handbags. After all, they went to the pictures with their boyfriends too.

'We must act natural,' I told my new accomplice, adding that kissing me was a better option than watching Reg Varney. Strangely, she made no comment.

Kissing someone whilst at the same time waiting for her leg to be tugged by a handbag thief felt a bit like fishing: you wait ages, hoping for a bite, then... bingo! Unfortunately, our fish never took the bait; we kissed and kissed until, quite honestly, we'd had enough. It's true. Kissing the one you love is one thing, kissing an attractive 20-year old in the course of your duty can be a right pain. And no-one tried to pinch her handbag.

Undaunted, I was back the following evening with the same woman officer. We tried a few token kisses, then concentrated on Reg Varney. Nothing. I decided there was nothing for it but to try again. *Never* give up! But, next evening, no WPC's were available. Whether this was the fault of Reg Varney or the way I kiss wasn't clear. So I went on my own, sitting towards the back where I could keep and eye on courting couples. I felt like a peeping tom and when, again, the thief failed to appear I decided I'd had enough. It was a good effort: there can't be many who can claim to have sat through *Holiday on the Buses* three times.

A few nights later the thief struck again. He was collared by some blokes who grabbed the stolen handbag. Unfortunately he made his escape, never to return.

Not all forces have a night-shift CID, but they should. Crime doesn't stop at ten o' clock, midnight, whatever. Okay, you can't investigate much at three o' clock in the morning, but prisoners still get arrested then, for burglary and violence mainly. Nowadays, some custody sergeants 'lie them down' for the night, give them their 'rest'. This is ridiculous: if they're out committing crime they don't need rest. Okay, there's not much you can do if they're drunk, they have to wait until morning then.

We kept ourselves busy nights, no problem. Even if it was quiet, you could get a young, eager officer to put on a civvy jacket and go on crime patrol in an unmarked car, a great learning experience. Plenty of criminals carry stolen property in the boots of their cars. When they move about they should do so with the fear of a 'pull'; police shouldn't wait for things to happen first. If things were quiet, we'd rendezvous with beat officers. Uniform-CID liaison is vital, yet it wasn't always possible. The two departments were kept apart, as though the CID were some kind of elite, which they are not, and the uniform section didn't matter, which they do. For the record, I always believed the patrol officer is the most important man/woman in the force, and still do.

Nights could be quiet. If so, it provided an opportunity to deal with the homos who frequented the gents' toilets. You'd see them hanging around street corners, looking for a mate. Cruising, they call it nowadays. Some people think there's no harm; personally, I think it's a bit much when you go for a pee only for some bloke to appear at the next urinal. Never mind there are plenty others, all unoccupied. At first he stands there, facing the wall, as though the purpose of his visit is the call of nature. Then his gaze slowly turns to you, and a faint smile appears (on his face, not yours). Slowly, he lowers his eyes, only to find himself staring at your warrant card. Horror of horrors!

They even cut holes into the partition dividing the cubicles. As you sit on the loo an eye appears at the hole. Or a note is slipped through. Once, a colleague, on duty, in uniform, had occasion to pay a visit and found himself staring at an erect penis, inserted through the hole for his benefit. As he explained, it was the only time he'd ever used his truncheon. They even installed brick partitions, only for the holes to reappear. Someone must have used a hammer and chisel!

The *Plain Clothes* department dealt with soliciting males. They'd usually be two-up in a cubicle, masturbating, sucking, going all the way (the homos, that is). Most were married men, presumably out for something different. They were from all walks of life. One, a prominent member of a local council, turned up at the enquiry counter one night, asking to speak to a detective, 'in confidence'. He said the impending court case was certain to attract the attention of the press, and could I keep them out to prevent his wife and family finding out about his arrest. I told him it's a free country and I could not. He was so distraught I would have, if I could.

Incidentally, as nightshift detectives, when I said 'deal with', I meant we'd nip into the loo, wait for the inevitable company and tell them to scram. In my opinion, these guys are a nuisance. But they aren't criminals. They seek a partner and, as I said, it's a free country, except public toilets are not the place to look. If they had somewhere else to go they wouldn't be in public toilets in the first place.

All this detective work, and I still hadn't been to the detective training centre at Wakefield. Finally, I went there in 1972. The course was intensive and lasted ten weeks. It was crucial to do well, both in the examinations and overall course work. We knew if we failed our careers as detectives would be over. I aimed to be top of my class, a tall order, but if you reach for something you can still achieve even if it's not the ultimate prize. I'd passed the Inspector's examination the previous year, so I was well clued up.

Not that everyone was bent on studying the finer points of the criminal law. To see some guys unleashed onto the fleshpots of Wakefield beggared belief. Shackled by their wives and the job, they were now free to get as much alcohol into their bellies as possible, and visit the local Mecca, where the women of Wakefield and District were waiting on what was cruelly but not without justification called 'Grab-a-Granny' night. The local ladies knew there was a new course, knew the names of the course instructors, knew whoever they teemed up with that night was theirs for ten weeks. Relationships developed right, left and centre. Men talked of leaving their wives, transferring to West Yorkshire, emigrating with their new-found loved ones to Bermuda. Talked, that is, under the affluence of incahol. Next day in class, throbbing heads gave way to reason, in most cases anyway.

The standard of instruction in criminal law and detective skills at the West Yorkshire Training School was superb. Studying was a natural response to the commitment given by the training school staff. In particular, I was helped by a book, a sort of Bible, on the relatively new Theft Act. Except, that is, in respect of Section 11 –

Removal of Articles from Public Display, a piece of legislation which, despite analysing every aspect of the Section, and even taking it to bed with me, was beyond me and everyone else I have ever known in my life. I should like to meet whoever drafted Section 11, preferably on a dark night when I happen to be carrying a machete.

Best of all on the course were the talks, given in the lecture theatre by experienced detectives. They showed us pictures of murder victims, told us why it was vital to preserve a scene for clues, gave detailed accounts on how such and such a murder was detected and so on.

You see drama on tv, but this was the real thing with real people. It brought tears to our eyes: on the screen a little girl, abducted, raped and strangled, and left on a rubbish tip, her decaying body found weeks later; a young woman, raped and strangled, her nipples bitten off, teeth-marks in her breasts providing the damming clue to her attacker's identity; charred bodies in a burnt-out house, victims of an arsonist. We learnt that most murders are committed by someone known to the victim, that if you haven't identified the offender in the first 24 hours the killer will be a stranger and it will be difficult to solve. We learned, too, of the harrowing scenes we would face sooner or later in our careers, if we hadn't faced them already. Like the plane that crashed at Stockport and burst into flames. The pilot had radioed ahead to say it was coming down, and police were waiting to witness the terrified and futile attempts of trapped passengers being roasted alive before their eyes. We were shown slides of the charred bodies lying on the runway, every one in a defensive, curled up position. I knew I'd see lots of death as a policeman, but my one fervent prayer was that I'd never witness anyone being burned alive. For the record, my prayer was answered, though other incidents over the years would be bad enough.

One senior detective expressed the belief that no murderer should ever be released from prison, no matter what. Maybe he was right, but you can get caught up with emotion, see revenge as justice. Maybe it is. I believe it's true that most police officers support hanging, at least for murder in the furtherance of gain, and possibly killing children. I never have, not because I feel anything for the perpetrators of serious crimes – as far as I'm concerned those who commit such crimes deserve to be strung up – but out of fear that maybe there was a mistake, that the person charged is innocent. To take the life of an innocent prisoner is as bad as taking the life of anyone, and I shudder at the thought of being an investigating detective in any such case.

There was much discussion at the time on the subject when, by chance, a newspaper revealed Myra Hindley had been permitted to go for a walk in a park with Lord Longford. This was just seven years after she and Ian Brady were convicted of torturing and murdering children. Public outcry saw her back behind bars. No, I wouldn't hang 'em, but I wouldn't let 'em out either. Not people like that. Yet paedophiles who, in more recent times, have tortured and killed, even sold video-recordings of their wicked deeds for gain afterwards, have long since been released, serving only a fraction of the time Hindley has spent in prison.

I came sixth in the final exam, only a few points behind the top man. Top *officer* I should say, for there were three women on the course.

*

She was old and frail, and to the best of my knowledge had never hurt anyone in her life. But Polly was attacked and left to die in a quiet lane next to the new stand at St James's Park. She was alive when they found her, and even hospital staff thought she'd simply fallen and cut her head. It wasn't until they examined her more closely they saw she'd been stabbed four times through the skull with a long, narrow-bladed knife. It was my first murder enquiry. What motive could there have been in killing her on that hot summer's afternoon? Her assailant must have been a madman. Or woman, I suppose.

Despite its proximity to the busy streets of the city centre, the lane was a backwater, used as a short cut by residents of St Thomas's area, university students from Leazes Terrace Hall of

Residence, and down and outs who called at the Cyrenian shelter for soup and a bed. The scene provided no clues. The lane was narrow, cobbled, hemmed in by the towering wall of the east stand of the football ground and a high wall opposite. There was no sign of any weapon. All we had to go on was the knowledge that Polly lived in St Thomas's, and the list of 'suspects': local residents, students and tramps.

It's usual on such enquiries to set up a 'major incident room'. In this case there were two: one at the police station, the other in the directors' box of the old stand at the football ground, available because it was summertime. (So *this* was the view they got of the pitch!). The work, particularly in the first weeks, was intense, the first time I had known constant twelve-hour shifts, seven days a week. It was the hardest I had worked in my life, the first time I had come to know the meaning of stress, although I didn't recognise it as such in those days. As for our suspects:

The local residents were mainly old people, naturally shocked at what had happened to Polly, a woman in her eighties. One old biddy had known her for years. As she stood barefoot on the bare linoleum of her gloomy parlour, she gave whatever info she could, at the same time stepping with great accuracy and purpose onto huge cockroaches as they traversed the floor.

'Polly was a lovely old soul.'

Crack!

'Never had a bad word about anyone.'

Crack!

'Wouldn't hurt a fly.'

Crack!

What about a cockroach?

Alas, other than murdering the hapless beetles, she was unable to provide anything useful, except a lingering memory.

From the local population, a suspect was identified. S had lived at the same address, and knew Polly. His room was searched, but there was no trace of any weapon or blood-stained clothing. He could not provide an alibi, but then many others couldn't either. Police put so much pressure on him he finally admitted it, but then so did a man in Exeter whose reason for doing so was to obtain a lift to Newcastle, courtesy of police, whereupon he retracted his story! R was released, but remained a suspect.

The students were helpful. We – the enquiry teams – began to suspect this one or that, without any real evidence to back up our claims. It might have been a woman, yet at no point did we feel it was. Again, no evidence to back up any theory.

We turned the Cyrenian shelter over nightly, hoping to discover the culprit or weapon. We never did. Some of the old tramps were men of violence, with criminal records or medical histories. One, known as 'Sir John' by the enquiry teams, stepped forward and sent my clipboard spinning through the air, then gave me a strange, faraway look! It seemed a fair bet that the killer must come from their midst, but there was no evidence to prove it, nor single out one from the others.

One feature of the investigation was a red lorry, allegedly seen about the time of the murder. Whether it actually existed is doubtful, but because we were so desperate for information, it took centre stage, with great efforts made to trace it and its owner. If nothing else, it served to prove just how easily police enquiries might lead down the wrong track, that almost everything seems to depend on one thing – as it might, if there's nothing else. Like the infamous 'Yorkshire Ripper' enquiry, when an unidentified man with a Sunderland accent telephoned the police. '*I'm Jack,*' he said, taunting the police. Everything went into trying to identify the man, whose voice was heard on the news. In fact, the Ripper was Peter Sutcliffe, who wasn't from Sunderland at all. As for our lorry, I wonder if there ever was one.

S was taken in again, and again admitted the murder, stating he'd thrown the murder weapon over the wall into the football ground. It so happened they were building a new stand at the time, and since the murder the entire area had been concreted. A decision, therefore, for the hierarchy: to dig it all up at great expense – or not. What if S had just *said* he'd thrown the knife over the wall? Prisoners who are repeatedly questioned are liable to say anything to get you off their backs. In the end they decided against it, let S go. Poor Polly: we never did work it out. But for me it was a great learning curve: the need to take comprehensive and accurate statements, for persistence, to continuously apprise others of how the enquiry as a whole is progressing – there's nothing worse than the right hand not knowing what the left hand is doing. Above all, perhaps, the need to keep an open mind at all times, that nothing is as straightforward as it appears.

One piece of information came to light on the enquiry. There was a nearby bingo hall, where we called one evening to speak to staff.

'Do you know a detective called Fred,' asked a woman member of staff. Tall, dark and handsome Fred. The detective who kept disappearing.

'He comes here evenings to play bingo,' she said with a smile.

Like I said: nothing is as straightforward as it appears.

*

Informants are the life-blood of a good detective. What better way can there be to detecting crime and arresting criminals than to have specific information? An offender's wife or girlfriend, an accomplice, someone who *knows*?

There was a red telephone in the CID general office. It was supposed to be for the exclusive and confidential use of informants, and took incoming calls only. I say supposed to be because, frankly, it seldom rang. In fact, I was taken aback when, unexpectedly, it rang one day. I picked up the bright red receiver.

'Is Bob there?' asked the husky voice of a female. Sounded around thirty. Bob wasn't in and there was no message.

The red phone rang again from time to time, and when I picked it up it was always the same woman. Some of the lads had taken her calls too. When Bob was able to take the call he always whispered softly into the phone. I wondered who she was until, one night, I caught Bob in intimate conversation with a woman in a city nightclub. When he saw me, he fronted their embarrassment by making a prompt introduction.

'This is Paul,' he announced, as though pleased to see me. She offered a tiny hand.

'Hi there!' she purred, her smile belying her equally obvious embarrassment. Where *had* I heard that voice before?

My own efforts at cultivating a 'snout' began with a young drop-out lass at the university. She'd failed economics or something, so (like others) had rescued her student status by taking art. I'd got to know her when I was investigating some thefts.

'If you hear anything about crime, let me know,' I said. She didn't know what I meant. I told her she'd get paid if she provided me with information. She told me she never heard anything. Just keep your ears open, I said, giving her the number of the red phone. All she did was offer me a free copy of the *Socialist Worker*. I didn't know what I was doing, went about it wrong. Someone said women make the best informants, and I can now say that in my case at least there was never a truer word. I always kept their identities a secret, even from my colleagues, and I guess I'd better do so now.

The first was Clare, a barmaid with form for burglary, theft, and assault, including assault on police officers. I decided she'd make a good 'snout', but how could I persuade her to talk to me? Walking alone into the pub where she worked wasn't something to be taken lightly. I knew the second my face appeared I'd be identified as old bill, my presence hardly welcomed by the patrons, most of whom, at one time or another, would have faced Sid and the line in the cell block. Anyway, having made eye contact with Clare, I made repeated visits to the pub, always alone. That way my face became familiar, not only to her, but also the locals who would no longer turn their heads when I walked in. If familiarity breeds contempt, it also breeds indifference: when you walk into a room, all eyes turn, but if you stand there long enough, everyone gets on with drinking and talking, you become part of the scenery. All I had to do was break the ice with Clare. I waited for the right moment; it came one quiet night in the pub.

As she poured me a half, I asked her if she would like one too, and what she thought about the record that was playing, *The Road to Inverness*. It was *always* playing! She said it was OK. I said she looked the type who'd be into classic stuff. And blah, blah, blah. It went from there. I didn't push it, left it at that, returned another time to renew acquaintance. Of course, this was far removed from her kindly providing the names and addressed of persons breaking into houses, but it was a start. To get her on her own was the objective. The chance came when she mentioned something about seeing a friend of hers up the west end the following afternoon, and what a pain it was cos she had to change buses to get home.

'What a coincidence,' I lied. 'I'm up that way tomorrow. Can I give you a lift?'

And Clare, who hated old bill, turned out to be someone who wanted to talk, wasn't such a bad stick after all. I quickly discovered two things: she knew lots of criminals, and when you meet someone on level terms and form your own judgements, people can be very different from what you were led to believe. If I'd had to arrest her in the first instance, she would have been hostile (though long-term might still have come round, as many informants do), but because I gave her a lift, because I talked to her, we got along fine.

But, just then, fate took a hand. They went and posted me to Special Branch.

4

"I know it's a secret. It's whispered everywhere"

William Congreve

The Vickers Viscount dropped noisily behind the terminal building, a sight I had seen many times from my position of advantage on the top deck of the No. 5 bus out of the Haymarket. It was the plane I'd come to meet, or rather its occupants, arriving in England on their flight from Belfast. In times of terrorism, it was considered vital. Sadly, the bus and aircraft timetables weren't compatible. Usually, by the time I reached Arrivals lounge, the only person I was likely to encounter was the cleaner.

The explanation was simple: they wouldn't give us a car. By us I meant the detective constables of Special Branch (Ports) who had to make their way by public transport. Or, if we were lucky, by the car we 'shared' with the drugs squad; but this was never an option, for, as I was told by the drugs squad detective sergeant, their work was more important than ours and he was a sergeant, so there.

This was far removed from what I was told on my course at New Scotland Yard, which I attended before going into action to protect the security of the United Kingdom of Great Britain and Northern Ireland. *Special Branch* sounded very important, as it must have been to send me to the Yard, with two weeks at the Port of Dover and Heathrow Airport to follow. When my wife asked me just why I was going away for a month the only information I felt I could impart was that it was very important work and I wasn't allowed to talk about it. Looking back, she must have thought I was off to spy on the Russians.

To a bloke in his twenties living in the north-east in those days, being dispatched to London was like being posted abroad. So it was with feelings of great importance that I emerged from the Underground at East Ham, where I would be billeted at the section house for the next fortnight. It was strange, being among people whose accent I could hardly understand. I thought they'd sound all posh, like in those old British movies; but this was the east-end, Alf Garnett territory. I liked the east-end: the people, the traffic, the *feel* of it. To me, it was the capital's equivalent of Newcastle: working class people, proud of their roots and their way of life, content with their world. And, truth to tell, the difficulty I had in understanding what they were saying paled against what they went through trying to understand me. I've always been proud of my roots, so I kept telling the natives and my course colleagues that *Get Carter*, the latest movie starring Michael Caine, was made in Newcastle. It was plastered all over advertisement hoardings and the sides of London's buses. Big deal!

We were taken to the Yard every morning in an old prison bus with bars at the windows. We pretended to be convicts, grasping the bars and making threatening faces at motorists. Without exception, every one looked away from what they thought were a bunch of gangsters. On the course, we were told the security of the country was in our hands. Even if where we worked was a quiet backwater. There must be no place in Britain where criminals, terrorists, drug pushers, wanted persons, missing persons, escaped prisoners, and abducted or runaway children could enter into or leave from, nor any way in for illegal immigrants and aliens. It was no use manning the busy ports of the south-east if they could sneak in and out through the back door elsewhere.

We were given talks by high-ranking officers from this security department, that such-and-such a branch of so-and-so. There was lots of stuff about Arab terrorists and the IRA, convincing me that a mad-brained idea I had at the time to transfer on secondment to Northern Ireland was a mistake. I confined the application form to a wastebin right outside the Yard.

I kept thinking about Newcastle Airport. I used to cycle there as a kid when it was no more than a shed though by now, admittedly, it had a modern terminal building. And the Quay at North Shields, where the ferry left the Tyne for the countries of Scandinavia. What, pray, happened there to merit the policing skills of a highly-trained officer such as me? You have to guard the back door, I was reminded, and these were my back doors.

The camaraderie on the course meant pleasant evenings once we got back to our section station at East Ham. There was table tennis, dominoes, cards... It was a long fortnight, broken only by the announcement that an evening out at a disco bar in the City had been arranged. We could go on our prison bus, so we could drink as much as we liked.

It was a great night, with scantily-clad girls dancing to *Baby Jump* and *The Resurrection Shuffle*, as bright lights flashed on their gyrating limbs. With a bellyful of beer I finished up on the floor with one in a tight skirt who, when the slow stuff started, was responsive to my firm, clinging grip, as I savoured her warm, soft body in the intimate darkness, penetrated by the shafts of light reflected from a revolving globe. Surprisingly, she drew the line when I tried to kiss her, gently pushed my eager lips away with the tips of her fingers, smiling provocatively in the glare of the spotlights. Finally, after making sure she knew my manly form was responsive to her being, I made my way to my mates in the corner, disappointed that our sexual liaison would go no further.

'Cock teaser, eh?' one of the Met lads remarked, as I resigned myself to an imminent return to the fleshpots of East Ham. 'Don't worry about it,' he said, sympathetically. 'She's a bloke anyway.'

84

There was no end of course exam so, like children who know they'll not be tested on a given subject, whatever we'd been told went in one ear and out the other. We made no notes, were given none and, to be blunt, remembered sweet fanny-adams about whatever we'd been told. It came as an unpleasant shock, therefore, on the last morning, to find the course tutor placing papers face down on our desks.

'Just a little test to see how much you've learnt,' he was saying. 'Don't turn the papers over until I say so.' Our faces drained with horror. This was below the belt, to be sure.

'Right,' said our tutor, consulting his watch 'you can turn your papers over... *now.*'

When we did we found ourselves looking at blank forms and a tutor with a grin as wide as the Thames.

I spent the next week at the Port of Dover, the one after at Heathrow. Where before, at the Yard, we had just listened, here we watched real SB detectives and immigration officers in action. I don't know how much the Official Secrets Act permits me to reveal, suffice to say the point of it all was to see who was coming and going. At Dover, they were looking for drugs, hidden in secret compartments of suitcases and cars and body orifices; at Heathrow, druggies again, and international terrorists. I kept thinking of North Shields and who I might find to haul in on sus of importing heroin. The back door theory prevailed; this was important work, a new challenge. Then I got back to my force where I discovered there wasn't a car. The challenge, it seemed, was getting to the airport before that bloody plane landed.

*

At first anyone posted to SB (Ports) automatically assumes an air of self importance. One or two of my former colleagues would say hello – we were stationed in the same building – but that was as far as it would go. To questions like 'What do you actually *do*?' I could only shrug. Not that many asked. For those dealing with burglars and thieves and filling in those crime reports there wasn't

85

time for small-talk. For me, however, time quickly became something I possessed in great abundance.

How to fill time was the problem. Take an average day at the airport. There was that Belfast flight which I sometimes met if the plane was late (or the bus was early). Then, around eleven the Amsterdam flights (in and out), and nothing more until they were taking off for places like Alicante, Gerona and Barcelona – package flights, with dad, mum and the kids, young lovers and honeymoon couples, and groups of young men and women off to the sun for a good time. Sometimes my services as a policeman seemed better directed to the airport bar, where prospective passengers got sloshed awaiting their flights.

Working at the airport was like working on a Hollywood film set, the outside world a million miles away beyond the automatic doors at the entrance to the marbled concourse. Smart chicks paraded in airline uniforms and stilettos. Young blokes, looking flash and very much in charge, took on an air of authority behind check-in desks. Now and again a pilot would wander across the concourse, brief case in hand, with an 'I've just flown a bloody great jet plane in' look. Male supremacy was absolute: the guys flew the planes and were in charge on the concourse; the gals were the gofers, always smiling, strutting their stuff. Look at me, smell me. I am beautiful. They were also very professional. Any sexual approaches by the all-male SB, customs and immigration contingent were met with smiles and firm rejection. So I was told, anyway.

Hanging around the concourse was the last place for a young, dynamic policeman to be. It was the antithesis of the busy divisional work I had done before. I wanted to be busy but there was nothing to be busy with. I couldn't even spend my time studying for the exams: I'd passed them! Still, all this free time did allow us to get to know the airline staff, especially at Dan Air, where *les girls* were always prepared to put the kettle on, and when we got bored with that we perused the magazine racks, where *Playboy* and *Men Only* featured still more unattainable chicks and made us even more sexually frustrated.

Apart from boredom and sexual frustration, doing nothing when others were working for a living was downright embarrassing. The check-in girls had their heads down, checking passengers' tickets and luggage; staff on the 'enquiries' desk always seemed to have someone enquiring; *les girls* at Dan Air, whilst accommodating with coffee, had more to do than simply entertain the likes of me; security guys talked of horseracing and security, which is all very well, it's just that after 1½ minutes you tend to run out of interest; the immigration blokes had endless forms to fill in, registration cards to check. With hours to kill between flights, I had to find *something* to occupy my time. And I did: I went to see mum and dad.

Catching the bus to the airport meant you were marooned at the airport, so we'd sometimes use our own cars, claiming the busfare towards petrol costs, permission to do so being kindly granted by the chief constable or somebody. This was all very well, but driving my car, a rusty, clapped out Morris Oxford, was fraught with danger: it was always going to be a matter of time before the driver's seat fell through the floor. Coppers couldn't afford nice cars in those days (or sometimes any car at all). For the record I sold the car to a scrappy for £10, then got a pull from old bill months later after it had been seen at a school where some nutter was eyeing up the kids. Gordon Bennett!

Sadly, my visits to mum and dad did not provide solace from my airport prison. It was okay at first, being greeted with such sentiments as 'Eeh, what a surprise,' and 'Lovely to see you.' But then the warm welcome you might expect changed to 'Oh, we thought you were at work,' accompanied by frowns from dad. He never said why – well he wouldn't – but I knew why. My father left school at fourteen, worked down a black hole, crawling about on his hands and knees cutting coal. He had a cheese 'doorstep' and a bottle of water for his bait, and in the early days scrubbed himself clean in an old tub in front of the fire. And here was his son, wearing a flashy suede jacket, kipper tie and platform shoes (as you did), sat on his arse all day at the airport, drinking tea round his ma's. If my pointless, lingering presence at the airport brought embarrassment, then my pointless, lingering presence at my parents' house brought shame. I never for a minute thought my duties as a policeman would lead to that. So I stayed put at the airport, or sought out ways to do paperwork in the office in town. I wanted out of SB, but I was still a *temporary* detective, and didn't want to spoil my chances of acquiring full detective status by rocking the boat. 'Nothing is forever' someone said, so I stayed the course.

One feature of our working relationship with H.M. Immigration was the arrest and detention of persons who had arrived at the airport without sanction. Illegal immigrants, in other words. Immigration detained them (pending consultation by telephone with the Home Office), we locked them up pending a decision and the availability of the next flight. We worked well together, although when it came to understanding 'detention' and 'arrest' we were on different planets.

One day I arrived at the immigration office to find it deserted, save for the presence of an Asian man seated in the corner. The immigration blokes, I knew, would have gone for coffee, having seen in the Amsterdam flight. But who was this bloke in their office? An 'illegal', that's who. They'd detained him and were awaiting a telephone call from the Home Office about what to do. But where a police officer would have stuck like glue to a prisoner, immigration had simply swanned off for their elevenses. All the guy had to do to secure entry into the UK was open the office door, walk through the now empty immigration and customs hall and catch the No. 5 on its way back to the Haymarket.

'You can't sit there on your own,' I said.

He shrugged, pointed to his mouth. Ah, he didn't speak English. But no, he didn't mean that. He pointed to his mouth again. You've guessed it: he was hungry!

He managed to convey the fact that he hadn't eaten for days and hadn't any money. So I did what anyone else would do: took him to the cafeteria and bought him some breakfast. There was no sign of immigration, who by chance were returning to their office by a different route, only to find their man had disappeared. When they turned up in the cafeteria, their panic-stricken faces were overcome with relief when they saw him. They said I should never have taken him from the office; I said they should never have left him there in the first place.

Our head of department was Chief Inspector Dear whose main concern was the *real* Special Branch, which concerned top-secret Home Office enquires and 'overstayers' – Commonwealth citizens who hadn't returned to their native lands – and covert security matters, which usually involved the Russians. He was full of his own importance, as anyone must be when answering the telephone at home with the words 'Chief Inspector Dear's residence.' Anyway, now and again he'd take it upon himself to pay us an unscheduled visit at the airport, to try and catch us out (it was rumoured we were up to no good with those ground hostesses). Unknown to him, a discreet telephone call by a mole in the main office always tipped us off, so when he arrived we'd all be busy checking passenger lists, or in intense conversation with immigration.

All, that is, except an SB detective called Arthur who, on being tipped off about Dear's imminent arrival, would covertly observe his arrival at the main entrance, then follow him around the terminal: to the police office, immigration, customs… Eventually, Dear would give up and leave. Naturally when he saw Arthur he'd have something to say.

'Where were you yesterday?'

'At the airport, sir.'

'I was at the airport yesterday, looking for you.'

'I know that, sir.'

'You know? How do you know?'

'I was watching you, sir.'

It gave Arthur something to do, and us something to laugh about.

Arthur came up with the idea that if we caught the Barcelona flight – on duty – we could enjoy a trip to the sun for an hour so before returning on the same aircraft. He pointed out that no-one would know, as there were no other international flights in or out of the airport in the time we'd be away, time when we'd be doing absolutely nothing. 'It'll make a change from going to the coast,' he said, pointing out we could bring back some duty-free when we were about it. Sadly, where Arthur was prepared to live dangerously, I was inclined to a more cautious existence. Suppose we got stuck in Barcelona for some reason. Dear could only splutter in frustration when Arthur told him he followed him around the airport. He'd have had a fit if he discovered we'd swanned off to Spain.

Then there was Norman, an immigration officer who was small in stature and big in his hatred of Germans. Now and again, just for fun (immigration officers were bored too) Norman would talk with an exaggerated German accent. You know: 'Ve haf ways of making you talk', and 'I'll ask ze questions.' It was racist, or would have been if he had allowed his prejudice to affect his work, but of course he did not. Except once, slightly.

One morning the inward Amsterdam flight was full, and a long queue formed at immigration control. One of the officers was Norman. The 'Amsterdam', as we knew it, always carried international businessmen, and one of them, a German, happened to be near the front of the queue. We overheard him speaking to a colleague.

'Typical Eengleesh queue, hmm?'

I glanced at Norman. Predictably, he was displeased. When the German handed Norman his passport, Norman flicked through it *ever* so slowly.

'Vot iz ze reason for your visit to zis country?' asked Norman quietly, mimicking a German accent.

'I vill be staying here on business,' said the German.

Norman checked every page of the passport in silence.

'Und how long vill you be staying?'

'Von month,' replied the German, not seeing the wind-up.

Norman wasn't finished. He looked intently at the passport, as though there was a problem. The German waited.

'Hmm,' said Norman, 'Vould you vait zare please?'

He indicated a seat at the side of the room, motioned the German to sit. The poor man did so, obviously puzzled. Then Norman saw the rest of the queue through, a lengthy process, as most were foreign. When it was cleared he beckoned the German to the immigration desk. He handed the man his passport.

'So sorry to haf kept you,' he said. 'It could haf been longer. It's as vell ve queue in zis country, eh?'

I didn't actually witness the German pass through control. By then I was in the gents. I had to find somewhere to be ill with laughter.

We took our posts routinely, along with the immigration boys, and checked the passports of anyone we considered suspicious: which, on those package flights, wasn't many. Still, as we reminded ourselves, one day we just might intercept a fugitive. As they said on the course, it's no use manning the major international ports only to find criminals could sneak in by the back door. Only two routes mattered: the Belfast and the Amsterdam. The year was 1971, when the IRA were very active, so we were ever on the lookout. For this reason I was keen to check the Belfast flight, and made out a case for a car to drive to the airport to catch that early plane. In vain, I have to say.

Not that the Belfast flight concerned immigration. It's a 'domestic', so checking passengers was difficult. After all, it was no different to flying in from Glasgow or London. We'd walk out into the 'finger', the long tunnel that stretches out to the apron, and just look at the passengers. It may seem like Big Brother, but considering the horrors perpetrated by the IRA it was more than justified. In a year of service in SB I checked only a handful. They all co-operated, as any reasonable person would when innocent people were being blown to pieces. But let one thing be clear: there was no lawful authority to make any demands of passengers, not even when people were being murdered in the city from which the flight had just arrived. Co-operation was the key-word. Two incidents are worth a mention.

The first was early on in my SB career at the airport. I was trying to calculate who might be a terrorist, when a likely-looking fellow came into view. I noticed him scowl and look away when the ground hostess smiled and gave a courteous 'Good evening'. (Hostesses always smile when in action). I had no concrete reason to be suspicious, but as we had to rely on luck and judgement, I decided to check him out.

'Scuse me,' I said, flashing my i/d. 'Just a routine check. Care to tell me your business in Belfast?' I smiled too. He looked at me in total surprise.

'I'm goin' home,' he replied in broad Geordie. 'Is there a problem?'

'No sir,' said I. 'Just we have to be vigilant these days, you know...'

He knew.

'So could you tell me your business in Belfast?'

His look of surprise turned to one of anger.

'Yes I could,' he said. 'I've been to Belfast to identify my brother.'

I was looking at a man whose brother, a soldier, had been murdered by the IRA. Of all the people to check out...

I expressed suitable condolence and asked him to agree that he, more than anyone, would understand the reason for police vigilance. I am happy to say he did.

On the other occasion I was checking Police Gazettes, which we held in our airport office, when the telephone rang. Permit me to digress. Police Gazettes contain photographs of nasty men wanted for murder and robbery, mainly in London or somewhere, and dead persons found in mysterious circumstances, mainly in Wales or somewhere. They usually include the ghastly features of some poor soul whose been lying dead in a swamp for ten months, with the caption: "Do you recognise this man?" And they are handy for drawing moustaches and specs on when you get bored. What relevance these criminals and dead bodies had to an airport in the north-east you might guess at, although there was that 'back door' theory I suppose.

Our office at the airport contained six aircraft seats, a small table, a telephone and several out of date calendars whose purpose in adorning the wall allowed us to gaze at the naked women featured their pages. I felt I knew them all personally. One was called Penny Irvine, as I recall. Anyway, the purpose of the office was threefold: it was somewhere to read the aforesaid Police

Gazettes, it served as a place from which we could telephone the Yard or anywhere else on an enquiry, and it was somewhere to hang our coats. What *never* happened was the telephone ringing. Who could this possibly be? I wondered, picking up the receiver.

It was the Control Tower. The pilot of the incoming Belfast flight had radioed ahead reporting a drunken man on board. Strictly, this was a matter for the boys in division, but they'd never have reached the airport before the plane. I said I'd deal and waited in the finger. He wasn't one of those nutters who try and storm into the cockpit or assault air crews. Just a young bloke who'd got ratted. With the help of a couple of stewards, I dragged him to the police office where he promptly slumped across the aircraft seats and fell asleep. When he woke he probably thought he was still on the plane. He surveyed the office with a glazed, faraway look. Then he addressed me in his best Geordie.

'Where the hell am ah?'

I gave him the run-down, adding that it was my duty to take him in. I asked him his name, which he gave, throwing down his soldier's identity card. He'd been serving in Belfast, he said, where he spent every day on patrol under the threat of being murdered by a sniper. Some of his mates were blown up or shot. So he'd got drunk and was off home for a few days leave before returning to the front line. I thought of my own days on patrol, walking up Northumberland Street, saying good morning to the girls. Okay, I'd had moments of violence too, but against guns and bombs...

I gave him an hour to sober up, called a taxi and told the driver to take him home. For several days afterwards I worried that I might be asked to report to my superiors about the drunk on the plane, that the authorities at the airport might have referred the incident to the chief constable or something. I heard nothing further. Just as well, although I'd have been more than happy to justify my actions.

I mentioned the Amsterdam flight. It flew in from Glasgow, when everyone had to get off and pass through immigration at Newcastle before getting on again for the flight to Holland. They were businessmen mainly, and Scottish industrial workers who were working abroad. Came the day: a passenger called Johnstone was wanted!

'Wanted?' I echoed, in a way suggesting there must be a mistake.

'Hmm,' the voice confirmed, 'except the name's spelt slightly different. J.O.H.N.S.T.O.N. Without the 'E'.'

'What's he wanted for?' I asked.

'Doesn't say,' said the voice. 'You'll have to phone the local police station.'

That was up in Scotland somewhere. There wouldn't be time. Even now the aircraft was taxiing up the runway for take-off. It was time for decisive action. I rang off and went into the now-deserted departure lounge to speak to my sergeant, Tosh, but he along with a colleague and the immigration boys had long gone for coffee. It would never have occurred to them there might be a wanted man on the plane. I called the control tower, to the best of my knowledge, the first time anyone in SB at the airport had ever done so.

'The Amsterdam flight,' I said. 'There's someone on board we want taken off.' I didn't qualify the 'we', except to say I was Special Branch. 'It's cleared for take-off,' came the reply. Either I requested the return of the plane or my wanted man was going abroad. The main thought flashing through my mind as I watched the aircraft manoeuvring was: what was he wanted *for*? It could be murder, or armed robbery. If so, when I submitted my report about his passing through the airport, wouldn't someone ask why I hadn't detained him? What was the point in our daily presence here if, when something came our way, we failed to act?

'Could you order the plane back,' I asked, more in hope than expectation. I knew there were costs once a plane was cleared for take-off, that it would be expensive to get clearance a second time once my prisoner was in custody. So I was knocked over by the instant, matter-of-fact reply.

'Sure.'

The phone went dead, and I found myself standing by the baggage conveyor, alone – I mean, *really* alone – and in silence. I waited, watched the plane, now a mile away at the far end of the runway, turn and slowly taxi back towards the terminal building. It seemed an age before the crash as Tosh, my colleague, the immigration boys, the airport manager, two ground hostesses, for the first and only time without smiles, and anyone else I can't think of, almost took the doors to the departure lounge off their hinges.

The airport manager was Jim Denyer, an ex-R.A.F. fighter-pilot. His face was crimson.

'Who gave you authority to order the return of that aircraft?' he demanded. I said there was a wanted man on the plane.

'Wanted?' said Tosh, his face screwed up in disbelief. Then, when he'd composed himself: 'What's he wanted for?'

'I don't know,' I replied.

Tosh is ashen. 'Are you sure it's the right man?'

'I think so.'

'You *think* so?'

'Well, his name's spelt different...'

There was nothing more to be done except wait for the plane. It was a long wait, I can tell you. When the steps came down I went into the cabin – alone again – and asked the steward to page Mr Johnstone. As I looked along the sea of heads a man stood up and presented himself to me. When he confirmed his identity I told him I was arresting him.

'What for?' he asked in a broad Scots accent.

I told him there was a warrant in force, and he would have to leave the plane. Strangely, it was only then I realised I was uncertain what authority there was to arrest him at all, as the warrant, whatever it was for, was issued in Scotland. I remembered some vague rule about having to have a Scottish warrant in your possession, and didn't it have to be backed by a magistrate if it was executed in England? It was too late to worry about such trivia now. If the chief constable got sued he got sued. If I got sacked I got sacked. If Tosh had a heart attack...

Fortunately Mr Johnstone co-operated. He looked a bit shaken up actually, which was hardly surprising: it's not every day people are taken from aircraft about to leave the country. We took him to the office and I telephoned the police station where the warrant was issued. It took ages to find anyone who could help, but in the end I got through. And yes, Mr Johnstone was wanted on a warrant, issued by the local magistrates.

'What's it for?' I asked, hoping it might be murder or some other heinous crime.

'Non-payment of maintenance to his wife,' came the reply.

That'll teach him, I thought, as the Scottish police came and took him home to face the music. And next day, guess what. There he was again, grinning from ear to ear. 'Bloody women,' he growled, passing through control, my greatest arrest as a detective in Special Branch (Ports). I bet he never saw the headline of a certain Scottish newspaper the following Sunday: *MAN HELD AT AIRPORT*, with special reference to special branch. His only claim to fame and he missed it.

There was only one other case of significance at the airport during my year in SB. Significant, that is, because it attracted the attention of the media, and even a Member of Parliament. It concerned a young Indian student, K, who arrived on the inward Amsterdam flight, seeking residence in Britain. This wasn't unusual. From time to time persons from the Indian sub-continent arrived for the same reason, but without clearance by the Home Office to stay they were refused admittance by H.M. Immigration. Our role (the police) was to detain them in secure custody overnight, then they were returned whence they came. K had no clearance, but at 17 he posed a problem for the immigration boys, or, more accurately, the Home Office.

Precisely what the Home Office do when considering applications I do not know, but whatever it is takes weeks. So, while they tried to work out whether or not K could stay, he had to be detained in a detention centre along with the local burglars and car thieves. K wasn't a criminal when he touched down on British soil; whether that remained the case by the time he left it again is debatable. Anyway, several weeks later came the Home Office decision: K had to go.

K declared he'd hated the detention centre where he'd suffered racist comments no end, although he *had* learned how to hot-wire a car. He didn't want to be deported. Said he'd refuse to leave.

Why, we asked, didn't he get permission to stay before flying in? He shrugged that one off. Then the telephone rang. It was the Home Office. They weren't sure any more, so we took him back to the detention centre.

Weeks later K was back at the airport, by which time he had learned how to burgle a house by inserting a wire through the letterbox. He had turned rather aggressive, presumably over his enforced confinement. Said he hoped the telephone would ring again and it did. The Home Office must have thought of something else. It was back to the detention centre again.

Even more weeks later, the airport yet again, where K extolled the wonders of forensic evidence, how burglars had to be careful not to leave any trace at the scene of their crimes. Fascinating subject, he said, eyeing the telephone. It was like an American film: someone is strapped to a chair in the gas chamber, the camera pans in on the phone. Will it ring? Not for K it didn't, not this time. It was time to go. He showed us a picture of his mother, said he wanted to stay. We said it was our duty to escort him to the waiting plane.

There were four of us: myself, Tosh, another DC and an immigration officer. Somewhere in the middle was little K. We crossed the apron where the smiling air hostess waited at the bottom of the steps to the plane. The airline didn't want any fuss, and there wouldn't have been if my companions had stayed the course. But at the bottom of the steps when I turned to ask Tosh something, there he was – gone! They'd *all* gone, leaving me and K and a bewildered but still-smiling air hostess.

'I won't go,' said K, refusing to climb the steps.

'You must,' I replied.

'I *won't*', he declared, looking me in the eye, as the passengers waited in blissful ignorance of the drama about to unfold. The firm voice of authority was needed. 'Gerrup up them stairs,' I ordered, and K stepped on to the first step, then the second. Then he stopped.

'I want to stay,' he said, in a pleading voice. It was no good. I told him I had to do my job, that he should have sorted all this out before flying to England in the first place. It was like talking to someone about to be face a firing squad.

I urged him upward. It was the start of the action as he gripped the rails with both hands in defiance. There was nothing for it but to force him into the plane. I dragged him up the steps, one at a time, until at last, at the top, exhausted, I pushed him into the aircraft. Earlier, we'd talked about our families, about India, about the Home Office, about detention centres. Now the hurt was written across his face. The hostess ushered him further into the cabin, and he was gone. I scurried down the steps, waited until they were raised. I had to wait, for I knew if I'd followed my colleagues he could be down in an instant and off across the tarmac. After what seemed an eternity, the engines roared, and K was bound for Amsterdam, whence he had come about six months before.

That night, I watched the local news programme, *Look North.* To my astonishment, there was the plane, there was K and me on the steps, and there were my colleagues hurrying off for their coffee. As the camera panned in, the population of the northern England was witness to a brutal policeman ejecting that poor little fellow from the country. Sometimes, as I might have said before, police work can be fulfilling. The incident with a 17-year old who left England in tears didn't fall into that category.

Another event concerning the airport, thirty years on, can (hopefully) now be told. Someone told me that if a friend flew out of the country and wanted to return with, shall we say, a bottle or two over the limit, you could tip the wink to customs who'd allow them to pass quietly through on their return, no questions asked. Whether this was true or not I didn't know. At the time, I'd never been abroad, not even on a package flight, so my interest on the subject of duty-frees was zero. Anyway, a friend, Geoff, and his wife were flying off to Ibiza for a fortnight. They asked if I'd see them 'okay' when they returned. To be honest, I was more eager to offer them a lift home as their flight coincided with the end of my tour of duty.

Two weeks later, their flight touched down and the passengers trailed into the arrivals lounge. It was after 10 o'clock, a cold night in Britain. It always amused me to see holidaymakers returning from the Med dressed in shorts and tee-shirts. They'd either forgotten about the British climate, or more likely were trying to impress with their sun-tans. Sure enough, Geoff and his good lady appeared with beaming smiles. I knew why: they'd half a ton of booze in their bags, but thanks to good old Paulus they'd declare nothing and pass quietly through customs. I felt embarrassed by the obligation I seemed to have had thrust upon me, but had a quiet word with a nearby customs man.

'Those two,' I whispered, indicating my friends. 'Could you look after them?' He gave me a knowing look and nodded. Sure, he said, no problem.

One of the things you learn about anyone passing through customs is to look at passengers' faces. Those without anything to declare look ordinary; those with, but purport not to, look too casual. Their faces say it all every time. Geoff's face had guilt written all over it, in glorious technicolor.

'Anything to declare,' asked the customs man next to the bloke I'd spoken to.

'No,' said Geoff confidently.

'And you madam?' he asked.

'No,' she replied.

Then came the words I will never forget.

'Please turn out your baggage.'

I was dumbstruck. I looked at the guy I'd spoken to, expecting him to intervene. But no, he just stood there looking.

Out came the booze. They'd cleared Ibiza out by the look of it. I'll never forget their faces, or my feelings of letting them down as they emptied their bags and paid the fines. And all the while the bloke who'd agreed to 'look after them' just stood and watched. When Geoff and his wife finally emerged I could only apologise. To their credit they placed no blame, and we all agreed we had no business colluding to beat the system in the first place. Just the same, I was angry with the man who had promised one thing and done another. I gave them their lift home, then broke the world land speed record on my return to the airport, where I made a beeline for the fellow who had let me down so badly.

'What happened?' I demanded, giving him the opportunity to explain before strangling him.

He looked at me, nonplussed.

'My friends,' I said. 'You promised to look after them at customs.'

'Oh,' he exclaimed, 'I'm only a porter.'

*

If the airport bored me stiff, the Quay at North Shields almost finished me off. On some mornings we had to be there before six, which meant scarfing off the drugs squad car at the risk of starting World War Three if it wasn't returned by 8.30. An early start was essential to check in the usual twenty or so Norwegians who'd made the trip to go shopping in Newcastle. Once, a woman carrying a paraffin heater told me she'd got it on special offer at Bainbridges or somewhere, I kid you not. All the way from Norway for a paraffin heater! There were a number of ferries plying between the Scandinavian countries, and of all the times we checked passengers in and out the most exciting moment was when I clocked a guy with a Filipino passport. (I'd never seen a Filipino before).

An exciting moment *might* have occurred one morning, just after the cargo had been taken off one of the Scandinavian ferries. I had just left the control when before my eyes I saw some men breaking into a crate with iron bars. They were clearly stealing some of the contents. I went off for assistance, only to be told a few 'bits and pieces' were their perks, that the company were aware and turned a blind eye. Leave things be, I was told, because any arrests would lead directly to strike action, which in turn would lead to the cancellation of the ferries. Imagine it: the ferry from Esbjerg cancelled because DC Heslop had nicked one of the men at North Shields for stealing a packet of Lurpack. I saw the point, but never came to terms with witnessing a crime and doing nothing.

Between sailings, the ferry terminal was dead. Once one ferry had arrived or departed, we could only hang around for the next one. Sometimes we operated the passenger control on board (when there were only a handful of passengers), otherwise it was in the terminal, which, like the airport, had its fair share of porn mags, but, unlike the airport no lovely hostesses for close liaisons. Still, as ferries *potentially* might carry more passengers than aeroplanes, we had to be there in greater numbers, which gave us the opportunity to play cards and learn about horseracing from Tosh.

Every day Tosh studied the form, said this horse or that was a racing certainty. Hitherto my only success at betting on the nags was in 1965, when my horse in the Grand National, Jay Trump, romped home at 100-8. I had no interest in whatever Tosh had to say on horseracing, but when you hear something all day every day you're bound to listen, and when Tosh walked in with a wad of money one afternoon and declared he'd won it thanks to events at Redcar my ears pricked up. To cut a long story sideways I decided to have a go myself, if only to pass the time.

I studied the form, checked the odds and placed my bets, on each occasion religiously keeping a record of the amount staked, won or lost, and a running balance. Surprisingly, I did okay. Better than Tosh who, despite the odd win here and there, lost more than he cared to admit, and most of what winnings he did collect went straight on to another horse, usually a loser. After seven months when I took stock the balance was minus 7 pence, which I considered not bad, although it convinced me there was no way I could beat the bookies, so I packed it all in.

The one day of relief from all this boredom was a Saturday when the *Leda*, from Norway, arrived in the afternoon. (One of her crew, incidentally, was a German who rejoiced in the name Horst Muck!). It was rarely on time, and rather than sit round the office, we – together with officers of H.M. Immigration – thought it a far better idea to sit around in the pub where we could play darts and enjoy alternative forms of refreshment. The problem was: how could we know when hordes of tourists would be streaming ashore with passports at the ready, only to face empty desks.

Where there's a will…

A carefully executed strategy was contrived, whereby the last person to throw a dart had to climb on to a chair and look out of the window, a manoeuvre which enabled him to catch a glimpse of *Leda's* funnel as she steamed upriver. When the funnel was sighted – and you had to know the funnel, or a ghastly mistake would be made – we drove like crazy to the terminal where, composing ourselves, we'd be just in time to greet the passengers, as though we had been seated there for hours, patiently awaiting their arrival.

Then, one day, came an opportunity to brush away the cobwebs and deploy ourselves as real detectives. It took place when a colleague and I responded to a report by a woman who lived at Tynemouth. She had been walking her dog, she said, when she had seen a group of men *emerge from the sea*, as she put it, and disappear into the night. From time to time I'd heard stories of Polish fishing vessels transporting Asian immigrants from Holland to offshore, UK, then transferring them to fishing boats, whose crews would bring them ashore, for a suitable 'fee'. (I never actually discovered any evidence of this, nor knew of anyone else who did). Could this woman have seen some as they were brought ashore?

The report was taken so seriously they allowed the use of a car to make enquiries along the coast. Northumberland's coastline is about 70 miles long, most of it deserted beaches and tiny fishing villages, so establishing where illegal immigrants might be embarking would be difficult if not impossible. We started at Tynemouth, made our way north to Whitley Bay and Blyth, checked out such dens of iniquity as Newbiggin-by-the-Sea and Seahouses, but drew a blank. Immigrants? What immigrants?

Here I must digress for a moment. Earlier, I mentioned coal miners; now I'll mention fishermen. As we headed north along Northumberland's lovely coast, we saw them sailing out of the little harbours, just as they do all around Britain (or as they did, anyway), earning their living the hard way. The weather was grand, but in just a few hours there might be gale-force winds, and stormy seas. There'd be no escape for them: no sliding off to the canteen (or their ma's), no going sick when the going got tough.

Risking lives for a few cod, mackerel, whatever. Police work is hard, stressful, dangerous at times – but always secure. So hey, you coppers out there, with your next pay cheque assured, your 28-days annual leave and inflation-indexed salaries and your subsistence over eight, remember the miners and the fishermen, and all those who have to *earn* their pay against *being paid*, whether it's earned or not.

Anyway, on our way to Berwick, we got the call: the coastguard at Amble had reported flashing lights out at sea.

We requested to be struck off from the usual duties at the ports to check it out. This could be serious crime: smuggling heroin or firearms or explosives, never mind illegal immigrants. I suggested liaison with all UK coastguard posts, alerting the Royal Navy, as well as a request for all police forces along the coast to contact us if there were any sightings. We'd be prepared to work long hours, day and night, to make an arrest (this was pre-overtime payment!). The response? Forget it, and stick to the ports. I was gobsmacked, but I was a detective constable with no option but to do as I was instructed. What went on remains a mystery, except I always believed there was something, and if you don't look you will not find. Thinking about it, the decision was probably made by somebody in admin or somewhere, who's idea of 'arrest' was something to take because it was Friday afternoon and thank God it's the weekend. Guns and bombs, indeed!

There was some relief from ports duties, albeit little. From time to time I was entrusted with a Home Office enquiry, usually tracing so-and-so from India or Pakistan who had arrived in the UK and hadn't gone home again. I'd deploy my detective skills to track them down, and file a report. Then the Home Office would consider the case all over again for a few months, during which the circumstances would not have changed one iota, before requesting another visit. Or, just as likely, recommend no further action which, in the cases I enquired into at least, should have been made in the first place, as the 'illegal immigrant' would usually turn out to be an elderly person who was doing no more than biding with his or her family. But one case was unusual, and made me realise how fortunate we are to be living in a free society. It concerned a Polish woman. Evidently she had failed to forward some papers to the Home Office who wanted her checked out. I went to see her at her home. When I told her who I was she was visibly shaken.

There was no problem, I said. It was just a matter of checking documents. She produced a briefcase, which she opened with trembling hands.

'My papers are in order,' she told me, producing her passport.

She was in such a state I felt like the Gestapo. If this was the reaction of an obscure woman in Britain in the seventies, what was like for the Jews before and during the war, or the political enemies of the state in China or Soviet Union, as it was, when the authoritarian state knocked on their door? She thrust a huge bundle of documents into my hand, urged me to check this and that as certain proof that all was well and I wouldn't have to cart her off to the Gulag.

I looked at the bundle, the equivalent in size to an encyclopaedia.

'Look,' she urged, pointing to various pages in the bundle. 'You see...?'

I saw. Didn't tell her I couldn't read Polish, but I saw. I handed her the papers, stood up, thanked her and left. Wherever she is now, I hope she feels she can answer her door without fear.

One day Chief Inspector Dear sent for me, and told me he had a special assignment. It concerned a senior member of the Indian High Commission, who was visiting the city. My job was to protect him. Against what was neither explained nor apparent. I knew my mission was important, because I could have the drugs squad car *all day*. Mind you, it was a Sunday, and the drugs squad weren't on duty. Dear only decided to entrust me with the assignment – or was it the car? – because I was now an experienced hack. Or words to that effect. He wouldn't have actually said 'hack'.

'Take him off at the Central Station,' I was told, 'and stay with him all day. Go everywhere he goes. Do not let him out of your sight. Do not leave him until he catches his train back to London.'

I took him off at the station, followed him here, there, everywhere. Even to the Gosforth Park Hotel for lunch. No-one tried to kill him, kidnap him or even ask for his autograph. It was after ten o'clock that night when, at last, he boarded his train. Until that point he had not spared so much as a glance in my direction, but now, just before he closed the carriage door, he looked at me and shook my hand.

'You are most kind,' he declared. 'Thank you.'

Then he was gone, a ship in the night who, for all I knew, was murdered before his train crossed the Tyne. Dear said nothing, so presumably I did okay. Monday morning saw me at the airport again. I'm not sure if I was in time for the Belfast flight. For some reason it slips my mind.

5

"Detectives are only policemen with smaller feet"

Marlene Dietrich

As the prison gates slammed behind McCann, I wondered briefly how he felt as he tasted freedom for the first time in months. The DCI had spelled it out.

'I know Eddie,' he said. 'It would be just like him to do twelve months for burglary, then screw a house on the way home.'

Apart from a test to show initiative as a Boy Scout when I had to follow someone around the streets of Newcastle for two hours, my experience at surveillance to date was nil. Now, a fresh face in the Regional Crime Squad, I'd been told to take McCann off from the prison. He was a wily so-and-so, a burglar who always worked alone. His movements were easy to anticipate: he'd catch a train to Newcastle Central station then make his way home. It was the bit between getting off the train and getting home that mattered.

I knew Durham well from courting days. Okay, that was a secluded spot by the river. But I knew roughly where the station was too. When McCann emerged through the prison gates, I followed as he walked off apace, hoping he wouldn't turn and see me. Meanwhile I had radio contact with Terry, my DS, not far off in an unmarked car. The plan was for me to stay with McCann – on the train – whilst Terry drove the 15 miles to Newcastle where we'd resume our game of cat-and-mouse.

The station platform was almost deserted: just McCann and me and a few commuters. There was nothing for it but to hang around, look casual. At least I hadn't fallen for that corny old trick of carrying a newspaper under my arm. No, I was just a young bloke in jeans, waiting for a train. Sure enough, McCann spared me not a glance. He'd never suspect anyone taking him off from the prison.

We occupied the same carriage, where I sat behind him, and relaxed in the knowledge that whatever happened I couldn't lose him, not on a train. But it would be critical to maintain contact at Newcastle Central. Would he catch a bus or take a taxi? Or buy a newspaper, maybe, and read it in a café over coffee? Whatever, I'd have Terry for back up.

Newcastle Central station. McCann stands up, turns towards me. I'm cool, averting my eyes. We leave the train. I follow him along the platform, not too close, keeping him in view. He goes into the gents, I stay back. I watch, as one by one men enter and leave. All except McCann. What's he doing in there? Suddenly, out he comes, glancing my way before hurrying out through the station portico to God knows where.

I hurry after, looking right, left, across the street. I scan the taxi queue, check the bars, restaurants, peer into shop windows. Zilch. I shoot up Pink Lane, circumnavigate the entire block, go back into the railway station in the forlorn hope of finding him again. Alas, in vain. There's nothing for it but to call Terry and break the news. Okay, he says, we'll go to where he lives. Might see him get off a bus. Sadly, all was lost. And if that wasn't bad enough, worse was to follow the following afternoon when two experienced detectives gave me a pull in the office. 'Was it you who took Eddie McCann off from Durham prison yesterday?' they asked, in such a way they knew it was and they had something to say about it. I nodded, accepting my failure had gone public. 'Just we saw him last night and he asked who that ginger twat was on the train.'

The last straw was a week later when I saw McCann in the *County* pub. I recognised the back of his head immediately. He turned, winked and gave me a look of utter contempt. Okay, my first attempt at foot surveillance had failed. But it might have turned out better if I'd had some instruction in the first place. Anyway, as I now know, you should never try surveillance alone. Surveillance is a team game. Once trained, you become better at it, although some become better than others.

Fortunately, it wasn't long before a few of us from around the region were briefed on the techniques of following someone on foot: how the person immediately behind the target could divert, leaving someone else to take over, and so on. It was called the A-B-C method, as I recall. You didn't even need radio contact, though if you had it was an advantage. Once trained in theory, they sent us to do the real thing, or at least pretend it was, at Stockton-on-Tees, the idea being none of us was known to the 'targets' – three young police officers – and we wouldn't know our way around. They showed us a picture of one of the 'targets', and told us she would be passing such-and-such a public house at 11.30 a.m. We were to take her off, and I was sent into the pub to take up 'eyeball'.

Even though it was only a training exercise, we were all geed up about it, determined to succeed and, above all, not to show out. When I got the call I decided to give her a couple of minutes to pass by, then hurried outside, emerging on the pavement *right in front* of her. She could not possibly have failed to see me, especially knowing she'd be followed by some strange blokes all day. I crossed the road, whispered something about her direction into my radio and hurried away, anxious to get out of sight quickly. I knew I'd blown it, and given the recent disaster with Eddie McCann, considered seeking out somewhere to kill myself.

We went on as a team to follow the 'targets', as one met the other and handed over a pretend parcel of drugs, rendezvoused with another 'criminal' and so on. Time and again we all found ourselves in direct line of vision as they deliberately turned heel or looked into shop windows where they could see from the reflection who was nearby. When it was all over we were called in for debriefing, and one by one, the 'targets' were asked to look at the officers who'd been following them along the High Street, in and out of Mothercare, through the park and into pubs and coffee bars. To my astonishment, not one identified me, including the young woman I'd all but knocked over at the start. It all went to prove that even though people look at you they don't necessarily see you. I learnt more from that practical exercise than from any text book.

Another surveillance course followed, this time using cars. The same principles apply, except it's done at speed and over greater distances, obviously. Ultimately, the combined use of foot and car surveillance comes into play: a target is dropped from a car somewhere, foot officers are dropped off to take up the 'follow'.

Following criminals, trying to catch them committing crime, or building up intelligence (identifying associates and so on) isn't easy. I'm not giving away any trade secrets in mentioning the subject: all active criminals know about police surveillance, and any who don't need only to switch on the telly to find out. Surveillance is exciting, good fun even. The hard part is being aware that a target will see you and the car you're in time and again, so you have to follow in such a way that he doesn't realise it.

Many criminals try various ploys to see if they're being followed. One guy would drive along a dual carriageway, then stop in the middle of nowhere and clock all the traffic speeding by. Obviously, you couldn't stop behind him. The same guy would park in a busy city centre car park, then, out on foot, double back to see if anyone following behind panicked, a sure giveaway. Yet though he looked, when he was eventually arrested he recognised none of the detectives or our cars.

Of course, sometimes things do go wrong. One target, realising he was being followed, allowed the game to go on for ages before deliberately driving down a cul-de-sac, where he waved cheerfully to the hapless crews of every car that followed. Another drove around and around a roundabout, pursued by all following cars, a Keystone Cops scenario. Sometimes we had good results, sometimes we followed targets who didn't do anything, sometimes we showed out.

Another quality you need on surveillance is patience. You can sit for days on end just watching someone's front door. Take your eye away for an instant and the target's gone, and you are watching an empty house. But it's a magic feeling when that patience pays off with an arrest, when you catch someone committing a burglary, say, or disposing of stolen goods. Naturally, there is often an amusing side...

We were onto a high-ranking (married) member of a borough council who was suspected of fraud. He wasn't your usual villain; he had no idea he was under surveillance. The info was he'd get loadsamoney from a development company in return for ensuring they were awarded a lucrative building contract to rebuild a town centre, no less. Witnessing the cash actually changing hands was stretching optimism to the limit, but you can only try. We – the surveillance teams – were sworn to secrecy forever, such was the political magnitude of the fraud.

This long, protracted operation lasted throughout the long, hot summer of 1976. We sat in our cars and sizzled, and followed our man everywhere in the hope that sooner or later we'd be there to nab him and whoever handed over the 'bung' in what would be a major corruption scandal if we could do it. This extended to a pub he visited, and many were the times I sat at the next table to him, listening as he chatted to his lady friend, a local magistrate. Never once did they suspect. I know they didn't because they always parked on a dark patch of waste ground for an hour or so afterwards, car windows all steamed up. I'm sure neither would have willingly done that if they knew half a dozen Regional Crime Squad cars were tailing them off. Whether or not the money was ever handed over isn't known.

In the squad, a **DS** and **DC** worked as a 'crew'. Consequently, you had to be compatible. Like marriage, only without the sex. Again, like marriage, you got to know the moods of your partner, and they got to know yours. It was important to get along; you could be cooped in a car or an obbo van together from dawn till dusk. By the time you'd worked with the same individual a few months, you knew whether he changed his socks every day, if he voted Tory or Labour. I'm happy to say my partners and I got along okay, with some minor irritations: Bill chain-smoked; Jack bit his nails to the quick; Charlie broke wind *after* he got into the car. Peter's song, as we headed back to the office after a long shift, to the tune of Alma Cogan's *You, me and us, we are my favourite people*...

> Aye, aye, aye, aye,
> Somebody's pissed in my sombrero;
> Some dirty twat
> Has pissed in my hat,
> And now I've got nothing to wear-o.

And they say *The Bill* is true to life.

One day Peter and I arrested a bloke named Albert. He was a market trader, a sort of Geordie Arthur Daley. Talking to Albert, it was all I could do to keep myself from laughing, as he always answered in the affirmative with the words 'by all means'. Our information was that Albert was in possession of some quality suede coats, which he was selling from his stall. Sure enough, when we went to see him, there were the coats.

'We have reason to believe these are dodgy,' said Peter, 'will you accompany us to the station?'

'By all means,' replied Albert.

Albert couldn't, or wouldn't, tell us where he'd got the coats. He was bailed to return at a later date. 'For enquiries', as we say. 'We'll have to hang on the coats,' he was told.

'By all means,' replied Albert.

There were about twenty, as I recall, and the only place I could find to store them was in a disused garage in the police yard,

111

where I hung them carefully on hangers, suspended from the ceiling. Weeks later, we were no further forward with our enquiries. We put Albert off, but in the end he turned up asking for his coats back. Fair enough. I went out to the garage to get them. Sadly, police buildings being what they are, a whole summer's rain had dripped on to the coats. They were soaked through, and utterly ruined. Albert would be able to claim £££'s for the loss of what was probably nicked gear. But I played an ace, telling Albert that, although we couldn't prove the coats were stolen, he couldn't prove he'd bought them, so he couldn't have them back either.

'Will you sign a disclaimer?' I asked, praying he would. Albert looked up and smiled.

'By all means.'

Needless to say, I then wasted no time in confining the coats to the scrapheap.

One day we were sent to a motorway services area. It was time to put a new-fangled system into practice, namely checking the registration number of motor vehicles using the Police National Computer (PNC). This was located in London, and every motor vehicle in the country was recorded on it, we were told. Hitherto, checking a registered number to identify the owner of a car was cumbersome, to say the least. Funny, even, to young coppers today, used to just calling in on their PR's and getting a result in minutes. In the old days, you'd have to go to the civic centre to search vehicle records: this would be done by a clerk during office hours, otherwise yourself, evenings, nights or weekends. Sometimes you'd be there at four in the morning, looking for a registration document for an officer in Aberysthwyth or somewhere, who was awaiting the result of your painstaking search. Or you might even get the call via the flashing police pillar, or by PR.

We selected ten numbers at random, of cars belonging to people now having lunch inside the motorway services. Ten numbers, from different parts of the country. It would have taken days to sort out before they introduced the computer. Now? Just a couple of minutes. Looking back, I think this was a definitive moment for all of us, as far as computers go. Now we could i/d

112

owners of suspect vehicles at the drop of a hat, a positive step in crime investigation, to be sure.

Where, in division, detective work had been *reactive* – responding to offences after they'd been committed, the work of the squad was both reactive and *proactive* – as well as surveillance, it included cultivating informants, following up with arrests and recovering stolen property. Although no different from 'ordinary' detectives, the name *Regional* carried kudos, with criminals and the media. We knew no boundaries, so we could go anywhere we pleased. And, instead of being dressed to the nines – suit, collar and tie – our clothes were casual. We didn't even have to shave. Anything, so long as we didn't show out. Not that jeans and an old T-shirt were any guarantee of anonymity, as I found out one day when I had cause to be in a car-hire office. As I waited to see someone, a young bloke I didn't know from Adam was waiting too. After a few minutes of silence he spoke.

'You old bill?' he asked.

How did he know?

'It's your shoes,' he said. 'Too shiny.'

Of course! I'd changed my clothes but still polished my shoes. Old habits died hard. I never polished my shoes again.

*

For the third time, I knocked, louder now. Then, suddenly, the door swung open. Clare blinked, wiped the sleep from her eyes, stared blankly from the hallway. She wasn't used to visitors calling as early as 8.30 in the morning. I maintained eye contact, partly to avoid sight of her huge breasts, left unashamedly naked by her loose-fitting, see-through nightie. Finally, she spluttered into life.

'You!'

Without further ado she disappeared into the depths of her flat. I waited, uncertain.

'Y'comin' in or what?'

I was comin' in.

She led me to her living room, turned off Radio One, looked at me with questioning eyes.

'At least it wasn't the *Road to Inverness*,' I said, seeking to melt the atmosphere. My biggest worry was that she might not be alone. Some toerag might be lying in her bed, wondering who she'd let in. She must have sensed it.

'Sawright. There's nobody here.'

She disappeared into the kitchen. There was the sound of the kettle being filled.

There was no wonder at her surprise in seeing me. During my time in SB (when I secured full appointment status as a detective), and a spell back in division, Clare had left the pub and disappeared. But then she got nicked for something and I found out where she lived.

Clare visited pubs still, mixed with criminals, was happy to have them buy her a drink or three, take her back to her flat and give her a few bob for her trouble. Whatever money she made, it didn't extend to paying for a telephone, so any time I wanted contact it would have to be a knock on her door with the risk of her having Johnny so-and-so for company. If I had any doubts that Clare might put loyalty to her male friends over her desire to make a few bob it was dispelled on that very first visit to her flat when I asked her if she 'knew anything'. She shrugged.

'There was this house in Gateshead,' she said, plonking down my tea in a mug so cracked it was leaking. I was all ears.

Three men had broken into the house in Valley Drive and stolen thousands pounds worth of jewellery. She gave me their names. How did she know? One of them spent the night from time to time after a session in the pub, came back to hers, bragged to her about it, even showed her some of the jewellery. 'You won't get the jewellery back,' she said. 'They've flogged it.'

I went to the office barely able to contain myself. A quick check identified the burglary, committed less than two weeks before. It didn't take long either to fully i/d the three offenders. The lads were intrigued.

'Where'd you get the info?' I was asked.

As I mentioned earlier, there was no formal training on informants. But what my common sense told me was the less anyone knew the better. It's not that I didn't trust my mates, but the trust I had so carefully established between Clare and me would be destroyed if she thought I had told anyone who she was. I had expressly told her I would not do so, that whatever she said was between her and me and one other – my boss. Her name on any documentation would be a pseudonym (there had to be one piece of paper, when claiming the reward for the information). Even the detective sergeant I worked alongside was in the dark.

All three men were arrested. All three asked who'd shopped them. I just shrugged my shoulders, a gesture confirming they had been shopped, but by whom they would just have to guess. In other words, they each thought it was one of the others. Clare's friend couldn't see the wood for the trees, whilst the others never knew of her existence. Arresting them was one thing, proving the case was another. Evidentially, there can be no help from an informant; you can't expect he or she to give evidence at court: they'd be 'blown', of no further use, not to mention their safety put in jeopardy.

Where was the evidence? There were no witnesses, the stolen property had been disposed of and none of the prisoners wanted to say anything. It all comes down to interviewing technique, detective skill, call it what you like. I'm not blowing my own trumpet; *all* detectives need these tools as part of their trade. Anyway, one of them 'went over' and spilled the beans, not out of remorse, but in the belief that if he co-operated it would be better for him at court. He even took us to the jewellers' shops, where we recovered the stolen property. They all admitted it then, each saying it was the idea of the others and they'd never have got involved if it hadn't been for him or him. Throughout my career as a detective 'honour among thieves' rarely stood up to its name. Once they look prison in the face, they usually look out for themselves. This lot were no different.

The most rewarding feature about that particular case, as well as the satisfaction of 'acting on information', was when I returned the stolen jewellery to its owner, a middle-aged woman who was greatly distressed by her loss. It had been in her family for years, and I never forgot the look on her face when she saw it. Such moments make the job worthwhile.

Now it was time for Clare's reward: payment. Informants don't provide information out of moral duty, not Clare's type anyway. It was my first 'claim', £30. 'There's more where that came from,' I told her. It wasn't bad for the mid-seventies. She must have been pleased as more success followed.

I'll mention here the 'culture' that exists, or used to, when detectives had the need to go to other force areas on enquiries, to make arrests, etc. Basically, as well as helping you out on their patch, the local lads would take you out for a few bevvies, arrange accommodation and so on. The guy who showed the stolen jewellery to Clare: at the time of the information, he was incarcerated in a Glasgow prison, but was due for imminent release. He must have been well pleased to pass through the prison gates and breath in the fresh air of freedom, only to be scarfed off to the local nick at the request of Regional Crime Squad officers on Tyneside. My DS and I went off to get him, naturally anticipating good Scottish hospitality before bringing him back to Geordieland. Unfortunately, the local DI had his own ideas about hosting visiting colleagues, and instead of heading for the nearest hostelry, we found ourselves at Maryhill, where, with the temperature around minus twenty, we were treated to the Partick Thistle versus Celtic football match.

Scottish football is dominated by just two clubs: Rangers and Celtic. The rest are there to give them someone to play against in the ritual of qualifying for the right to take part where the real money is – Europe. Partick against Celtic was like David against Goliath, so the crowd would be well pleased with a score of 0-0, which was akin to climbing Everest blindfold, or a successful traverse of the polar icecap with your legs strapped together. Unfortunately, with just ten seconds remaining, Celtic scored. You couldn't help feel sorry for the Partick players as, to a man, they lay prostrate on the pitch, gutted by the blow dealt so late in the game. Or, indeed, the crowd, which until that moment, had sang and cheered on their team, but now, with no time left to equalise,

116

fell into muted silence. When the ref blew for time, they filed out of the ground, headed for home through the darkened streets, filled Maryhill with a sense of melancholy which laid its cold hand on everyone's shoulder, including our DI escort. Still, we were off for a pint – weren't we? Well, no, we weren't. As the DI reminded us: we couldn't go for a drink as the pubs in Scotland closed at 10 o'clock then. Great night, though.

In those days, the squad was utilised regularly on murder enquiries. That is, where lots of manpower was needed, especially in the early stages. Some murders are premeditated, most aren't. As the squad covered a vast area, we were dispatched far and wide on murder investigations. Some are worth recounting, albeit briefly.

A man and woman meet in a pub after which he takes her to a secluded lane where he rapes her, throws her from the car then runs over her, backwards and forwards several times to make certain he's finished her off. He has. The tyre impressions of his car, left in the mud and across his victim's body, secure conviction

New Year's day. An old lady in her 80's is found dead in her house. It looks as though she has died of old age, but a post mortem reveals she's been raped and strangled. There's a broken window, the point of entry, with a fingerprint. Over 2,000 males in the locale are fingerprinted on a voluntary basis. When half a dozen or so won't come forward they are flushed out and checked, revealing the identity of the murderer. This was a particularly difficult enquiry, as most people in the north-east have a good drink at new year, and visit each other's houses. No-one could remember who was where when it came to alibis. The offender's family swore he was with them all night long. They admitted later – after he was charged – they were protecting him.

A man discovers his wife is having an affair. He turns up at her place of work next morning and runs a sword through her body over sixty times. He then changes into a different set of clothes and tries to maintain it was someone else, not he, who did the murder.

A black man is subjected to racial taunts in a city pub. He takes as much as he can before leaving, only to return with a knife and stab his tormentor to death in a frantic series of thrusts about the body. I was first officer on the scene. Everyone was just standing, looking at the dead man's body in drunken disbelief. There were over thirty witnesses.

An old man is out walking in a quiet coastal village. A young absconder who is passing at the time throws a lump of rock into the air. It lands on the old man's head, killing him instantly. A bizarre killing, it was a tragedy born out of an irresponsible act.

A small boy is sexually assaulted and murdered, his body hidden high in the undergrowth on the banks above the River Tyne.

In each case, the offender was arrested and charged, yet will now be free. Just a thought.

*

During my time on the squad they sent me to learn about firearms.

Hitherto my experience with guns extended no further than mimicking Roy Rogers and Hopalong Cassidy, and rifles with twisted sights, designed to prevent you winning a teddy at the Spanish City. Some of my colleagues had mentioned gun clubs, but I'd never been interested. I used to say all firearms should be tossed into the sea. Still, only by being able to use them could I expect to deal with armed criminals, so I went on the course.

We were shown how a Smith and Wesson revolver worked, how to clean it and most importantly, how to fire it. *Pulling* the trigger distorted the aim, the instructor said, as we missed the target from 25 yards. We weren't sure what he meant.

'Don't pull it,' he said. '*Squeeze* it.'

Better, but still not very good. He slowly waggled his forefinger,

'Gently.'

He waggled it even more slowly.

'Like it's your girlfriend...'

No one missed after that.

Against the clock we had to load, fire twice at the target, move position, fire twice more, move again, twice more. *Re-load!* Then do it all again. If there was a click you'd miscounted, a definite fail. This put pressure on you: the time, the need to move and take cover. Where some could hit the target cold, they failed when it came to the action stuff. We practised with rifles and shotguns too, and just for good measure allowed ourselves to be fastened up in an old shed to see if we could resist a dose of CS gas. We couldn't! It debilitates in seconds, leaving your eyes streaming, a ghastly experience.

We trained on an army range, where hidden targets appeared in the bracken. You had to be quick, as well as accurate. Then we had to watch a film, our reactions tested by people who unexpectedly appeared behind cars, in doorways and so on. The point of this was to look first before you fired, as my instructor pointed out when I 'shot' a woman pushing a pram. Hesitate and you were dead; the next figure was pointing a sawn-off at me.

I passed the course, so now I could carry firearms for real. As an RCS officer, this meant a *Ruger* pistol, in an upside-down holster under my armpit. Like Kojak without the lollipop (or the bald head). I was in for a new experience: the feeling of power a firearm gives. The first time this power-thing happened was when we turned a house over one morning (i.e. searched it with a warrant). The occupant was a well-known criminal, with convictions for firearms offences.

'Show him the gun', the DS said. 'Let him see we mean business.'

We crashed through the front door around 6 a.m. We were looking for a shotgun, as I recall. At first chummy taunted us, then offered a cup of tea (without saying what he might have put in it), and generally took the piss. Things changed when he saw the *Ruger*.

He cut the crap then, said he was sorry and there wasn't any shotgun (there wasn't). So, the gun actually *gave* you power. The desire to use it seemed a logical reaction. Just give me an excuse, that's how you feel. I have long since held the view that this same psychology motivates people who carry guns to use them, like

119

those who killed at random at Hungerford and Dunblane. I accept that 99.9% members of gun clubs are law abiding people, but I was pleased when they passed the law closing them down: just that one remaining 0.1% is too many. Only by denying access to guns can we hope to prevent such tragedies. Some argue that most criminals – armed robbers, gangsters – can always get access to firearms, but how many of them go around shooting kids?

As a firearms officer, I was sometimes called in on special enquires. One example was when police were searching for the 'Black Panther', Donald Neilson. He learned about guns during his national service, after which, back in civvy street, he became one of life's failures who developed a hatred of society. Neilson kidnapped the heiress Lesley Whittle, and demanded a £50,000 ransom of her family. He hid Lesley in a drainage shaft, providing a mattress and sleeping bag for her comfort until the ransom was paid. Tragically, it all went wrong, and Lesley was discovered hanging by a wire which was tied around her neck, having fallen or been pushed down a deep shaft near to the place where she had lain. She died as a result of 'vagal inhibition' – meaning she was literally scared to death, not strangled as might be supposed. Neilson also shot three postmasters dead during the course of many armed robberies. He was identified as the same man who had kidnapped Lesley, after shooting a worker who disturbed him loitering on railway property one night. The bullets were identified as coming from the same gun used in the murders of the postmasters.

I sometimes found myself helping to check out addresses in the north-east, in the search for this evil man. Several times I found myself sticking my head through loft hatches, which is not the way to look for somebody who might have a gun! In the end, as often happens, the fugitive was arrested by uniformed patrol officers. Neilson said Lesley had fallen down the shaft, and on the three occasions he shot the postmasters the gun had gone off by accident. The jury didn't believe him, and he was sentenced to life imprisonment.

Another call for my firearms expertise was the time when President Carter visited Newcastle. After the assassination of John

Kennedy, Northumbria Police didn't want Newcastle to suffer the same infamy as Dallas; there would be an armed police presence. I went as a firearms officer, but they didn't give me a gun! Instead, I was posted on St Thomas's church roof and told to keep a look out for snipers. Quite what I could have done about any snipers I wasn't sure. Perhaps I should have had a catapult. Meanwhile my colleague, George, a practical joker, followed the President through the crowd and shook hands with him twenty times. George wasn't armed either, but he proved anyone who was could have popped him off at a range of three feet.

*

I'll mention a case which proves that meticulous, painstaking work can culminate with a great result. It concerned a burglary at a post office in Yorkshire. The stolen property included cash and postal orders. Local police had managed to get a part-registration number of the car used by the thieves, and after joint enquiries between them and the Tyneside RCS office we knew their identity, and details were circulated. At the time I was working with a detective sergeant, Jack, and when we saw the wanted car in Newcastle we arrested the occupants. All we had to do now was prove they'd committed the crime. It wouldn't be easy; we knew they would say absolutely nothing when questioned.

We searched their houses, but none of the stolen property was found. I had the pleasure of searching through the garbage in the dustbins. Nothing there – at first glance. But among the discarded tins of baked beans and Chinese takeaways were tiny fragments of charred paper, so flimsy the breeze was liable to sweep them away. We put them carefully into an envelope. To the naked eye, the charred remains were burnt beyond recognition. But we suspected what they were, and we were right. A forensic scientist turned out to examine the burnt pieces of paper, which he did by placing them underneath a microscope with tweezers. Under magnification were revealed the serial numbers of the stolen postal orders, damming evidence which was used to convict the man at whose home they were found. He went on to admit a number of other serious offences.

There's an amusing sequel. Jack and I took our prisoner to Yorkshire, to hand him over. The prisoner and I were handcuffed as we entered the police station, where the local station sergeant, a sort of Ernest Borgnine with a Yorkshire accent, was expecting us. He opened a huge register and picked up his pen.

'Name,' he said, pen poised.

As my man would only mess him about I gave his name, followed by address, date of birth and so on. The station sergeant wrote it down, slowly and methodically, crossing the t's, dotting the i's. When he'd finished, he put his pen away and closed the register.

'Right,' said Sergeant Borgnine, 'you're gonna be sorry you ever came down here robbin' our little post office,' whereupon he grabbed me by the coat lapels, and began to drag me off to the cells. To me, this proved two things: I had achieved creating the appearance of someone who wasn't a policeman, and that I should let prisoners do their own talking.

Jack and I went off on one of those trips I mentioned, this time to Liverpool. They sent me to Liverpool on a drugs course once, to Mather Avenue. We spent our nights at the *Grafton*, where you had the choice between the inevitable Grab-a-Granny, or, at the Grafton, Grab-a-Scouse Under-age Kid. Anyway, the reason for our visit was to arrest a man who'd stolen a car, from Whitley Bay, as I recall. Jack and I were entertained to a night's booze (the Liverpool lads really looked after us!) after which I found myself apologising profusely to the natives for Newcastle United not giving Liverpool much of a game in the 1974 FA Cup Final, the most one-sided travesty I ever saw. After all that, we took our man back to Tyneside where he was promptly bailed for further enquiries, which probably enabled him to nick another car and return to Liverpool. You couldn't make it up!

There were busy times on the squad, and times when things went quiet. Sometimes surveillance paid off, sometimes it didn't. My belief always lay in the value of informants. Clare and I maintained contact, but she could only do so much. I needed someone else, some*where* else. Sure enough, I got the break I needed. It came about when I arrested a man for burglary. As usual, I sounded the prisoner out about info. He seemed interested, clearly tempted by the money. We arranged to meet in a pub. His name was Tony, and because he didn't want anyone to find out he was about to become a copper's grass, I promised to turn up alone.

As I drove into the pub car park the following evening, I began to have misgivings about what I might be letting myself in for. I knew nothing about this bloke, except that he was a local villain with form, hardly the sort you would expect a detective to spend a cordial evening with. The pub was located somewhere in the badlands of County Durham: what if he was waiting there with his mates, all fired up to wreak revenge on their common enemy? Belatedly, I realised I should have asked for back-up, someone outside to act as the cavalry if I needed help. It was too late to change things now, so I entered the quiet bar ready to do business. In the event, there were no problems: he was alone, eager to earn a few bob. He even bought me a pint.

He gave me what he could, bits and pieces really, useful for intelligence purposes. He couldn't actually name names for specific jobs, but he knew someone who could. Her name was Joan. 'She'll do *anything* for money,' he said, adding 'but she hates coppers.' Joan had form, and Tony advised me not to call at her house. 'It'll be full of villains,' he said, adding that I could find her at a local club.

I identified her as she danced among the broken glass in the middle of the floor. I went over, and shouted above the loud music.

'Your name Joan?'

'Eh?'

Louder still.

'Is your name Joan?'

'Who's asking?'

The music stopped suddenly. The silence was deafening. I turned on the charm.

'Fancy a drink?'

How could she resist?

At the bar I broke the news. 'Actually, I'm a police officer.'

I braced myself, expecting World War Three to erupt. Instead, once convinced she wasn't going to get nicked, she asked what I wanted. I told her we couldn't talk there. She invited me round for coffee, presumably when the coast would be clear. I was in. My man was right about her love of money, but, as I would discover, it wasn't just money. Like many who 'snout', Joan got a buzz out of talking to old bill, especially *Regional Crime Squad* old bill. She only blabbed about her old man, who was breaking into offices at weekends, posing as a window cleaner.

'No-one ever susses,' she said with pride.

I asked her if she realised he could be arrested, telling me all this.

'Oh, he's inside at the moment,' she said. Actually, I wouldn't have arrested him at that stage anyway, as I considered it might blow her cover. It was a bit close to home!

She told me she'd keep her ears open, and to call again, pointing out it was safe to do so 'through the day'. (Like Clare, she had no phone). When I did, the front door was open, and I sauntered into her living room to find she had company: her girl friends, now looking curiously at the stranger in the jeans and dirty shoes. Their faces said it all. They knew Joan's old man was inside, so who was this? 'It's the man from the insurance,' said Joan, quick as lightning, and in such a way it was obvious I wasn't but at the time planting a false scent in the minds of her mates. In other words, I was her bit on the side. Knowing looks accompanied my discreet exit from the room. Joan was in her element, acting out her role as copper's nark in a complicated plot of intrigue. She told me to come back in an hour.

I came back in an hour.

'There's this factory,' she said. 'Two blokes are having the safe away.'

It would be a Thursday night. She couldn't give a precise location or specify which Thursday, so I couldn't stake it out. A couple of weeks later, a Friday, I spied a teleprinter message: a factory had been burgled and the safe containing wages had been stolen. I went and saw Joan. Yes, that was it. Two of the men were coming to her house later; she would keep them there so we could swoop and make the arrests. But she didn't know where the safe was, so we'd have no evidence.

I was concerned about Joan's welfare, so when we arrested the men we gave some story about them being seen near the factory. We gave Joan a hard time, just to make it a bit more convincing. She turned on a hell-raising performance to make it more convincing still; it was worthy of an Oscar. Neither man admitted anything, but when I said Joan would be arrested for conspiracy they rolled over. Men will often admit things when they see their women might get arrested. How gallant! They led us to the safe. They were charged and convicted. It was a great result. Joan was delighted with her reward; didn't give a damn about the guys she'd shopped. They had protected her, but loyalty was a one-way street, obviously. Tough titty!

More info from Joan led to arrests for burglary, thefts of and from cars (one man admitted over fifty), criminal damage, and three guys who'd stolen a bus! The local CID, whilst appreciating the clear-ups on their patch, were tearing their hair out. Where was I getting the information? I never told them. Things became difficult when Joan's old man got out, so we arrested him (on Joan's info, naturally) for burglary, and he got another custodial. When I went to see him in prison (to see if he would clear up other crimes – he did) he asked me the question I knew would come.

'Who shopped me?'

I couldn't tell him, of course. No doubt he smouldered on his bunk every night wondering which of his mates it was. Meanwhile, Joan played the part of a good wife, visiting him in prison. I knew she did; I was giving her a lift.

One day Joan showed me a load of cassette players, car radios, calculators and some credit cards, all piled up in a cupboard. She said her husband had been getting rid of stolen property before he was sent down, and the guy who was stealing it was still bringing it round to her house. Most was stolen from offices and cars locally. A plan was needed to entrap him. This was slightly dodgy ground. After all, here was I a police officer looking at a lot of nicked gear. But, as Joan explained, it was intended for her old man.

I was worried that the man might suspect that Joan had tipped us off, so when he arranged to see her again, with more gear, we planted a squad officer (not known to him) in her house. He would purport to be 'Mr Big', i.e. someone who would merit the attention of the dramatic-sounding Regional Crime Squad. When chummy arrived with the gear, we swooped, ostensibly to arrest Mr Big, who gave us a load of verbal, called us pigs and so on. We told him – in the presence of the guy with the gear – we'd had him under surveillance for days, that we were arresting him for armed robbery, and carted him off, along with chummy, who thought it was just his rotten luck to be in the wrong place at the wrong time. Once again, an Oscar-winning performance from Joan, as she acted out the role of an innocent woman, tragically caught up in a situation all the fault of her husband. Someone asked if this was *agent provocateur* – where police instigate someone to commit an offence (not allowed under the rules of justice). It wasn't: our man had stolen property without any help from anyone.

About this time, I knocked a bloke off for a high-value burglary at a butcher's shop. He'd broken in one night, with others, and stolen a lorry-load of frozen meat. We recovered all the property and they all went down. But quite a few things about this guy stuck in my mind afterwards. I'll call him Alf.

Alf was an ordinary chap who had turned to crime as a kid, and got sort of indoctrinated. The old proverb might have been written especially for him: *No child is born a criminal...* Chatting over a cup of tea with Alf, you'd never have imagined he'd driven that lorry-load away that night. He was the most tattooed person I ever saw, covered in blue all over his body, arms and legs, face and head, neck, everywhere. (Yes, there too, adorned with the words: All For You. A treat for the ladies, he said).

Alf seemed quite happy to accept his fate – a prison sentence. Some criminals are like that. It's the rules of the game. You commits crime, you takes your chance. Fair cop, guv. Prison to Alf was a way of life. He'd do his penance, be a model prisoner, and do it all again after he was released. I thought he'd make a good 'snout', so I went to see him in Durham.

Just to digress. Prison visits are commonplace for detectives. It doesn't all end when the offender is sentenced. There are other crimes to clear up, information to glean. I visited many prisons, but there was something about Durham, something about those gates when they slammed behind me and I was in that courtyard, fastened in by those grim, stone walls with those tiny, barred windows. How Alf and his ilk can ever keep coming back for another dose is beyond me.

Alf couldn't speak to me in the presence of other prisoners. He had a reputation as a hard-man, and to be seen talking to the filth just wasn't on. So, as soon as I sat down at a table opposite to him, he stood up and walked off, even though earlier we'd got along fine. Later, after negotiation with the prison authorities, we met in private. I asked him if he could give me any useful info, and after offering him a fag (all good detectives should carry a packet of cigarettes when about to talk to a prisoner, unless that's classed as an inducement nowadays) we had a chat.

It was what Alf had to say about the police that interested me. He said he always moved at night because, as he explained, the police never give you a pull. They *used* to, he said, but not now. 'They just sit on their arses,' he explained, adding that many times he'd had stolen property in the boot of a car but had never been stopped. He'd been quite happy to drive from that butcher's with all that meat without interference by police patrols.

Once, he and others were breaking into an office complex when the alarm went off. They fled, but Alf, who had been climbing up the drainpipe, fell and broke his ankle. He managed to crawl away and hide behind some dustbins, although he feared imminent capture. But he wasn't captured because the police never took the trouble to look. Instead, they had a quick recce of the building and scarpered. 'Another thing,' said Alf, 'is when your boys turn out to an alarm they always turn up with their headlights blazing and park at the front door.' In other words, they give warning of their approach, so there's always a chance of escape out the back. This saddened me. A few short years before, as a young recruit, I had learned how police should turn out to an alarm. I had spent four hours checking doors one nightshift, and was making my way into the nick at 2 a.m., when I encountered PC Ken Richardson.

I learned a lot from Ken in the early days. He was known as Muscles, thanks to his phenomenal physical strength. I believed then and still do now that he was the most formidable person I ever knew, and a great copper to boot. Ken would walk around a corner on nights, just as somebody was breaking into a shop. Some said he was lucky. He wasn't; he made the arrests because he looked for them. A classic example of Ken's vigilance came about one night when he spied a bloke standing at a bus stop. He and I were on patrol in the G.P. car.

'Look at him, mucka,' said Ken. Ken called everyone mucka.

He sensed I could see nothing untoward.

'His sack.'

I looked again. There was a large sack on the ground at the man's feet. It obviously contained something very heavy. Ken pulled the car up, and we got out.

'What's in the sack, mucka?'

He had a way of being reasonable about it all. Either that, or his physical presence persuaded folk to co-operate. The guy gave an answer, which was drowned out by the rumble of a passing lorry. All we heard was one word: 'Hoist.' That's slang for nicked.

Ken grabbed his arm. I looked inside the sack. It contained a heavy block and tackle, chain and all. A hoist! We all laughed. Even the bloke. But that was Ken. Ever on the lookout. No wonder he scored so often. But I was talking about my encounter with Ken at 2 a.m. one morning...

'Come on, mucka,' Ken shouted, running to the GP car.

'I'm due in for bait,' I called out, climbing the steps to the back doors. Ken called out across the yard: 'Get into the car.'

I couldn't argue

We sped through empty city streets until, about a hundred yards from the premises, Ken turned off the ignition and headlights and car radio, and cruised to a halt fifty yards from the front door. No-one could have known of our approach. We got out

– without slamming car doors – and hurried on in silence. Ken pointed to an alley, meaning cover the back. I did so, waiting for burglars, if there were any, to pour out the rear. None did; in fact it was a false alarm. But that's how you turn out to alarms. Not with sirens wailing, not by pulling up at the front door, not by using giveaway flashlights. It all seemed like common sense, yet Alf was spelling out what was a bad show. If criminals perceive the police as lazy or inadequate, they are bound to see greater opportunity to commit their crimes undetected.

I often wondered over the years whether Alf finally got himself on the straight and narrow. Maybe he did; he said he would, but then, so do many when they're behind bars. 'Never again, guv.' Yeah, sure. And see you next time.

As I said earlier, the magic word *Regional* carries kudos. It paints a picture of ace detectives, super sleuths whose knock on your door means big-time. Sure, there were lots of good blokes in the squad (no women then), but they weren't all Eliot Ness. Far from it. Take Bill, a detective sergeant I worked with. Bill was a lovely bloke, not to look at – Bill's face looked as though someone had been chopping wood on it – but he was hardly suited to the rigours of the squad. I remember the first time we crewed together. It was a Friday, on lates.

'We're goin' to High Pit Club,' Bill declared.

It was one of those workingmen's clubs, typical of the north-east. It didn't seem a likely place to find thieves. I asked why. 'I always go there Fridays,' Bill explained. Fair enough. He was the sarge. If it meant drinking Fed Special, so be it.

Then, on another Friday afternoon, a phone call came in about a man who worked for a company manufacturing curtain material. Their security suspected him of stealing material from the premises, and today he'd been seen leaving with a sack-full, too late to give him a pull. They gave his address, and Bill and I went to see him. (I don't know why, it was a divisional job). He went ashen when he opened his door to two Regional Crime Squad officers. Bottle gone, he admitted us to his living room, where a mountain of brand new curtain material was piled high on the centre of the floor. Bill asked him if he'd stolen it that afternoon from his employers, and the man admitted he had. He could hardly have denied it!

Bill's face betrayed his mood. Obviously, arresting the man would mean missing out on the ritual of High Pit Club.

'Are you free Monday evening?' asked Bill. He was free. 'Right,' said Bill, telling him to present himself on Monday with the stolen material. The man was only too happy to say he would. Oh, yes, sir. Most definitely. I'll be there.

In the car, Bill sensed I had a problem. 'Something wrong?' he asked.

'Any particular reason we didn't arrest him?' I enquired, knowing full well what it was. Bill considered his reply. 'D'you think we should have?' he asked.

I am happy to relate the man kindly presented himself, as arranged, together with the stolen property. He and two others involved were later convicted of theft, pleading guilty at crown court, where would you believe, Bill and I were commended by the judge for 'attention to duty'!

Bill would talk of his days in the Royal Navy, where he served on submarines during the Cold War. What they got up to behind Soviet lines was frightening. He said if anything happened they'd be 'disowned' by the government. He couldn't say more, he said, because of 'official secrets'. Obviously these missions were more dangerous than arresting someone for stealing curtains. I respected Bill. You couldn't begrudge him his pint in the club, not after what he'd been through.

There was one aspect of squad work where, I must admit, I was hardly successful. It was carrying out what is known as a 'buying job'. This is where a detective poses as a dealer, who is introduced to someone who is in possession of stolen property. I only tried it once.

I was sent to Middlesbrough, where I was unknown, to meet a guy in a nightclub. The info was he had a load of stolen car radios for sale, and my task was to agree a price and get him to meet up somewhere for the transaction when – wham! The troops would swoop and arrest him with the gear, whilst I disappeared into the night. (Not for nothing was the scarlet pimpernel the motif on squad ties). This sort of work is dangerous. I would be in the club on my own, and could expect a smacking if the man or his mates sussed I was a cop, or if by some chance I was recognised. We were introduced by the snout, our conversation drowned in the cacophony of disco music.

'This is Paul,' the snout yelled to his mate. The man nodded.

I then attempted to engage him in conversation, to invite a deal. It was impossible in the din, which frustrated our attempts at dialogue. Then a young thing in a mini-skirt sidled up to the man and started licking his earhole and fumbling with his tie, and he began to lose interest in me for some reason. When she slipped her hand underneath his shirt it became clear his interest in disposing of stolen radios had died completely. This annoyed me, as failure would mean the local squad guys might think me a bit of a washout. I decided to take a tough line.

'D'you realise I've come all the way from Newcastle?' I said.

'I don't care if you've come all the way from Exeter,' he sneered, 'you can fuck off.'

Then he was gone, along with his passionate woman friend, leaving me and the snout and the dancing folk of Middlesbrough to the music. It's strange, but at no point did I feel at ease as a 'buyer'. Not because of the danger – there are plenty of other dangerous aspects to police work – but rather because I just didn't feel I could carry it off. I decided to stick with informants instead. They are dangerous too, but more my line of work, so to speak.

During my time on the squad it was inevitable I'd finish up working in the north-east's other metropolis: Sunderland. With the aforementioned Bill, I arrested three Sunderland lads for burglary. We stopped them bang to rights with a carload of gear, stolen a couple of nights before from a house in Roker. Yet this turned out to be a case where the police, through no fault of their own, bore the brunt of the public's anger.

Naturally, the injured party in this case was pleased when we turned up at his door with his property. He was more pleased still when told all three offenders had been charged. 'What happens to them now?' he asked, in such a way he expected to see them hung, drawn and quartered. When I told him they'd been bailed he went ballistic.

'You mean you've let them go?'

I told him they were 17 or less, that they had fixed addresses, and the property had been recovered. Their brief had no problem persuading the magistrates they were entitled to bail. It did no good. In his eyes the police were soft on criminals, and no wonder no-one supports them any more. But if his reaction seemed unfair, it paled into insignificance when they were given non-custodial sentences.

'What's the point of catching the bastards if you don't lock 'em up?'

The rules of justice allowed their bail, the court passed sentence. Yet no amount of reason could placate his anger against what he saw were deficiencies on the part of the police.

I was amazed at how busy Sunderland turned out to be. The chargeroom teemed with prisoners – car crime and burglary, mainly. One burglar does much the same as another you might think, but here I detected a subtle difference. Where burglars usually break into other people's houses, in Sunderland they were breaking into *each others*! Gas and electricity meters mainly, on housing estates. The detection rate must be high in Sunderland, I reasoned. Nick one and he'll happily name everyone who's done his place.

*

It was nine years since I passed the promotion exam, and I was still a constable. All my endeavours on promotion selection boards had been failures.

The problem was twofold: one, there were dozens qualified in Northumbria, so there was lots of competition for only a few places; two, being seconded to the squad hadn't helped my cause. As someone said, out of sight is out of mind: senior officers sitting on boards were looking at a stranger. Hitherto I hadn't cared; I enjoyed surveillance, arresting villains and squad work. But, as any working detective will tell you, when it comes to promotion it isn't arrests that matter, it's how you are 'assessed', who is batting your corner, what words say on pieces of paper, how you fare in front of the selection board, the latter meaningless unless they are considering you in the first place. Then someone pointed out I owed it to my family and myself to get promoted. I realised he was right.

I'd noticed one or two of my colleagues always slipped away early on Tuesdays – 'freemasons' night. As one admitted, he was in the masons for promotion. Fair enough, he was honest about it – to me, if not the grand master. This was sad: he was a good policeman who was worthy of promotion without having to join a secret society to win favour.

Around this time I happened to bump into Tom Douthwaite, a smashing bloke who years before had been my scoutmaster. Tom was a self-made chap who as a youngster had bought a pair of ladders and a bucket and started cleaning windows. No big deal, you might think, but he went on to form his own business and became a highly-respected member of the community. Tom was a freemason, and had long advised me to join up. 'It's the only way you'll get on,' he explained, meaning promotion isn't a level playing field. Finally, I was persuaded. Okay, I told Tom, I'll join. What happens now?

What happened now was he would propose me and I would be seconded. An inauguration date was fixed: 3 March – my birthday!

As the weeks passed I became more and more ill at ease with the whole idea. Apart from the utter hypocrisy of it all, I just couldn't see myself going through the swearing-in ceremony, rolling my trouser-leg up and wearing antlers and things. Mostly, though, I couldn't come to terms with what would be an admission of failure: unable to win promotion fair and square, joining an organisation in which I had neither interest or respect would be demeaning, something I could not live with. I phoned Tom and told him I'd rather fail to achieve promotion outside freemasonry than succeed within it. He respected my decision and wished me well – but said I might as well forget about promotion. He might have been right, but I'll never know because another police force was advertising for sergeants. Hertfordshire, it seemed, had a dearth of qualified officers, partly due to its proximity to the Met, where you are paid a higher salary with the result that many officers who lived locally worked in London. I applied and was granted an interview.

The idea of living in what I perceived to be a pleasant, rural county appealed. But here I must digress, and admit what I now regard to be a monumental mistake in my failure to consider the wishes of my kids. They were young, but without asking them what they thought I told them they would be moving to the south of England – away from their friends, their school, their grandparents, everything. I never anticipated the torrid time they would have when their Geordie voices brought guffaws from their new classmates, never thought for a moment what they would think of moving to a new town. When I passed the board, I accepted the post.

6

"I am their leader. I really should be following them"

Alexandre Auguste Ledru-Rollin

(famous French politician)

They were staring at the police car, two little girls whose attention for once was distracted from the ducks in the nearby pond.

'The policeman is your friend,' their mother was saying, and she flashed me a smile as she dragged her charges along the footpath.

I watched them go, innocents in a wicked world far removed from the tranquil setting of a sleepy village in Hertfordshire, where I awaited the imminent arrival of PC Speed. Ah, here he came, legs slowly depressing the pedals of his bicycle as he approached on the other side of the village green, my first rendezvous with a policeman wearing a helmet since I was pulled on sus of stealing apples, twenty years before.

'Afternoon, skipper.'

Skipper. That's what they called sergeants in Hertfordshire.

Anything to report? No, all quiet. I signed his book, he said something about the weather. All was well.

If you think I'm being facetious – about the village bobby and all – don't. I've always acknowledged his or her value – on patrol, foot or cycle, town or country, high street or council estate. See and be seen. It would make a good motto. They should try it today.

How different: PC Speed cycling around the Hertfordshire countryside, me patrolling Newcastle's Bigg Market years before. But that was in my past now, and I had made a mental note to remember not to keep mentioning my past. Not like another 'intake' on a course at headquarters. Devon and Cornwall this, Devon and Cornwall that ... Someone passed the inevitable remark: 'If it's so bloody perfect in Devon and Cornwall, why don't you go back?'

I had been a little concerned about how the arrival of a 'foreigner' would be received by my new colleagues in Hertfordshire. Years before, the transfer on promotion of an officer of another force, Grimsby, to my own, had not gone down too well. As someone observed: 'the only use he'll be is for identifying a noisy trawler.'

My Geordie 'marras' had forewarned about the folk of the 'sunny south'. 'They are reserved and stand-offish', I was told. And 'they think folk up north keep pigeons and whippets and smoke tabs.' (As if!). All I can say is the people of Hertfordshire, colleagues and public alike, made me welcome, dispelled the myth, as it were. I was accepted from day one: officers of all ranks were courteous and helpful, shopkeepers on 'Ricky' High Street approached me, shook my hand, welcomed the 'new sergeant' (proof, incidentally, that the public want their police men and women on foot).

I was anxious about the form. Where, up north, years before, we'd started on street corners, I was given to understand officers now paraded formally for inspection. Evidently this meant the production of pocket book, truncheon and handcuffs (which I'd never carried). I'd been out of uniform so long I didn't know what to expect. So, on a dark December night in 1977, having put on a helmet for the first time and sought directions to Rickmansworth police station, I marched purposefully into the Parade Room to face the nightshift.

How many would there be? Five? Ten? In fact, the number of constables parading before the new skipper at Rickmansworth totalled precisely *one*. Considering the size and population of the area he had to cover, I took PC Mark Crampton to be one helluva guy. There was no formal parade – how could there be? – and he didn't show me his truncheon and things. Instead, he 'read up' the Occurrence Book, where constables' handwritten entries, accompanied by snotty notes from sergeants and above, provided a record of events of the past 24 hours, then went off in something called a unit car and wasn't seen again until midnight when the enquiry officer made the tea. Tea in a police station was something unheard of to me. In fact, when Mark appeared I was on the point of ordering him out, but then I remembered I was in a different force, and over the years lots of changes had taken place. Anyway, he was company...

Later, I was introduced to the superintendent, who gave me a whistle-stop tour of the nick, which was helpful, except he kept introducing me as Sergeant Heslop from *Dar-ham*! I presumed he was saying Durham, so I kept telling him Northumbria. It did no good: next office, it was *Dar-ham* again. The chief inspector, Cyril, was intolerant of carelessness or mistakes, and liable to let fly at what seemed the most trivial error, such as failing to enter the date in the Occurrence Book. *Bloody* this, *bloody* that, that was Cyril. But I respected him, because he cared. If something wasn't right, he'd see it. That's what's needed in the police force: someone to make sure the job's done properly. Management's the key-word these days. They should try supervision.

Cyril took me to North Watford police station where I witnessed a bollocking he gave to a PC who'd made a mistake with an entry in the property register, then on a tour of Loudwater, Chorleywood and Moor Park, where I viewed, wide-eyed, some of the most expensive properties in the country. (It was a far cry from Sunderland. I bet they didn't break into each other's houses here).

Strangely, he left out the Meriden estate, which was much the same as the estates of the north-east, only the windows had glass in. But we did make Oxhey, where we found every *bloody* officer on duty skulking inside the nick.

PC Treadway welcomed me to the force.

'Where are you actually from, Skipper?' he asked, donning his coat and helmet (having been told to get out on *bloody* patrol by Cyril).

'Newcastle upon Tyne,' I replied, pleased at such a courteous reception.

He checked at the door.

'Well I never,' he declared. 'I've got relatives up your way.'

'Really?' I replied, in awe at such a stunning coincidence. 'Whereabouts?'

'Dunstable,' he replied.

Then he was gone, a ship in the night, leaving me with the sound of laughter from behind, and yet another *bloody* from Cyril.

My accent was a problem. I recall my swearing-in before the Watford magistrates. There were a few of us (the others were young recruits), and as we each gave the oath to serve Queen and Country the beaks gave nods of approval and smiles of encouragement. Except when it came to me their faces made it clear they hadn't the faintest idea what I was saying. But I was wearing the uniform, so they nodded and smiled for me too.

As far as change was concerned, I'd have faced the same problems if I'd stayed in Northumbria. Things had moved on everywhere. The role of police *women* was the most obvious example. Instead of being fastened in, they were out there on patrol, just like their male colleagues. For me, the notion of women patrolling alone slipped into place like the final piece of a jigsaw. Now and again I noticed some of the older guys still stood back when it come to making the midnight cuppa, that their woman peers still carried out the ritual. I countered the old order one night by waiting till a woman officer was about to put the kettle on, and at the last second asked to see her about something. This left her male colleague with no choice but to step forward and do it. The message got through: all officers are equal. Period.

Apart from helmets for caps, there were differences between the two forces. Take shifts. As I recall, as a PC, I'd never worked more than five straight shifts without a day off. In Hertfordshire, I was astonished to find they worked *seven*, a situation prevailing at the time of my retirement. To my mind, no-one should work seven consecutive shifts routinely (except detectives on incident rooms!). And I found myself having to calculate the overtime, both for individual officers and the entire shift. So many hours at time-and-a-third, time-and-a-half on rest days, double-time Bank Holidays. But hang on, PC so-and-so had two hours off that day, and what's-'er-name wants to carry five hours forward to next month. Oh, and Bloggs was at court off his night-shift, so he's entitled to 4¼ hours time off…

Operational police officers shouldn't be messing about with this sort of thing. The duty sheets should have been sent off to admin for a clerk to complete, leaving police officers to police.

As station sergeant, I had to accept prisoners into custody. This was a direct reversal of roles: until now, I had always taken prisoners in. This meant assessing the facts, ensuring prisoners knew their rights, and ensuring the investigation into alleged criminal offences was being undertaken diligently. Today's custody officers have a far more difficult task, with the stringent rules of the Police and Criminal Evidence Act; one mistake can see an entire case thrown out at crown court, and never mind the evidence. The only problem I had was a prisoner who was PQMS (person of questionable mental stability), who decided to defecate and decorate his cell in monotone-brown. (Actually, his mental stability wasn't 'questionable' at all; he was barking). The gaoler got a bucket and started cleaning it off. As I always said I would never ask anyone to do anything I wouldn't do myself, I joined him. Then we got the council in to decontaminate the place.

Like anyone newly-promoted, I had much to learn. About local procedures, as well as the role of a supervisor. They sent me on a 'management course', where I learned that management courses teach you little except that you need real and practical experience outside. Thanks to being out of uniform for so long, in some respects I found I knew less – sometimes much less – than those I supervised. Take the breathalyser.

As a detective the breathalyser was a thing to be avoided at all costs after a binge in the pub. So, being a stranger to this wonder of modern technology, I read up dutifully, had a good look at the little glass tube and learned how to attach the plastic bag to it (which you did then). I did a deal with a probationer: I'd show her how to take fingerprints if she'd show me how to use a breath test kit. Fair enough. I took her prints, she took mine. Unfortunately, before she could keep her part of the bargain, traffic brought a prisoner in when I happened to be station sergeant. The guy was ratted.

'Blow into the tube,' I said, adding he must blow for ten seconds.

He failed miserably to inflate the bag. The traffic officer waited patiently whilst I checked the kit, handed it back to chummy.

'Try again,' I said firmly, adding, 'if you don't inflate the bag it will be classed as a fail.'

He took a deep breath and *BLEW*. Nothing, except his face had turned crimson. Then the traffic bloke seized the tube, took one look and handed it to me with a look of pained resignation.

'You're supposed to break the bloody ends off first,' he said.

I should've stayed in CID.

I was astonished at the importance officers placed on arresting people for driving over the limit. Where before road checks were set up on nights to try and catch criminals, now eager PCs stepped forward with a breath-test kit, never mind there might be stolen property in the boot or drugs secreted in the dashboard. Still, as one explained, driving over the limit was a danger to peoples' lives, which is more important than recovering stolen goods. Another said no-one in Ricky ever carried stolen goods, but I soon put him right on that score.

As sergeant, I was expected to take the lead when dealing with sudden or suspicious deaths. I'd seen death up north, but it was usually a bloated wretch from the river, or some poor soul who'd collapsed in C & A's or somewhere. Only once had I been present at the identification of someone who had died. He was a 39-year old guy who had taken a civil service examination at the Guildhall. He'd stepped outside and dropped dead. We led his wife into the mortuary. She didn't seem too upset. Maybe she thought there was some mistake, that the body on that cold slab couldn't be her husband. Even as she looked upon his face she seemed reluctant to believe. But then she buried her head in her hands and was led away in tears. Witnessing someone's grief is a sad thing, to be sure.

I'd been lucky when it came to people dying. Like when I went off duty just minutes before a pregnant woman fell underneath the wheels of a bus, which ran over her head. Another time I had just passed the spot where two electricians were servicing a generator, which exploded in their faces. The officer who attended the incident ran to the scene to find them ablaze in burning oil. He could only watch helpless as they died in agony. He was off work for months afterwards. Anyway, now I could expect to be sent to where people had died in their homes. Young constables would look to me for leadership, so I told myself I'd best find out what to do. It's straightforward enough, of course. The doctor refuses to issue a death certificate, but it's usually a heart attack or old age in the end. And if it's suspicious, you call in CID. The coroner's officer deals with the deceased's family.

The call came one Sunday afternoon. A 90-year old woman who had never been ill in her life had cooked Sunday lunch, sat down to watch the afternoon film on tv and died. She was still sitting there, the telly cackling away.

'Such a shame,' said her son, a slip of a lad aged about 70.

'She had a good innings, anyway,' I remarked. Not very original, admittedly.

'I meant she missed the end of the film,' he said, as the music played out Clark Gable or somebody.

Suspicious circumstances? Not a mark on her. It was just a matter of making sure the PM didn't turn anything up (like a dose of arsenic). Others followed, one of which merits recall.

An old boy had died in his bed, also on a Sunday. As his wife explained, he'd been ill for years, so he'd slept downstairs. Why police were called in the first place escapes me now, but this was one of those cases which proves 'there's nowt so queer as folk'. As we awaited the undertaker, I saw the man's wife staring out the window. I went over to do my bit of counselling, to keep her mind occupied until her late husband could be removed.

'Garden's lovely,' I said, adding, 'he certainly had green fingers.'

She turned, looking angry.

'I'm the one with green fingers,' she snapped. 'That bugger never lifted a finger all his days.'

I could only apologise. But she wasn't finished.

'Have you any idea how long this is going to take?' she asked. 'Only my daughter and her husband are coming for lunch and I don't want *him* lying there when they get here.'

She could see I was upset.

'I'll put the kettle on,' she said.

I believe there is much truth in the philosophy that police officers have to see the funny side of some situations, that if they didn't they'd go potty. That's why I make light of it sometimes. But not all death can be treated so lightly. One tragedy comes to mind. It was a big, detached house, and they'd built a swimming pool in the extensive garden. One sunny Saturday, the family begged dad to fill it with water for the first time. He refused at first, pointing out a safety fence he'd planned had not yet been erected. But, in the end he gave in; the pool was filled and his daughter, aged 5, was allowed to play in the water, under close supervision, of course. Then she was ordered out, and that was that. Or so he thought.

When the early evening news came on tv he slipped inside to see it, only to emerge to the screams of his wife who'd found their daughter face down in the pool. I saw her in the ambulance, a mite wearing brightly-coloured wellies, her little face still tortured by her dreadful death. The worst bit was having to visit the pool and her bedroom, where they'd tried to revive her. You have to look at the scene, clear things up for the coroner. Understandably, pressing questions didn't go down too well, but there was nothing more to be done. The little girl's face I will never forget. You can never make light of events such as those.

One man managed to cheat death. It happened at a pop concert at Knebworth Park, where police mingled among the hordes of young people, gathered before a huge, outdoor stage over a long weekend of music, sex and drugs (for them, not the police). People peed here, there and everywhere, couples copulated in sleeping bags (also here, there and everywhere), and passed the reefers around. Fair enough: the music was loud but contained within the park, the sex was their affair, and there were far too many to deal with over the drugs. On the last night, when the music stopped and they turned out the floodlights, disaster struck. Show over, this guy had decided to sleep on the ground in a man-sized polythene bag. He was indistinguishable from the abandoned debris covering the entire area. Which is precisely why he almost met an untimely end.

A bloke who'd been selling hot dogs from an old van decided it was time to leave. Unfortunately, his van wouldn't start, so he asked a mate for a tow. In the darkness, the driver of the other van thought it would be okay to just drive right across all that garbage to get his mate's van going – and drove right over our friend who, as he would later explain: 'felt the front wheels then the back' as they thundered over his sleeping form. As he was carted off to hospital, the two van drivers were past themselves with worry over what everyone thought must be a fatal. But then the word came: the injuries amounted to only a broken leg and lots of broken ribs, along with multiple bruising and severe shock. Only!

Incident over, the drivers went on their way. Hours later, at dawn, I glanced up to see our injured friend, who'd caught a taxi to the arena. He hobbled over on crutches, leg in plaster, rib-cage strapped up, looking like a casualty from the Somme. His face, black-and-blue and grimacing with pain, betrayed his mood.

'Where are the bastards?' he demanded, scanning the rubbish, now blowing over the ground like sagebrush. I tried to cool it.

'You were lucky.'

His jaw dropped.

'Well, *relatively* lucky. After all, you could be dead.'

'I wish I *was* dead,' he groaned.

We took him off for a cup of tea. As the accident happened on private property, there was nothing more to do. I advised him of his options, like suing the two men for negligence. God knows if he ever did. For all I know he shot them.

As anyone with a CID background will admit, you always want to get back to the 'department' after you've been promoted. With this in mind, I was ever eager to make a mark, and made certain I was 'involved' in arrests for crime and interviewing prisoners. This included my role as station sergeant – in fact, especially as station sergeant – where I could get my teeth into prisoners (not literally), helping the arresting officer in interviewing and, to some extent, directing the course of follow-up enquiries. A far cry from today's custody officers, who must remain detached. It makes sense, but there was merit in the old method too: young officers learnt from experienced sergeants, and the rapport between the station sergeant and prisoner was more often than not useful.

Another way to make a mark, I decided, was to cultivate a good informant. I soon identified a suitable candidate. Debbie had come to the police station to make a complaint about her boyfriend. He'd given her a beating, she said, and had the marks to prove it: her face and her arms were black and blue from the night before. He was a small-time crook. She could begin by shopping him, I told her. She wasn't sure about it until I added there'd be cash involved. She said she would, and I arranged to call on her the next day.

If I'd managed just fine with my informants in the north, it wasn't quite so straightforward at Rickmansworth. Debbie lived on the main Uxbridge Road, and as she did not possess a telephone I had no choice but to walk directly to her front door, resplendent in uniform and tall hat. All it took was her boyfriend or one of his buddies to clock me entering or leaving Debbie's, in which event it wouldn't take them long to work out where the info was coming from if they got arrested.

When I called about the promised info on her boyfriend, she announced she'd changed her mind about supporting a prosecution for the assault. (A typical 'domestic'). She gave some snippets about the goings on at a local pub, where stolen gear was being passed across the bar. (I arranged for some obbos, but the DC's specially drafted in were clocked in five minutes flat!).

Later in the year, three of us paid a visit to that same pub, just to show the flag. As we sat in the far corner over three half-pints, a man walked in with a carrier bag containing a bulky object. He sat on a stool at the bar, ordered a pint and placed the carrier with its mysterious contents on to the bar counter. He was just taking a first sip from his pint when, lifting his gaze, he saw us eyeing him with great curiosity. He froze, his pint held close to his mouth as he recognised old bill.

We awaited his next move. It was some time in coming. But we knew, as he knew, he was in a pickle, that it was obvious the contents of that carrier were dodgy. And we knew, as he knew, that if he made for the exit he'd be pulled. So we watched, as his desperate mind sought to find a way out of the situation.

Nonchalantly, he placed his glass on to the bar. Then, ever so nonchalantly, he picked up the carrier with its bulky contents, and ever-ever so nonchalantly, he somehow slid it behind his back and leaned back, still seated, so that his body wedged it tightly against the wall. Then, ever-ever-ever-so nonchalantly, he sat in obvious discomfort and picked up his pint. But when he raised his eyes, he saw old bill was still looking, must have seen what he'd done. And, of course, we had.

We let him stew awhile, talked to one another in such a way he must have known it could only be about him. It was a precious moment. Then we went over and asked for a look inside the carrier. What carrier? *That* carrier! When he reluctantly handed it over, it was found to contain, of all things, a blue flashing light, the sort you see on tops of emergency vehicles. It belonged to a disc jockey, and chummy had nicked it not twenty minutes before from an unattended van. You couldn't make it up.

One good job backfired on me. Slightly.

A probationer constable had arrested this guy for indecent assault on some schoolgirls. He'd been at it for some time, stalking them on their way home from school. It was a tricky situation: as well as dealing with the prisoner we had to keep angry parents at bay. Naturally, as station sergeant, I got in on the interviewing. He admitted all the offences, was charged and bailed, job done. A few days later, file submitted, I was instructed by radio message to attend Rickmansworth police station to see DCI Pickard. Ah, I thought, this'll be about that job with the indecency merchant. I was right, but Mr P wasn't impressed.

'That job merited the involvement of a detective,' he said. 'You should have handed it over.'

'But I was a detective for years,' I countered, pointing out that the man had admitted every offence he had committed over the past weeks. But Mr P, as I would discover, never took kindly to losing anything, including an argument. So, after a pause…

' 'Ow many burglaries did he 'ave then?'

'We didn't ask him about any burglaries.'

'There y'are,' he said, point proved.

*

A year later I was back in mufti. They posted me to Hemel Hempstead, where two armed robberies had occurred. In one, a security van had been held up in one of the highest value robberies ever in the country, and in the other a security guard was shot near a bank in the town. Also, shortly before, a man named Graham Young won national notoriety by systematically poisoning some of his work colleagues. It was a tragic case.

Young was employed at a photographic instruments company, where seventy workers went down with what became known as 'the bug'. Two died. It was all thanks to Young, who had been slowly poisoning their tea with thallium. This, after poisoning his stepmother, father, sister and a schoolfriend nine years before. I don't know who authorised his release, but I hope they were able to live with themselves afterwards. Anyway, it seemed a good place to work as a detective. First, though, I resumed my firearms role.

Sadly, the Smith and Wesson 5-round revolver issued to detectives in Hertfordshire I found unacceptable. Compared with the *Ruger*, it seemed little more than a toy. I went up to the firing range at Royston, and decided there was no way I wanted to face a man with a gun with one of those in my hand. The whole thing became academic anyway when my DI complained about my absence on firearms training days. In any case, to put it bluntly, the novelty had worn off: all that cleaning the firearm and so on. I called it a day.

It wasn't long before I identified my next informant. Ivy was the mother of some local lads who were forever in trouble. I'd heard she hated old bill, so I knocked on her door one day. She stood in the doorway with a steely glare. Her look said it all: who are you? Or, more accurately, who the *fuck* are you? Ivy was the world's swearing champion. To save about three pages, I'll delete the expletives.

'Police,' I said simply, giving her a smile and a shrug.

Surprisingly, she stepped aside and let me in. I came straight to the point.

'Look, I know your boys are always getting nicked...'

'By you bastards...'

'...but they're not the only ones...'

'So why d'you always pick on them all the time?'

'That's why I'm here. It's time the others got nicked.'

'Just what I've been sayin' to your lot at that cop shop.'

'And you can help me nick them.'

She looked surprised, as though she'd never actually had dialogue with a policeman before. Well, she hadn't. She'd always just sworn at them. I decided I was looking at someone who displayed a hard shell to the outside world, but in reality was a reasonable soul whose life was hell because of her family. I said so. She'd found a friend, someone who'd listen, someone who'd understand. She smiled, put the kettle on, started talking. There was no stopping her: she had plenty to say, had wanted to say it for years if only she could.

Ivy's grievance against the police was founded on the repeated occasions her sons were arrested, and had no legitimate basis. It hurt her, obviously. But then, youngsters who are constantly in trouble with the law never consider their parents' feelings, do they? Suffice to say it wasn't long before we arrested a local toerag for robbing a milkman of his takings, and some young

147

blokes for burglary. In the end we got on so well I'd pop in for a cuppa, even if she'd nothing for me. Truth to tell, Ivy was no different from any other mum who stood by her kids. She was kind, she was friendly – once you got to know her. She was also a victim: an old man who was useless and kids who ran riot. There but for fortune, eh?

Then I met Marie.

Nature did Marie no favours: her face was worn through years of abuse by her husband, and a lifestyle of fags and booze. As one of the lads observed: if beauty is skin deep, Marie was born inside out. Her house was one of the worst I had the displeasure to visit as a policeman; you had to wipe your feet on the way *out*. My big mistake was accepting her invitation to sit down on the settee, next to her son who was barely out of nappies, only to find it damp with urine which filtered through my Marks and Spencer trousers. Then, if the little blighter didn't get up and deposit a steaming turd on the carpet, right in front of me. This was completely ignored by his mother, who carried on talking as though it was nothing out of the ordinary. I suppose it wasn't – to her.

Marie's husband had escaped from prison, and turned up at her door one evening, having walked over a hundred miles to get there. Now that's what I call loyalty. He told her he'd be back the following evening. Unfortunately (for him), someone else was staying for breakfast, so she telephoned the police, and a few of us went round to await his arrival. Waiting in Marie's house ought to have merited some sort of special allowance, except I don't suppose anyone ever thought conditions could ever be that bad. Anyway, when her old man slid in through the back window, we were waiting. We told him he would be going back to prison. He wasn't too pleased but, as we explained, at least he wouldn't have to walk.

Marie mixed with the dregs, knew plenty, no doubt about that. And, yes, she agreed to 'snout'. Time and again I'd brace myself and knock on her door for the promised info. Sadly, in vain. She provided little of use. Looking back, I think she just wanted company. In the end, having run out of clean trousers, I gave up. I've never seen her since.

As a detective, I noticed a major difference between prosecuting offenders in Hertfordshire, and my former force. For serious crime, that is. Northumbria had a *Prosecutions Department*, a sort of crown prosecutions service ahead of its time. It was unpopular with detectives because cases tended to be switched from solicitor to solicitor, with the result that several knew something about it, but none knew very much. Moreover, the solicitors had a high workload, having to deal also with minor criminal cases and summary offences, with less time to focus on yours. (Does this ring any bells with detectives dealing with modern-day CPS cases? Don't tell me, I already know!). And there was a perception, perhaps unkindly, that solicitors employed in the Prosecutions Department weren't good enough to get a position with a private company. In Hertfordshire, on the other hand, in a serious or complicated criminal case, the DCI would give the authority for it to be handled by a solicitor from the private sector. I found this strange at first, not least because those same people often acted for the defence. But, for me, Hertfordshire's was by far the best system: the officer and solicitor discussed the case thoroughly, met at appropriate times to discuss its progress, and worked together as a professional team to see it through. As a bonus, young (and not so young) detectives learned much from first-hand contact with first-rate solicitors; and mutual respect between officers and solicitors developed, when the latter acted for the defence in other, unconnected cases.

Unlike working in a big city centre, at Hemel Hempstead I found myself dealing with crime committed by an indigenous population in an expanding, so-called new town. There was a high level of domestic crime, along with the usual theft of and from cars, burglary and so on. As nearly all offenders were locals, we were usually able to develop a suitable repertoire. But as familiarity breeds contempt, so complacency leads to cock-ups. Take the case of a young bloke arrested for burglary.

He would have none of it at first, but after several hours' incarceration he changed his mind and made a full admission. As ever, we asked him if there'd been any others. No, he said, there had not. We were certain there had been, so returned him to his cell to make 'further enquires', and to allow him time to reconsider. After a few more hours we asked him again with the same result. So he stayed where he was.

After what to him must have been an eternity he asked to see us. Yes, he said, he had committed other burglaries and could he clear his slate? Of course, he was told, and we took him to the interview room where he made a statement in which, he said, he had broken into about a dozen houses in the town. He was then taken out in a car and given the opportunity to point them out, before being charged and bailed. He had excellent recall, pointed unfailingly to every address, most helpful to investigating officers. Next day, we discovered that not one had been burgled. What had happened was a lesson for all police officers: fed up with being locked up, our prisoner had made admissions solely to secure release. It proves you should check *everything* out (as we did), and not just take someone's word.

Sometimes, interviewing prisoners produces an amusing side, even though at the time the consequences of your actions might have been serious. One day, Detective Constable Stuart Marvin and I went into a cell to have a chat with a prisoner. (You can't do that sort of thing now, with interviews tape recorded according to certain procedures). The man was amicable, and as we chatted the gaoler brought his tea: sausage and chips. The prisoner said he didn't want it, but it was placed on his bunk anyway. As we chatted, Stuart asked the prisoner if he could have one of his chips. Help yourself, he was told. Stuart did, and by the time we'd finished all the chips had disappeared, along with the sausage. (I never had any, honest). In the end the man was charged and bailed, and that was that.

Only it wasn't for, would you believe, he complained that when he had been in custody, the meal he had been given had been eaten by one of the officers. Thus, later admissions, he maintained – through his solicitor – were made solely to secure release because he was hungry. Stuart admitted devouring the meal, pointing out he'd had no break due to an intense workload when he was about it. OK, it was wrong, but the point is: you can never be too careful, and this story supports the need for stringent supervision of prisoners. A straightforward matter might have failed in court had the jury believed the man only admitted his crimes out of hunger. In reality, it was just the defence trying any trick they could think of to get the case thrown out. It happens all the time (not necessarily over scoffing prisoners' meals).

Stuart was an ace detective, a man who always had a smile, whatever the pitfalls and difficulties. He died of cancer, in his early thirties. It was the first time in my career I felt the loss of a close colleague, and the feeling of 'there ain't no justice' that goes with it.

One morning a young woman came into the police station and said she'd been raped. If you think it strange that I've not mentioned rape yet, there is a very good reason. Rape in the 70's, and before, was almost unheard of. Which is not to say it didn't happen. It must have, but either it wasn't reported to police or, if it was, it was often brushed aside.

I shudder when I think of the way police responded to a complaint of rape in those days. Okay, if a woman came to a police station in a demented state, with physical injuries and her clothing torn, and said she'd been raped, she must have been. But if she had entered the building a week (or even years) afterwards, apparently composed and uninjured, you doubted her story. Of course, it's right to seek the truth, but not by in the first instance implying she's lying, or making it obvious you don't believe her. That's what used to happen.

Rape is often seen as an attack by the man who jumps from the bushes, or appears in a dark alley with a knife. But most rape is *domestic*, that is to say, the offender is known to the victim, who usually doesn't have any visible injury. In law, rape is sexual intercourse by a man with a woman (or, nowadays, with another man) *without consent* or *by force, fear or fraud*. There's nothing about bushes and dark alleys. But, without evidence or witnesses, it is difficult to prove the crime. This is the case even if the man admits intercourse, if he says she consented. Thus a woman who said she'd been raped and didn't have the visible scars to prove it usually found herself back on the street, whether officers believed her or not.

If there is one thing police got wrong over the years it was this response to what is, after all, violation of one human being by another. I had a dose of violation myself once, when a bloke touched me up in a park. I was 15. He had a feel on the outside of my clothing, then made off. I found myself shaking and in tears afterwards. That's nothing compared to rape, you are saying. Damn right it isn't. Yet, as a young detective, when I saw how women who reported something far worse were treated, I said nothing. I should have known better.

Detectives aren't clairvoyant, so they must ask pertinent – and personal – questions. It should be done sympathetically and without prejudice. They should gather all the evidence they can find to establish the truth: early complaint, a medical examination of the victim, an examination (if possible) of the scene, an interview with and examination of the alleged offender. It should all be done with sensitivity, the woman given tangible support, even if her story seems doubtful. Nor does it end when the offender is charged: she will need support at court and even afterwards, possibly for years.

The woman who reported being raped that morning lived in south London. She'd gone to a club the night before, she said, where she'd met a Chinese who'd taken her back to his bedsit, where he'd forced her to have intercourse, and refused to allow her to leave the flat. She wasn't physically injured, but said she had succumbed to his demands out of fear.

The Chinese bloke was still in his bed when we called to arrest him. He sat up abruptly on sight of detectives, raised him arms, as though he was going to put up a struggle. In fact, his reaction was born out of fear. He was scared to death, it was obvious. It was difficult to reassure him, as his English was poor. He 'came quietly', evidently more relieved not to be beaten black and blue than concerned about losing his liberty. It made me wonder if, perhaps, he'd been in trouble in China, that maybe there he'd had a going over by the Red Guard, or whoever. Anyway, with gestures we could communicate – just – and, having seen we weren't brandishing iron bars, he was only too willing to talk.

'Did you meet a woman in a nightclub in London last night?'

Yes, he did.

'Did you give her a lift to your flat?'

Yes, he did.

'Did you have sexual intercourse with her?'

Yes, he did.

'Did she consent to intercourse?'

Yes, she did.

The issue was consent. Who would *you* believe?

It's important to remember police officers aren't judge and jury, but there comes a point when you have to make a decision: do you pursue the complaint or not? On one hand, you owe it to a rape victim – if she's been raped. But you mustn't lose sight of the alleged offender's welfare either: after all, if she's lying, you've arrested an innocent person. Ultimately, it may be right to put the facts before a jury. But, equally, police can be criticised, not least by judges, for wasting a court's time. In this case, the woman admitted lying. She'd got drunk the previous evening and finished up miles from home without any money. She wanted the police to get her home, that's all. We had to consider charging her with 'wasting police time', but if we had we'd have been wasting time ourselves. The case would have had to be referred to the Director of Public Prosecutions, who'd be unlikely to pursue what he would have regarded as a trivial matter; and the Chinese bloke would have emigrated before entering a courtroom (as a witness), or had to be dragged there. Reports of rape may be false, for all manner of reasons, which is not to say they should be treated with doubt or scorn.

Far from it, as another case proves. This one concerned a schoolboy, but the principle remains the same. He turned up at the enquiry counter one morning, accompanied by his mother. She told police he had gone missing the previous day, a Sunday, and stayed out all night, turning up around six in the morning. When she asked him where he'd been he said a strange man had picked him up in his car and wouldn't let him go. What's more, he had 'interfered' with him.

I spoke to the boy, who admitted his parents had always told him never to go with a stranger, and especially never to get into a stranger's car. So, had he made up a false story of 'interference' through fear of retribution by his parents? My own judgement – kept to myself – was that his story was false, that he'd been larking about and was too scared to go home. I was wrong. That he'd been abducted was not only true, but a medical examination revealed he'd been buggered by his assailant. This part of the story had been too embarrassing for him to divulge, so here we had a victim falling short of giving a full account of events. It's a tricky business!

The man had offered the boy a lift in his car, and as he was worried about getting home late he'd accepted. He was then taken to a secluded country lane and sexually assaulted. The man kept him in his car all night, refusing to let him go. Finally, around six in the morning, the boy had fled.

He was able to give a reasonable description of the man, and the car. But we had little to go on, except it didn't look as if the offender was local. He said the man had bought a pint of milk from a milkman around dawn, which they'd shared, before the man threw it into a hedgerow. He was uncertain of the location, but accompanied police on a search of lanes and byways, and the bottle was found, lying in the hedgerow, as he had described. Fingerprints on the bottle turned up the name of a man who lived in London. He had previously committed a similar offence, and been given a long prison sentence. But, of course, no-one does the time. Now he'd done it again. He got life. I wonder how long he actually served.

On of my 'responsibilities, as detective sergeant in those days, was 'Property Subject of Crime' (PSOC). This involved checking the PSOC register at frequent intervals, along with 'property' which had come into the possession of the police and which was or was believed to be stolen – cash, bicycles, cars, television sets, anything really, or otherwise connected with crime: drugs, jemmies, knives and so on. The stolen property was retained pending the outcome of a case at court, before being returned to its owner; or where the owners were unknown, and in the case of burglars' tools, sold at auction or destroyed. I considered this to be a civilian post (as it now is), but I was lumbered with it anyway.

Naturally, during busy periods (which is most of the time, if a DS is doing his job properly), checking the PSOC took second place to investigating crime and arresting villains. I simply hadn't the time (or the inclination) to tour the division checking property stores, cupboards and police yards. Still, I made the effort when I could (usually waiting until a formal check was long overdue, in which I would have to work overtime to do it). Anyway, one day, when my shift and I had a shed full of prisoners, my divisional commander, probably bored sitting up in his office, demanded an impromptu check of the PSOC store.

Registers in hand, we commenced a check of the main store. A jemmy, in police possession since whenever. Where was it? Oh, yes, there it is. Good. What about these trainers? They're going mouldy in that polythene bag. A burglar wore them when he broke into a house? Hmm. And that radio-cassette? Stolen property, guv. Case is going to crown court. And so it went on, until we came to the fishing gear.

It comprised a fishing rod and reel, and bits and pieces, including two small tobacco tins. Found by the canal, owner not traced, as I recall. It should have been disposed of about three years before, but languished in the store anyway. Tut-tut.

The chief super picked up the tins, each of which had a piece of paper stuck on the lid, with the word 'Maggots' written on it in biro. As he handed one to me, I realised he wanted to look inside the tins.

'You first, sarge,' he said.

I looked down at the tin, my imagination running riot at the thought of writhing maggots inside. Were they still there, I wondered?

The chief super was waiting.

I took a firm grip, slowly unscrewed the lid and looked inside the tin. Apart from a few small particles of grit, it was empty. No maggots! Now it was the chief super's turn.

Just as I was preparing myself for the joyous moment when he would, to his horror, discover his tin to be crawling with maggots, he hesitated, then handed it to me, bottle gone, clearly nauseated at the thought of what he might be holding in his hand.

'You might as well do the other one, sarge,' he said, in such a way there would be no discussion about it. Then he declared he had other, pressing business, and fled from the room, leaving me to get on my work. He never asked, and I never did tell him, but for the record the other tin was empty, too.

Missing persons always give rise for concern, especially those classed as 'vulnerable'.

One day, a young Pakistani woman was reported missing by her parents. She was about to become a bride in an arranged marriage, but she'd never met her husband-to-be, and wanted instead to marry the man of her own choice. So, when her family refused to consent to her wish, and insisted on the arranged marriage, she fled with her lover – a check with the airline showed their names on an outward flight to Karachi. Her parents were distraught when they heard the news.

I suggested she might return one day, that she might find happiness, that family ties might be redrawn. This was met by a stony silence. I guess she probably never did come back home. I offer no opinion about the culture of the people of another race, except to say that young people of that race, when brought up in a country of different cultural standards, are liable to be influenced by what those cultural standards are – in this case, freedom to choose one's own partner.

My fair share of suicides continued, including on the railway, where we picked up the pieces of some poor soul who'd ended it all by standing in front of the Euston-bound express. His remains were splattered all over the line and even the station platform, where early-morning commuters mingled in blissful ignorance. We were there ages, searching for a missing leg, whilst all the time mainline trains thundered through the station. In the end, his leg wasn't missing at all. It was in a polythene bag, along with all the rest of him. Except for the gunge on the platform, of course. Looking back, I can't ever recall accounting for his head. Maybe it's still there.

Another suicide I'll mention, not least to show tragedy of suicide itself.

An old boy had walked out of Woolworths with a packet of onion seeds, valued at 19 pence, without paying, and was arrested for shoplifting. He had no criminal record, and was a respected member of the community. Maybe he forgot to pay, maybe not. Whatever, he was next seen hanging from a tree in, appropriately, Hanging Wood. Evidently the shame was too much to bear.

*

In 1980 they sent me on another detective training course, this time to the Metropolitan Police training centre, at Hendon. It was an 'advanced' course, supposedly a step up from the 'initial' course at Wakefield, years before. I can offer no opinion on 'initial' courses at Hendon, then or now, but if Wakefield was Premiership, as far as the 'advanced' course was concerned, Hendon was non-league. Where before there'd been first-rate instruction on criminal law and procedure by dedicated tutors, now there was second-rate instruction by dedicated detectives. In short, the tutors at Wakefield *wanted* to be tutors; at Hendon the detectives were tutors because they'd been told to be. I spent six weeks at Hendon, which, as far as furthering my professional knowledge was concerned, was a waste of taxpayers' money. The only test I can recall was the preparation of a project, a load of tosh that we presented to a bored audience at the end of the course. When will those in authority realise that without tests, those who have been 'taught' won't have learnt anything?

Actually, it wasn't all a waste of time, for we went to the Yard to learn about terrorist groups and their leaders. We were shown different types of explosive devices, including some the IRA was using. One was a simple alarm clock, attached to a bomb; when the pointer reached a thin strip of metal it completed the circuit, triggering the blast. Another device, with a phial containing mercury, was fixed to the intended victim's car. The mercury would swish around the tube when the car was driven off, making contact with electric points, detonating the charge. This was the type of bomb that killed the MP Airey Neave outside the House of

157

Commons in 1979, exploding as he drove out of the underground car park.

Other bombs were more sophisticated, and to demonstrate what the bomb disposal people had to face we were shown a series of wires and switches on a make-believe device, which we were asked to examine, and calculate which wire to cut to render the circuit useless. If we were right, the 'bomb' would have been defused; wrong and there'd be a loud bang. Easy for an ex-electrician. One glance at the circuit and I cut the wire. *BANG!* That was the first and only time I attempted to defuse a 'bomb'.

Again, the inevitable night out, this time to a club in the City, where our money paid for entry, bangers and mash and an evening of entertainment. When I say I was taken by surprise by the latter, I mean it literally. A woman, stark naked, appeared and led me, out of over seventy blokes, on to centre of the floor. To a loud cheer, she was joined by two others in similar attire, and they began undoing my tie and shirt and trousers. Being quick-witted, I realised they were going to take *my* clothes off too. Trouble was, they'd caught me a bit too early, i.e. before I'd poured enough booze down my throat. I bottled out, allowing some other stooge to take my place. A lot of harmless fun went on before they walked off to grand applause. But they weren't finished.

After a break they returned, and another willing stooge was undressed. Then, to steady handclapping, varied sex acts were performed: cunnilingus, fellatio, masturbation, mostly all at the same time. You might think there'd be eager volunteers to take a turn, but, strangely, there weren't. Either a state of genuine shock prevailed among those present that night, or no-one else had the will or bottle to take part. Everyone got ratted, including me. Later, after crawling into my bed at Hendon, the door was opened and one of my colleagues was unceremoniously dumped on to the floor in the mistaken belief that it was his room. Somehow, I managed to drag him into the corridor, where I left him for dead. (It's OK, he survived. Made superintendent, actually).

7

"I saw no-one.
That is what you may expect to see when I follow you"

Sir Arthur Conan Doyle

As usual, the streets of the capital were chokka. As we threaded our way slowly to our 'plot', the car radio crackled into life.

'Cancel all operations. Proceed to Heathrow and await further information.'

And there we were, mingling with the crowd at *International Arrivals*, where passengers off the flight from Johannesburg emerged onto the airport concourse. One of the passengers, we were told, would have two suitcases stashed with heroin. The problem was: we didn't know who. Then came the message from Customs: the two suitcases had been taken off the plane, and had been allowed through for collection.

Who would pick up the suitcases?

The more you look, the more you see. Or think you see. Was it that young bloke in the flash suit? Or maybe that smart couple in their thirties? What about those two big guys, the ones who looked like Chicago gangsters? We were all wrong: it was the woman in her seventies, dressed in black and smiling gratefully at the kindly porter now pushing a fortune in heroin on a trolley towards the exit. Who'd have guessed?

We hovered, anxious to see if she'd be met. She was. Another passenger, a tall, debonair gent, hurried forward as she arrived at the taxi rank outside. He looked handy. Might be armed even. It became academic as half a dozen detectives pounced, forcing him to the ground. He struggled against the combined weight of those who now restrained him, fought desperately for his liberty, grimaced at the well-aimed swipe from my briefcase. As he succumbed, the old woman stood smiling, her baggage momentarily unattended as the porter looked on, goggle-eyed. It was all over: two arrests and a fortune in drugs recovered. As I have said time and again, *information* is the key to success in the fight against crime.

It was a clever, if ultimately failed tactic by the man and his courier. Customs would never have checked out the old woman. Instead, they'd have checked matey and found him clean. He did it for profit; the old woman did it for a free ride. She said she'd always wanted to visit England. Well, now she could enjoy her visit as a guest of Her Majesty. She got two years.

We knew from intelligence most of the addresses for which the heroin was intended, and it would have been better to have allowed delivery to prove involvement of all concerned: the pushers, the manipulators. But the risk of losing the targets in the London traffic was too great, so we took what we could – the international couriers.

'We' were the Regional Crime Squad, detectives seconded from forces of the northern Home Counties. Sometimes we worked with colleagues from the same office, sometimes with detectives based in other towns. Whatever, we almost always finished up working in London. That meant surveillance in London. 'Why don't you work in your own counties?' someone asked me once, pointing out loyalty should begin at home. So it should. Our targets lived in London, sure, but they were driving out into the shires to commit their crimes. Modern motorways provide rapid escape routes (except the M25, I suppose).

Surveillance on Tyneside was easier than surveillance in the Met, where the volume of traffic and the sheer size of London provided a far greater challenge. If you aren't much cop at surveillance in the first place, trying to follow someone in London finds you out.

As before, sometimes surveillance paid off, sometimes it didn't. It didn't on Operation Royale. Our target lived at Earls Court, but he was burgling houses in Hertfordshire. According to intelligence, anyway. There was no pattern, no regular routine. And our informant could only provided information *after* the crime! There was nothing for it but to sit on his flat, follow him everywhere, every day. Yet he always seemed to drive to nowhere in particular. If, due to other operations, we missed a day, you could bet your bottom dollar he'd strike. One day he broke with the usual routine, and jumped on to the tube at Earl's Court station. This is it, we thought. He'll be met by someone with a car, and drive out to the sticks. Game on!

Surveillance on the Underground is different: you can't get radio reception (we couldn't anyway), and the inevitable crowds make it difficult to maintain contact with the target. So you work as individuals, in the knowledge that your colleagues on the street above – in their cars – won't have a clue where you've gone. By the time they've got out of Piccadilly, you could be tailing the target along some leafy avenue in Bexleyheath.

A few of us bundled on to the train. As we thundered beneath the streets of the capital, I held on to one of those dangling straps, watched chummy further along the crowded carriage. He never suspected the presence of half a dozen detectives, and when he took the escalator to the street, we were right behind him – all the way to the Odeon, Leicester Square. The following day – when not under surveillance – he was arrested on a rooftop by local police, guided in by the Met helicopter. So, all the hours spent watching his front door, and following him to nowhere except the pictures were a waste of time. Some you win, some you lose.

One job that came up trumps concerned two young blokes. We knew they were 'busy', committing day-time residential burglaries. We took them off after they'd reported to the local probation office and set off, on foot, in their wake. (Probation was doing them a world of good, obviously). Foot surveillance around a quiet housing area is far from easy. You are likely to show out with just one glance from your target. Unlike, say, a busy town centre, there's no cover, nowhere to 'blend in'.

They ambled along, looking for likely houses. As I explained earlier, people look but don't necessarily see, even when they're up to no good. On that particular follow, as one of the targets glanced in my direction, I responded by walking up to a detached house and knocking on the door. It was opened by a woman wearing a dressing gown and a friendly smile. You have to be cool. I apologised for the intrusion, and asked directions to a street I knew perfectly well was just around the corner. She put her hand to her mouth, they way you do when you know the answer but just can't think of it. She looked left, right, then paused for thought. Then, just as she seemed to find the answer, I walked off, leaving her thinking I must be some kind of madman.

That was nothing compared to the reflexes of one of my colleagues. Realising he, too, might show out, he did no more than walk straight into someone's front garden for a pee. Outrageous, you might think, but we were after burglars, and that's all that mattered. To us, anyway. Whether the householder at that particular address would have condoned his actions is open to conjecture. Finally, our heroes sneaked down an alley at the side of a house. I stood at the front, listened as they smashed in the reinforced glass of the back door. Caught 'em bang to rights, as they say. I don't know about you, but that's what I call a good morning's work, made even better when they admitted every house they'd broken into over the past weeks.

The expertise (or otherwise) of the *region's* detectives at surveillance was put to the test one day on a mock-kidnap/blackmail exercise. The idea was to be ready for the real thing if and when it happened. In a genuine case, it is imperative not to show out to the kidnappers, whilst at the same time police must make arrests without endangering the life of the victim. It was given the full monty, with detectives from Oxford to Cambridge taking part.

Especially for the operation – no expense was spared – each crew was supplied with two brand new hardback atlases: one of Great Britain, the other of London. Each had a laminated grid inserted, enabling us to identify a location by a given map reference. So, instead of broadcasting give-away locations, like the identities of towns, map references would be transmitted instead. That would fool anyone eavesdropping on confidential police messages.

Doug and I were instructed to proceed to map reference so-and-so in the Britain atlas. It turned out to be a tiny village somewhere in Oxfordshire. We drove off up the M40, and parked by the village green to await further instructions. There we watched the world go by: a different world, a sleepy, dreamy world, where the birds sang and the ducks made their way lazily – and safely – across the road for their morning dip in the pond. Hard to believe we were but an hour's drive from the busy streets of London. We waited a long time. Too long. We felt something was wrong, but we couldn't ask, as the whole point was radio silence. But in the end, after many hours, we drove back to the Smoke, where we found everyone else in an equal state of bewilderment. What had gone wrong?

Some clever-dick had inserted the laminated grid for the *Britain* atlases in to the *London* atlases, and vice-versa, that's what. When I inserted the correct grid into the *Britain* atlas, I discovered we should've been parked up in Slough! After that, I made a mental note not to call the police in the event of any of my loved ones being kidnapped!

My first job on the Regional (in the south-east) was to arrest a man for handling stolen goods. He worked at a club in Luton, where he had been receiving stolen property, brought to him by men who had been committing burglaries in Hertfordshire. George had no form. He was just a guy who'd succumbed to temptation. It was easy: the burglars stole the property, brought it to him at the club, he got rid. We took him from his bed and interviewed him about his wicked ways. He might have been a stranger to police tactics, but he was no fool. He admitted nothing over two days of interrogation.

This, of course, was before the Police and Criminal Evidence Act, 1984. Today, we'd never have been permitted to interview George for such a protracted period. Instead, interviews and holding prisoners in custody are done against the clock. It's a sort of game, like one of those quiz shows. 'You've so many minutes to prove the case, starting – now!' To me, this isn't justice. I'm not suggesting police should be allowed to hold suspects indefinitely. But if criminals would say something, like the truth, they would find themselves questioned for not nearly so long. Innocent people are likely to tell the truth in any case.

We charged George with handling a stolen tv. He pleaded not guilty at crown court. I was in the witness box ages, during which time his defence really had a go, virtually accusing me of fitting him up, saying he'd said things which he said he hadn't. But the notes were written at the time, and were accepted as the truth. George didn't admit anything, and I never said he did. It was just the defence trying to cast doubt in the minds of the jury, and to hell with the evidence of the officer, even though honestly given. That's part of the game, too.

George was convicted, and as he was just one of many arrested on what was a big police operation, a prison sentence seemed certain. But, just prior to sentence, his barrister, now wearing a patronising smile, said he wanted to ask a question of the officer. I returned to the witness box.

'Would you say my client is the sort of man who would never have turned to crime if temptation hadn't been put to him by others?'

I looked at George, now staring at the floor of the dock. At that moment, I knew, his immediate future, and that of his wife and family for that matter, lay in my hands. Who was I to play God? I considered the question, and said George had been the victim of temptation, which I believed to be the truth. He was put on probation. A few years later I chanced to meet him in a pub. He shook my hand, bought me a drink. And no, he'd not been in trouble since.

Incidentally, George was another reason for one of those trips to another force area. This time it was Bristol. I'd never been to Bristol before, so after a beer or three the local lads granted my request to be taken to the Clifton Suspension Bridge. I knew it was high, but how did it feel to look down from it? I walked half way across, then peered over. Suffice to say I'll never do it again. It's a perfect spot for suicide, of course, and it came as no surprise to find the Samaritans have their name and telephone number at each end of the bridge. Amazingly, one woman failed in her attempt to end it all. In 1885, Sarah Ann Henley, who'd had an argument with her lover, failed when the crinoline hoops of her petticoat acted as a parachute. She lived to be 85. (I bet they still called the DI).

Talking of wives and families – as I was when I mentioned George – it was around this time my own marriage finally hit the rocks. I say finally because, as in most cases (I suppose), when you're on the slippery-slope, it takes time to grind to a permanent halt, at least when there's no 'other woman' involved, which there wasn't. Friends asked if the police force was to blame. I really don't know. Sure, detectives work long hours, often without notice, and they don't see as much of their loved ones as they should. Maybe the job changes them, turns them from what they were to what they ultimately become. Anyway, no longer your Mr Average family man, I found myself living in a one-bedroomed flat, with a three-ringed electric cooker and a Hotpoint freezer for company. I quickly learned two things: one, living alone when you've spent nearly twenty years with your wife and kids isn't all it's cracked out to be; and two, television is utter crap.

Still, confident of my ability to survive, I got to grips with the day-to-day chores of living on my own. Like cooking for one. Hitherto, my culinary expertise had extended little further than fish fingers and chips, so I decided it was time for new horizons, as far as the kitchen was concerned. Hence a whopping great pizza found itself being inserted into the oven one evening, prior to a nights obbos. I enjoyed it too, although it was, I had to admit, rather crispier than I imagined it would be. A mere mouthful or two only remained before, belatedly, I realised I had consumed the cardboard base. It repeated on me all night, I don't mind admitting. Frankly, I've not been too partial to pizzas since, although, in fairness, I can hardly blame the Italians.

Living alone whilst seconded to the Regional was a lonely experience. Alone at home; alone at work, where, if there was company, it was usually male. At least in division I could have fluttered about the nick, wandered into the typists' office, perhaps, for a natter and a sniff of Chanel No. 5. Never mind, I told myself, there was always the Metropolitan Police Sports and Social Club, where the squad went to wind down after long days on surveillance. They even had me playing cricket for the first and only time in my life. Heady summer's evenings spent on the boundary, a grand recipe for relieving stress after a long day. It's a great game. Makes you wonder why a country like England can't field an international team worthy of the name.

*

5 a.m., somewhere in east London. A lone car appears, and the driver pulls over, finding himself surrounded by armed police. He cannot know that they are waiting by the roadside on that dark morning just for him. He lowers his window, is taken aback when I speak his name.

'We are Regional Crime Squad officers. I am arresting you for armed robbery and burglary.'

Told he was being nicked for armed robbery, you'd think he'd have said *something*. But Ted wasn't saying anything: not in the car, not in the police station, not anywhere. Except to give his name, address and date of birth. Like a soldier, captured by the enemy: name, rank and serial number, and that's it.

It all started with a 'supergrass', D, who, months before, after being arrested for armed robbery, 'rolled over', telling police all about his crimes and, more importantly, the crimes of associates – naming names, giving all relevant details. Facing a lengthy prison sentence, he had decided to co-operate, and the interviewing officers recorded all the facts: listing the offences (nearly all in London), building up an intelligence bank. For his trouble, D was given preferential treatment on remand, hoping that ultimately he would get a lesser sentence. The downside was forever after his life would be in danger, and a false identity would be necessary to ensure his safety. He had fantastic recall. Every detail of the activities of his and his fellow-criminals was written down. The robbers' MO was to hold up a security van at gunpoint, or maybe walk into a bank or building society with a sawn-off, fire a round into the ceiling, and when staff were suitably terrified and handed over the money they'd flee, going to ground in a 'safe house'.

Having gleaned the information, police proceeded with arrests, but securing convictions needed corroboration – independent evidence to back up D's testimony. There was virtually no hope of recovering stolen property – the robberies had taken place years before. This meant police needed admissions from hardened criminals who were unlikely to admit being born, let alone robbing banks five or ten years ago. But the philosophy of Brian Ward, the detective chief inspector who ran the enquiry, was sound.

'They'll be queuing up to admit their crimes, and point the finger' said Ward, adding that every one of those arrested would want to get in first before somebody else 'rolled over', as D had done. Their fear would be not rolling over in time, finding themselves charged and facing long prison sentences.

Operation Carter, Phase One, was the arrests of criminals named by D. Just as DCI Ward had predicted, one of them 'rolled over'. S admitted every robbery he'd done over the years, and named every accomplice: from gangsters who would shoot to kill, to getaway drivers and the locations of safe houses. He became the next 'supergrass', and over the following months, as he provided the 'intelligence', DC Brian Sansom and I were charged with collating it.

It was a long, painstaking job, requiring careful collation of all the facts provided by S: names of offenders, particulars of every crime they had committed and with whom, what vehicles they'd used, and so on. All relevant crime reports, most of them years old, had to be recovered, mainly from the Yard. Each offender, or target, was given a number, and a file prepared so that when the time came the arresting officers would be in possession of as much detail as possible about him, his associates, and details of every offence and the part they played.

When all that S could tell us was complete it was time for Operation Carter, Phase Two. Investigating detectives, armed with their intelligence files, had to 'house' their targets, and build on the information they had been given. Brian and I had a target of our own: Ted was Target 19.

S, in his statement, named Ted as a man responsible for a number of burglaries, twenty years before, and later, taking part in armed robberies in north London, like the hijacking of a security van, when Ted, with others, had climbed into the rear of a lorry fitted with shutters. When the security van was sighted it was rammed, and the robbers, armed with guns and pickaxe handles, threw up the shutters and poured from the rear of the lorry.

As Brian and I beavered away at S's statement, and colleagues went about their work in the incident room at Reading, a BBC film crew drifted about the police station, recording what we were about. It was part of a documentary, *Police*, to be screened later in the year. It was strange at first. You'd be talking to someone when, glancing behind you, there'd be a guy holding what appeared to be a fishing rod, at the end of which a microphone dangled above your head. Then you'd look elsewhere and there was someone else pointing a video-camera. At first I found it intrusive, but in time got used to it, accepted it as part of the background. Just the same, I was somewhat tongue-tied when, after that early arrest of Ted, I found myself cornered in the incident room, facing the camera. What had happened, I was asked? How had the arrest gone? Eager faces awaited the answer, which would be broadcast to every television set from Land's End to John O'Groats.

It wasn't that I had a problem with the mike and the camera. I knew the television people wanted something exciting; after all, it's their job to entertain. But the arrest was so ordinary, with Ted saying nothing and coming quietly, I felt silly saying so. It would have been better if he'd made a run for it or pulled a gun or something. The arrest of the tramp, William Hutchinson Stewart, all those years before, was more exciting.

All we had to do now was get Ted to admit to his crimes.

Reading police station couldn't house all the prisoners arrested that night, so we took Ted to Henley-on-Thames. I must say it seemed bizarre: a robber from London's east-end now languishing in a cell in sleepy Henley. I don't think they were used to housing prisoners: the cells were so decrepit the locks didn't work properly.

As someone who'd been in and out of prison all his life, Ted knew the form. There was no stolen property recovered, no forensic evidence, no witnesses – other than S, his accomplice. So he maintained his steely silence. After breakfast in Henley's Wimpy bar, Brian and I went off to interview Ted, seeking the admissions we needed. He was shocked at the accuracy of the allegations being put to him. He shook his head, wondering who could possibly have grassed. In the end he asked us point blank. We told him. 'No way,' said Ted, meaning he knew someone had shopped him, but not a hard man like S. Not the man he'd known for all those years, the man he'd stood shoulder to shoulder with on so many armed robberies. He had nothing more to say, except to request a wash and a meal. Good idea, we told him, returning him to his cell, inviting him to think about what we'd said. Brian and I went back to the Wimpy for a coffee.

When we returned Ted refused to come out of his cell. No matter, we went through the precise details of every burglary, every robbery, describing in detail the parts he had played. Ted must have known S really had 'gone over', for the facts put to him he would know to be true. He sat stony-faced, staring at the floor. We thought S's statement was our ace card, the one thing to persuade him to admit his crimes. He wouldn't stand back and allow S to take the rap alone, surely. But Ted stayed silent, except to state that S's statement was a fake, that S had never signed it, that it was a 'fit-up'. He told us to leave him alone, so we went back to the Wimpy to let him think about it. An hour or so later, we returned to find Ted had changed his tactics. Instead of allowing us to talk, he was shouting at the top his voice:

'C.O.M.P.L.A.I.N.T.!!!'

The station sergeant appeared, and asked Ted what his complaint was. All Ted could tell him was that he wanted Brian and myself off his back. It became impossible to communicate, so it was back to the Wimpy.

Later, Ted changed tactics again.

He was lying face down on his bunk, blankets pulled over his head. He refused to look at us, said he wasn't listening. However, as I pointed out to him, he could refuse to speak, but not to listen. So we went through S's statement again, reading out one by one the offences he had committed over the years.

'I'll leave the statement with you, if you like,' I told him.

'You needn't bother,' said Ted, 'I won't read it.'

We repaired to the Wimpy again.

Returning to Ted's cell, we found him staring at the wall. He told us he'd not read the statement, but we knew he had.

'You're wasting your time,' he declared.'

'The statement is true,' I told him.

'Oh, yeah? Well, bring him here and let him say it to my face.'

Ted thought there was no way his friend would shop him in the presence of any police officers. But he was mistaken. At that point we wheeled S into Ted's cell. As S went through his statement, Ted listened in disbelief. It was enough: he made a full confession.

Once Ted started there was no stopping him. It was almost with pride that he took us through the armed robberies, the burglaries. Later, he joined us upstairs for tea and biscuits. He was a different man, as though a tremendous weight had been removed from his shoulders. He said it was good to get out of his cell. We said it was good not to return to the Wimpy bar.

He talked of his upbringing on the streets of the east-end of London, how he'd turned to petty crime when young. He'd never been violent, not even on the robberies. He was a man easily manipulated by others, men like S. He hated police, because, as he explained, he had served a prison sentence for a robbery he did not commit. There seemed no reason to doubt him, for what he said now had nothing to do with his present incarceration. The robbery, he said, was committed by a man disguised as a postman, in a provincial town he had never been to in his life. Yet police knocked on his door one morning and arrested him. All they had was an identikit of the offender. 'It looked like me,' said Ted, and on the strength of that alone he was charged. He stood trial at Oxford crown court. 'Those juries, out in the sticks' said Ted. 'They think if the police arrest somebody it must be them.' The jury obviously thought Ted was guilty; he was convicted, and sentenced to two years.

If anyone was living proof that you are what you are because of your background, it was Ted. Over the weeks that followed I came to regard him as a proud individual, someone you could trust. He was fiercely loyal, and I do not believe he would ever have 'gone over' on his mates, no matter what. But fate had not dealt him a kind hand: he had been brought up against a background of petty crime, so maybe it came as no surprise when he succumbed to crime himself. He was 'institutionalised', as he proved one morning on one of his remand appearances at Reading.

They were short-staffed, with no-one available to ensure the prisoners got some exercise. I told the station sergeant we'd see to it, and escorted Ted outside to the small exercise yard. No sooner had he emerged from the building than he proceeded to march around the yard, striding purposefully into every corner, making the most of the opportunity of fresh air and the chance to stretch his legs – just as he did in prison. Ted agreed he'd been treated fairly. If ever I saw him again I'd be more than happy to spend time over a drink. Whether he would is debatable, I suppose. Maybe being institutionalised doesn't extend to socialising with old bill. Anyway, Ted got ten years.

Operation Carter wasn't finished. Just as S had 'rolled over' on Phase One, so did Y on Phase Two (thus creating a Phase Three). Y's information concerned a team of professional criminals who had committed burglaries in London and the south-east. They would target gold and silver, and even had a smelting plant in a private house. Their 'business' had been so lucrative, they'd bought properties with the monies from their ill-gotten gains.

Their identities (provided by Y) and current addresses, had to be firmly established, and required observations and surveillance, to 'house' the targets and prove association between them. It was no good swooping without this knowledge, only to find some had moved. Once again, securing convictions would not be easy, as most of the burglaries had been committed years before. Brian and I were given the task of housing Bert. He lived at Catford, in south-east London, a pig of a journey from Watford (then our base). Brian claimed he knew his way around London. So, when it came to the usual traffic snarl ups, he would suggest a short-cut. As he explained, 'it's what them London taxi drivers do'. Sadly, for all his good intention, Brian's shortcuts turned out to be duds. Take the Holloway Road.

'Turn off here,' said Brian, 'we'll cut through the back roads.' Fair enough, I said, relieved to have an expert in London's streets as my partner. We drove through narrow streets and back alleys, in and out of culs de sac – emerging on to the Holloway Road again, about 150 yards from where we'd left it! Still, I was getting to know London.

As usual, our equipment wasn't too brilliant. Brian and I had use of a small Ford Escort observation van, the idea being to skulk inside near Bert's home, and photograph him (for a positive i/d). To mask its real purpose, the van contained part of a washing machine – the side with the glass door. Have you ever tried looking through the glass door of a washing machine? No, we couldn't see either. So how could a camera? But they'd thought of that at headquarters. What you did was slowly raise the glass door bit – it was on special runners – then peek out below.

'A bit awkward for taking the pictures,' said Brian. Meaning when the glass door was raised it would be an obvious show-out. I agreed.

'Look,' I said, 'you lie in the van and I'll be a passer-by. See if I notice you.'

Somewhere in deepest Catford, as I approached an insignificant Ford Escort van, there, before my eyes, was what appeared to be a washing machine being slowly raised, with Brian's contorted face appearing, behind the camera. Unforgettable!

In due course Bert (and others) were arrested. We were able to recover some stolen property, thanks to knowing the addresses they frequented, and the information provided by Y. Two of these addresses were in Essex. It was a marathon journey that morning: Watford to Reading to Catford to Southend, then via the M25 and M1 to Luton. Given that we'd started duty around 5 a.m., and didn't finally arrive at Luton until mid-afternoon, we were knackered before we even got to the interviewing stage. And, if that wasn't enough, we were well peed off for another reason. I suppose Bert's bottle must have gone when we banged on his door that morning, but whatever the reason, his bowels chose that long, grinding drive at the proverbial snail's pace to react in the most unpleasant way imaginable. Methane gas was expelled from deep within Bert's tormented guts every inch of the way as, all four windows down, we crawled along the cluttered roads of England's green and pleasant land. The occasion was and remains the one and only time in my life I've been glad to arrive at Luton.

One target slipped the net. Whether Bill had somehow got wind of the enquiry isn't known. Whatever, he was abroad on the morning of the arrests. Then, some months afterwards, the message came: Bill was returning to England. He probably thought police interest had cooled, that we were now busy with other things. We were. But we hadn't forgotten Bill. We knew the date; we didn't know the time.

We took up positions around Bill's home in Hampstead. I was incarcerated in the little Ford Escort van, with 'eyeball' on Bill's front door (the washing machine long gone). The moment I spotted him, I would radio my colleagues who would then swoop. Alone in the van, I watched and waited. Surveillance should always be in pairs, one watching, the other relaxing, able to go to the loo, etc. But the van was too small for two, so I had eyeball all to myself, with only a large bottle for company.

The day was a scorcher, and as the morning came and went, and the afternoon dragged on, I got hotter and hotter. Bit by bit, I divested myself of my clothes until, at last, I was down to my pants. When Bill did turn up, he was spotted by my colleagues at the end of the street and arrested. So, my tortuous vigil was in vain. You hear of people leaving dogs and even children in cars in hot weather, sometimes with fatal consequences. Looking back, I might have become a statistic myself.

We interviewed Bill for three days, during which his only reply to our questions was 'yes' when I asked him if he took sugar in his tea. His silence didn't do him any good. Thanks to the evidence of Y, and the recovery of stolen property from accomplices, he was convicted and sent down. Thus ended Operation Carter, and with it my own experience with supergrasses. I don't think the police can use them now. I guess it must give them an unfair advantage.

*

Len was no hardened criminal. He wasn't used to being interrogated, was dead and buried the moment I said the magic words: *Regional Crime Squad*. He worked in the scrap-metal section of a company specialising in precious metals, a position demanding trust. I passed him a copy of the ad.

'Have you ever sent metals to this company?'

He nodded.

'What, precisely?'

'Just a few scraps.'

'Scraps of what?' I asked, although I knew the answer.

He sighed, looked away. I waited. Eye contact again. He nodded, resigned to the inevitable.

'Gold.'

The ad had been placed by a company in Manchester. Police had raided the premises, turned up addresses all over the country. We were investigating those in Hertfordshire and London. Len admitted he had no authority to take gold from his employers' premises, but stressed again it was only scrap. 'Just bits and pieces', he said. Considering the level of security – or, perhaps, lack of it – we were intrigued. How did he get the 'scrap' out? Wasn't he searched at the end of his working day? He slipped a finger down the inside of one of his shoes.

'They don't check your shoes…'

Obviously!

Whatever happened, he was facing the sack. You don't work at a company dealing in precious metals and take gold out without permission. Not even scrap gold.

Had he taken any home?

'A few bits,' he admitted.

Could we have a look? He nodded.

'It's not very tidy,' he said, adding that his wife had left him. No matter, we told him, and we went to look. He had few possessions, obviously lived hand-to-mouth: unwashed dishes on the drainer, oddments of clothing draped about chairs. Looking wouldn't take long.

We found the 'few bits'. Gold in the kitchen drawers, the kitchen unit and the kitchen cupboards; gold in the sideboard; gold in the wardrobe and chest of drawers. Enough to start another Klondike. It looked worthless, fit only for the dustbin. But scrap gold melts down, has value. We carried it out in sacks so heavy we could hardly lift them. It was all smuggled out, piece by piece, in his shoes. Amazing how a company so big, with such levels of security, had failed to notice. We got the experts in to value it. It came to quarter of a million, give or take. And that was just the pieces we recovered. What about the 'bits' sent to the company in Manchester? How much money had he made? He didn't know.

Where was the money?

Spent. On what?

A house in Hong Kong. A new car.

'There's a bit in the bank,' he explained. So there was. A few grand.

We charged Len with theft. He responded by giving the money in the bank, and the house and car, to his employers. As the gold at his home was recovered, his solicitor was able to say that nothing was missing. He got twelve months. Fair? Maybe, but the company had something to answer for. Whilst not condoning theft, the temptation for a man on labourer's pay must have been overwhelming. Then again, union rules forbade the searching of employees' shoes. A pity; if he hadn't been able to steal the scrap gold, he wouldn't have ended up in prison. Incidentally, if ever there was an opportunity for coppers to go bent, this was it. We could have retired, all of us. Those who level accusations of corruption at your ordinary coppers, please note.

Apart from surveillance and other, allocated enquiries, I always felt the need to generate my own work. I needed a new informant. Alan lived in north-west London. We arrested him for a burglary, which we couldn't make stick, and he was released. I asked him if he'd care to make a few bob snouting for old bill.

Alan had never worked for a living. In fact, he was unemployable! His lifestyle was signing on, playing pool, booze and crime. It was clear he wouldn't mind making a bit more by shopping some of his mates – so long as it didn't bounce back on him, of course. The trouble was, everything he could give was Met crime. We could have passed his info on, but this wasn't satisfactory. First, no detective likes passing information on to another (although there are times when it is prudent to do so – protecting the informant, for example). Second, the recipient would be some harassed DC with enough on his plate without trying to respond to information given by someone else's informant. Anyway, one of Alan's jobs looked a runner, with a possibility at least of a connection outside London, so we decided to give it a go.

Alan said a guy I'll call Max was in possession of a large quantity of valuable coins, stolen by means of burglary, although he didn't know where from. (He did really. He was on the job with him). Alan said the coins were hidden underneath Max's settee. Why the settee? I asked. How many times does old bill look underneath a settee? asked Alan. Fair point, when you think about it. Max was a big bastard, said Alan, with plenty of form for violence.

We went to Max's house at six one morning, with the usual warrant. Just to digress…

There is, or was, nothing like the early morning knock to get you off to a good start with a prisoner. It's a sort of shock tactic, designed to stun the enemy. Your burglar, handler, whatever, is tucked up in his cosy bed, when the quiet of dawn is broken by the sudden, battering on his door by old bill. As Corporal Jones used to say: 'They don't like it up 'em'. Nine times out of ten they made admissions then and there, especially if you found the gear. Now, I'm not so sure. Criminals today, aware of modern procedures, know if they keep schtum they'll soon have their solicitor by their side, and if police haven't found the gear they'll have to find some other evidence to make it stick. More than ever, it's vital nowadays for police to have as much intelligence as possible *before* arresting a suspect.

Anyway, our big bastard, Max, wouldn't answer the door, no matter we were just about knocking it off its hinges and the neighbours were opening theirs. But I saw the curtains move, so I went around the back where my colleague, Detective Sergeant Keith Crowder, stood with a beaming smile. 'He's not in,' Keith said, meaning we should go for a fry-up breakfast instead. Then he pointed to the kitchen window, indicating it had no glass in. There was my point of entry. I had just bashed in the makeshift boarding and climbed through the window when Max appeared in the kitchen. Alan was right: he *was* a big bastard.

'What's goin' on?' he asked.

I should mention I wasn't that bothered about his size as I was carrying a pickaxe handle. I let Keith in, and we went into the living room, and stood next to the settee. It was time to go through the formalities.

'I have reason to believe,' I said in my best formal voice, 'that you are in possession of a quantity of valuable coins, and I have a warrant to search this address.'

The procedure would then be to ask him if he had the coins, whereupon he would shrug and say he had no idea what I was talking about, then we would search the house from top to bottom, not discovering the booty under the settee until the last moment (to find them straight away would make the source of information obvious). But if our early morning visit had caught him by surprise, now it was turn to surprise us. He did no more than lift up one end of the settee.

'You mean these?'

There, on the carpet, lay the coins. Everything from doubloons to pieces of eight. If ever we considered a charge of handling stolen goods (which you sometimes do if you can't prove burglary), he'd already chalked up a neat bit of defence work by readily admitting possession, as opposed to lying or secreting the goods in the loft or somewhere.

We took him to a Met nick where the station sergeant, a pedantic (but procedurally correct) individual insisted on listing the coins, one by one, a process which would take hours. I wasn't prepared to interview the prisoner until this was done, so he was placed in a cell. So far, Max had been co-operative, a nice guy even. Not a word of complaint or protest uttered since we met in his kitchen.

'You'll have to wait until we're ready to formally interview you.' I told him, adding we had other enquiries – omitting to add these included asking staff in the canteen if they did bubble and squeak. (Keith was already finding out). The response?

'That's alright, officer. You've got your job to do.'

I allocated the task of coin-counting to someone and went for breakfast. Soon afterwards, the station sergeant came looking for me.

'That bloody prisoner of yours,' he said. 'He's causing mayhem in his cell. Sort him, will you.'

I could hear loud banging and Max's voice before I even entered the cell block. As I opened the little hatch of the cell door my protests about his conduct were sharply interrupted as he turned and pointed to another prisoner, a man who had been put into the same cell after him.

'I don't mind being banged up,' said Max, ' but not with *him*.'

A black man, small in stature, sat quietly in the corner of the cell, looking apprehensively at Max. Alan hadn't mentioned that Max was a racist bigot. I sorted alternative accommodation, to the relief of the man and the satisfaction of Max. Better to keep Max sweet than alienate him. I wanted to tell him what I thought about his prejudice, but police officers sometimes need to keep their thoughts to themselves.

In the end we couldn't prove burglary or handling the coins. At least Max agreed to disclaim ownership. Then, again seeking out an informant, he said was interested. I met him over a drink in due course. His info turned out to be bits and pieces, a few names mentioned, including, surprise surprise, Alan's. Honour among thieves, eh? It was all Met stuff again, so I let Max go. I stuck with Alan for a time, the problem being, as usual, he was a snout without a telephone, and it wasn't always possible for me to respond quickly to any message. One day he managed to ring me from a payphone. As it was in a seedy pub in Wealdstone, he couldn't speak. I said I'd see him at his flat first thing the next morning.

'I can't talk there either,' said Alan, explaining his sister and her husband and God knows who else would be present. So I arranged to call early with other officers, on the pretence of arresting him. This meant dragging colleagues from other jobs, and setting up a bogus 'operation' to make it look real when we arrested Alan. To support the sham, he gave me a load of 'grief', mouthing about this and that (the way he normally did to police). Unfortunately, so did his family. In fact, World War Three might have broken out had Alan not backed off a bit. I then 'arrested' him, thanked my colleagues for their valuable time, took him a coffee somewhere and asked him what his information was.

'I was wonderin' if you could sub me a few quid.'

That was it. End of dear Alan. It would have been anyway. Shortly afterwards he was nicked by the Met. So, it was mostly down to surveillance. Never as effective as good information, but a means to an end. Though not always: one guy we took on was 'surveillance conscious', and more than once we ended up with him waving cheerily as we trailed him around roundabouts. Another followed us back to base to say hello in the police station yard! Another burgled houses after checking the doorstep for milk. Milk on the step is a dead giveaway, meaning the occupants have gone to work before the delivery, and the house is unoccupied. We followed him all over London, into Surrey even. He did nothing. Plenty milk; I saw it myself. In the end he clocked us and that was that. He was arrested soon after – in Hertfordshire – burgling a house with milk on the doorstep!

Then there was a job in Oxfordshire. Every day we drove miles to take off a lorry driver who, we were told, was stealing tyres. We sat on him for ages. Nothing. Someone said he might be active at night, so we changed our shifts, followed him for miles around Oxfordshire, Buckinghamshire and Bedfordshire, all to no purpose. One night, to try and get a close look at the target's lorry, my partner and I sneaked around the back of his house. Suddenly, a door opened somewhere and a light was switched on. Thinking it might be the target, we did what any couple would have done: got to grips. That light stayed on ages, so we had to grope for ages. Still, I didn't mind doing my bit for Queen and Country. Incidentally, my partner was a woman (in case you were wondering).

Another surveillance operation came up trumps. He drove one of those huge petrol tankers you see delivering at garages and fillings stations. It was always the same garages who reported shortages: from Basingstoke to Cambridge, they were checking their meters, checking their accounts, checking their underground tanks. So many gallons had been delivered, yet they were short, and they were losing thousands. It was always the same tanker driver. That much had been deduced by the petrol company before Regional Crime Squad officers were called in. I hesitate before recounting this story. The man's game was so ingenious I wouldn't want others starting to get at it (tanker drivers everywhere poring over *The Job* in transport caffs!) But he was able to do it because of failure in basic procedures by filling station staff, too busy or too indifferent to supervise deliveries, so maybe they should be aware too.

It was always the same half-dozen. One or two were small, privately-owned companies, whose owners were approaching bankruptcy. Losses were unsustainable. We spoke to garage staff.

'Could it be a faulty meter?'

No, meters at all garages are checked by HM Customs. They're dead accurate.

'Are your accounts reliable?'

They were, moreso since the losses appeared. Now they were checked and double-checked and even triple-checked. They'd been in business for years, knew what was what.

'Are you certain you are receiving the correct amount of petrol?'

They were, insisting staff were present to supervise the dipstick check of the petrol tanker *before* and *after* delivery. Always full, always empty.

'Could staff be involved with the driver?'

No. It wasn't always the same staff. And some owners checked themselves.

'Is the driver supervised throughout the entire period of the delivery?'

Those who were never short-dropped: 'yes'. Those who were: 'no'.

So, the driver must be doing something when no-one was looking. But the tank was always dipped full, then empty...

In the end we took the accounts back to the office, studied them till the cows came home, and agreed they didn't add up. X-gallons of petrol delivered on such-and-such a date, and sold at such-and-such a price didn't work out. We'd have to catch him bang to rights, that's all. That meant surveillance.

Early follows were negative, the problem being we never knew in advance where he was going. Contacting the depot would have blown it if he had an accomplice. But it was always going to be a matter of time.

One day, as we followed him up the M1, we realised he was heading for one of the 'target' premises, a motorway services filling station. We watched as the tanker's compartment was dipped full by a member of staff. Then, unsupervised, the driver was seen messing about on top of the tanker. Doing something procedural or irrelevant was not known. Delivery completed, the member of staff dipped the tank empty (confirmed as soon as our man drove off). To all intents and purposes, the entire quota of petrol had been deposited into the storage tanks.

But we knew our man would have short-dropped. This meant there must be petrol in the tanker still, and as he could hardly return to base with it we had to follow him to where he must be off-loading it. How he'd actually *done* it remained a mystery at that stage. He headed off down the M1. We followed.

Further down the motorway, he unexpectedly turned off and parked on a bridge, directly in the line of vision of the car with 'eyeball', a manoeuvre which suggested he'd spotted us. But no. As we held back on the hard shoulder, 'eyeball' reported him on top of the tanker. 'Eyeball' was unable to see exactly what our man was up to, other than after a short time he drove off, rejoining the motorway. Finally, he took to the country lanes – off-route – driving to his ultimate destination. This was the most difficult part of the 'follow', as to get too close would surely blow our cover. But experience, determination and luck were with us as he pulled on to the forecourt of a garage in a country village.

We couldn't arrest him then. What would we have? A tanker driver who'd just popped in to see his mate? That's no crime. And the petrol in the tanker? Must have been some sort of mistake, and the bloke at the garage did a dry drop himself. So we waited, and from the window of a convenient pub I watched as the tanker's hoses were connected to the underground tanks of the garage. Yet my greatest memory of the moment was glancing up to see a DC, Mark, standing in a field, looking like a scarecrow who'd suddenly taken an interest in the garage over the road. I guess no-one involved with the shenanigans with the petrol would have thought about checking for scarecrows.

We steamed in then, arrested the driver and the owner of the garage. The latter tried to get rid of his paperwork, but we were too quick! But how had the driver deceived garage staff?

It was simple, yet brilliant. Each tanker had five or six separate compartments (filled with petrol), each with a long, vertical tube inside, and a small opening at the top to allow the long dipstick to be inserted. The tube is open-ended at the bottom, so that when the compartment contains petrol, it is forced up the tube. When dipped, the dipstick accurately shows the depth. When empty, the dipstick remains dry. When our driver drove on to a forecourt, the relevant compartment was dipped full. No problem. He then commenced the procedure of transferring petrol to the garage tanks. If supervised, as he should have been, he was unable to put his cunning plan into action, which was...

Unsupervised, he would fiddle about on top of the tanker, apparently checking this and that, but secretly inserting a long aluminium tube into the vertical tube within the compartment. It was an exact fit. The inserted tube had a sealed base, so that even if the compartment contained petrol, the dipstick when inserted would emerge dry, as the petrol was unable to flow up the tube. When delivery was complete – a quantity of petrol unofficially remaining in the tank – a final dip *inside the sealed tube* showed 'dry', i.e. tank empty. But, of course, it was not. He would then drive off, removing the aluminium tube en route to his unofficial drop – as he did when he stopped on the motorway bridge.

We still only had him for one theft. What about all the others, going back months, in which he and his accomplice had made thousands? We checked the records of the garages he had targeted. It was long, painstaking work. Fortunately, the driver had kept his own 'record' of the drops, as had his accomplice at the garage (to enable him to know how much tax to avoid paying to customs!). And, of course, we recovered the aluminium tube. Both men went down. You might think this job was no big deal. Not against burglary, say, or other fraud. In fact, it was a cruel, selfish crime. Small companies had been driven almost to bankruptcy. For them, there was no profit on their petrol sales, only losses, and for their staff the prospect of unemployment.

Another operation, involving surveillance, concluded with a great result. It concerned two burglars, Thomas and James. Both men were known locally for their violent conduct, mainly against other criminals, and were suspected of carrying firearms on occasion. They were committing house burglaries in west London and out in the sticks. Unfortunately, we didn't have an informant close enough to tell us where and when. Indeed, this was impossible, as their criminal activities were largely spontaneous: they might go off one afternoon, one evening or maybe not at all for a few days. With limited resources – we couldn't follow them 24 hours a day, seven days a week – we had to play a guessing-game, sadly without success.

Frustration set in. What was the point in following them for hours when, after we'd gone to the pub to play 'Nom' (Nomination Whist, a card game played at police stations all over Herts and London whenever a target was lost – we became expert), they went off and did a burglary? Or if we were on them at night if they'd done a burglary earlier the same day? We stayed on them for weeks, knowing time and resources were being spent to no avail. Finally, one afternoon as we followed them through north London, we decided to give them a pull and leave the rest to lady-luck.

With Thomas and James held at traffic lights, Ruislip resembled the Bronx as we dragged from their car, forced their hands on to the car roof and spread their legs. They quickly succumbed to sheer weight of numbers and the sight of pick-axe handles, and we recovered over £40,000 of jewellery from the car, stolen the previous evening from a house not too far away. The irony was not lost on us, for we'd followed them that day, only to withdraw at 6 p.m.!

The jewellery was quickly identified. But, as any experienced detective will tell you, this stage of any enquiry is only the beginning. What about the other burglaries down to these two?

They rolled over, admitted everything. Not out of repentance, but to try and impress the judge: how helpful they had been, how they had co-operated with the police. They led us to addresses where they'd broken in and stolen property. Their MO was simple: park along the street, knock at the front door and if there was no reply they'd break in, piling stolen property – jewellery, ornaments, televisions, etc – behind the front door, then load it into their car.

Once, driving back after one of our 'tours' into the sticks, Thomas glanced over his shoulder at a car travelling in the opposite direction. 'Oh, there goes so-and-so,' he remarked, all matter-of-fact, meaning another 'team' was on its way to burgle houses in deepest Buckinghamshire.

The magistrates were keen to remand two persistent burglars into custody, which, you might think, was only right. But we had other ideas. Both had indicated they would 'snout' – and I have made my feelings clear on the value of good informants. Neither would be any use incarcerated in Brixton, so I told the bench police did not object to bail. Their worships were understandably perplexed. Why were the police willing to see burglars back on the streets? I couldn't tell them the reason, not least because their criminal friends were sitting in court. The magistrates remanded them into custody anyway. It was the right thing, really. But then they applied for bail to a judge-in-chambers. I went to the hearing at the Royal Courts of Justice in the Strand, to tell the judge (in private) how desirable it was that they should be released. He listened attentively, nodded his head slowly and announced his learned decision:

'I'll take the risk,' he declared, granting bail.

Afterwards, as I made my way along the Embankment, my mind clouded with doubt. What had I done? Having worked so hard catching two prolific burglars, I had just gone and got them out. Was it worth it? They provided bits and pieces, nothing spectacular. I do believe they packed the burglaries in, at least for the time being; I'd have hated myself if they'd broken into someone else's home after that. They got three years, a relatively light sentence as they had 'co-operated'. They said they'd never offend again. They say a leopard never changes its spots. I leave you to form your own opinion.

After four years it was time to return to division, not least because, once again, a posting in the RCS meant being passed over for promotion. Someone once said a man who makes the same mistake twice is a fool. Fool me, then – but I have no regrets about serving two stints on the Regional.

8

"Times change, and we change with them"

Anon.

The chief superintendent welcomed me back to Hemel Hempstead. 'We keep a low profile,' I was told. Damn right. I lived in the town and hadn't seen a uniformed constable on foot patrol for months. This policy was obviously a great success as it prevails today, nationwide.

The Squad had arrested a woman just before my return to division. A typical heroin addict, she resembled a walking skeleton. As she lived in town, I reasoned she would make an ideal snout. I'll call her Sally. Yes, she agreed, drugs are evil. Yes, she condemned the pushers, the ones she blamed for getting her hooked in the first place. But grass them up? No way. She couldn't do that, not for money. She understood me asking, acknowledged it was part of my job, wished she could help. But she couldn't. Next day she was on the phone. 'Can we meet?' she asked, in a trembling voice.

As we sat in my car in Gadebridge Park, Sally told me she had some information about a woman who was dealing from her home; she also told me that she – Sally – needed a fix (heroin). Like straight away, and when could I get the money for her to buy it? She was clenching her fists, biting her nails. What had been an outwardly calm, decent young woman the day before was now a broken specimen of humanity.

Getting money for an informant takes time: there's a process to follow before the money comes through. I promised I'd get it ASAP, so the sooner she told me what the 'info' was the sooner she'd get the money – if it was accurate, of course. I had no doubt it was. She was in the know. First, though, I made an attempt at giving her some advice, like telling her to get help to kick the habit. Some hope!

She provided the name and address of a local woman, a known 'pusher'. 'I don't know where she'll have it,' she explained. 'But she'll have it.'

We crashed in through the back door that evening. The front door was secured by specially-fitted iron bars. Fortunately, we knew about them. Sally told me. We'd have needed the SAS if she hadn't. You have to crash in on a drugs bust. It's no good knocking at the door and waiting politely outside for an answer. By the time it's opened the drugs will be flushing along the sewers.

We spent ages looking for the packet of powder. Young constables, each eager to be the one to make the discovery, searched everywhere. I checked underneath the settee. Alas, after searching every room and the loft, there was no sign.

Outside, her car was emptied of its contents, again without success. Or so it seemed. Then, just as all seemed lost, the jackpot. In the boot of the car was a one-litre can of engine oil, the sort you pull off a foil strip from the top to allow the oil to be poured out. The top had been removed, yet the can was full of oil. Or *looked* full. In fact, a disc-shaped piece of metal, the exact size of the interior, had been inserted just an inch from the top of the can, leaving anyone looking with the impression that the can was full, but in reality only the top inch contained oil. Below, encased in the main part of the cylinder, was our heroin. Bingo!

It was a great hit, not least because we had information from another source that this woman was selling drugs to kids. She was convicted of possession with intent to supply, and a prison sentence looked certain. But when her brief told the beak her children would have to go into care if she was locked up, they let her go with probation. At the time I thought it might be better if they did go into care. Even that was better than witnessing their mother using and supplying drugs.

It took a few days for the money to come through for Sally, during which she was never off the telephone. As I handed it over, I urged her to spend it on food, to get help. She said she would, but I knew she wouldn't. The money would be spent on a fix within the hour. A few days later, she was on the phone again. Another name, another address. I went with the night shift, turned another house over. The occupant, a woman again, denied having any drugs. I knew she was lying. She had probably supplied Sally with a fix that very evening.

We turned the house inside out, searched everywhere from the loft to the insides of Kelloggs corn flakes packets before we had to admit failure. With everyone resigned to defeat I took one last glance beneath the bed in one of the kids' bedrooms. Lo and behold, I spied three white bundles. They looked like towels, but turned out to be soiled nappies. Somehow, we'd missed them first time around. The woman held out her hand, offered to take them away. Then she realised what I was thinking, and stood back, awaiting my next move.

One by one I laid the nappies on the floor, unfolded them carefully, examined their contents, nightshift constables and their sergeant looking on at the painstaking and determined efforts of the DS. I fingered the contents carefully, eagerly seeking the packet of white powder. It must be there, it *had* to be there. Alas, they contained what any soiled nappy would contain, and nothing more. Sally rang me the next day. She was in an angry mood, as failure to find the drugs would mean no reward.

'We turned the place inside out,' I told her. 'She was clean.'

'It was buried in the field on the other side of her fence,' said Sally. 'I saw her digging it up this morning.'

Sally came again. This time it was a guy who was supplying from his house. We burst in, caught him bang to rights: scales, wrappers, the lot. He was charged with possession with intent to supply, and pleaded not guilty at crown court.

There is all the difference in the world between *possession* of drugs, and *possession with intent to supply* drugs. The former is for your own use, the latter for the use of others. Not surprisingly, supplying carries a far stiffer sentence. This man was trying to tell the court the drugs were for his own use, even though he had carefully weighed and wrapped each deal separately. He was convicted of possession with intent to supply and sentenced to twelve months. But long before the trial I stopped using Sally as an informant. Sure, thanks to her, we were catching drug dealers. But Sally was being pushed further into drug abuse, thanks to financial inducement by the police. I didn't consider arresting druggies, desirable though it was, merited being an accomplice to the destruction of someone's life. Whether or not Sally still has a life I do not know.

I also became 'acquainted' with a local burglar and car thief. He was a hard case, the last person anyone would think would 'snout' – but he did. I never revealed his i/d, safe to say my peers at that time would have been amazed. We'd meet in the park in broad daylight. I'll call him Ben. It was a bizarre situation. There we were, strolling by the river in the lee of the Old Town, like two old pals who'd known one another for years, sworn enemies engaged in a sort of truce: I found out who was committing crime, he got paid. In case you're wondering how Ben was brave enough to run the risk of being clocked with old bill, the answer is simple. He didn't give a damn.

Once, Ben gave me some gen on a man named T, said he'd broken into a garage, with another man, and that he had wads of stolen test certificates at his home. The face value of the certificates was small, but their real value, what they could be sold on for on the black market, ran into thousands. I got a warrant, and spun T's home. The test certificates were hidden behind the tank

189

in the airing cupboard. He was charged with burglary, alternatively handling, and convicted. He never revealed the identity of his accomplice. He didn't need to. I'm sure you can guess who it was.

For getting the info, recovering the stolen property and seeing the case through to conviction, I had the satisfaction of seeing T put on probation. That, to a burglar, is the same as getting off. You have to ask yourself why you bother sometimes. I really wonder if the magistrates know what's going on in the real world. Then again, how or where the information comes from doesn't come out in evidence, and in any case cannot be relevant to sentencing a criminal. I suppose putting my pretty face on the line isn't relevant either. Caught in a bad mood, Ben might have smacked my ear just for the hell of it!

One day, a detective constable's informant provided info that led to the detection of an armed robbery. Three masked men with shotguns robbed a sub-post office of cash and postal orders one morning. They could have been anyone, a fact not lost on me as I surveyed the tyre marks of their getaway car on the lush grass nearby. We thought they were probably from London, out committing crime in the sticks.

We were wrong. The DC's contact named the robbers. One lived on our doorstep. I'll call him M. To prove contact, and hopefully lead us to the stolen property, we kept obbos on his address. It led us nowhere, but we arrested him with no evidence except the information of the 'snout' – 'reasonable suspicion', as the law requires. This was before PACE, so we were able to interview him for hours, refusing him a solicitor on the grounds that it would 'defeat the ends of justice' – as it would if anyone else, solicitor included, knew of his detention whilst armed accomplices were still free and stolen property was still missing. Obviously, knowledge of M's arrest would enable them to destroy or dispose of vital evidence.

Why do they want a solicitor anyway? They've already been told they 'are not obliged to say anything,' and today PACE ensures investigating officers are unable to access their prisoner without strict supervision by the custody sergeant. The police can 'fit up' the prisoner. That's what they say. Yet in M's case we couldn't, even if we tried: without his co-operation, we were unable to recover anything, or (without our informant) identify his associates. They want a solicitor to get 'em off, that's why. The first things a solicitor wants to know are: what evidence have the police got, and what have you told them? If it's not a lot, it's keep schtum and we'll be looking at a 'not guilty'. Criminals seek acquittal for their crimes and solicitors seek payment to help them get it. It's a game, like Snakes and Ladders. All that's missing are the dice.

M admitted the robbery. What's more, he led us to a quiet spot in a wood where he showed us the burnt remains of the clothing he and his accomplices had used. Just as a solicitor would have advised, I don't think!

His two accomplices were in a different league. The first, when arrested, said not a word, other than declaring he'd been treated fair and square by police. It was almost as good as a commendation. The second man went on the run, but was tracked down (with commendable help by the Met) and arrested at an address in London. He was armed, and was arrested after a siege situation. I saw it all on *News at Ten*. They all went down.

Much crime is 'domestic'. Domestic violence, as it's known. Man v. Woman. Husband v. Wife. Whether it's over drink, sex or because one partner asserts physical control over the other simply because he (or she) can. In one case, it was a combination of the first two. Woman goes out with her friends, gets drunk, has sex – *not* with her husband. But husband finds out. That's when we get our domestic. She's still drunk as he drags her to his car, drives into the country where he carries her to the river and holds her head under water until she's nearly drowned, a process which he repeats until he's satisfied she won't do it again.

Typically, she did not seek police action, and that would have been that, except she had a few brothers who, on discovering what had happened, decided to take the law into their own hands. That's when hubby decided the police should be involved. It was all sorted in the end, with the status quo restored. And so it is – or was – over the years that police have treated 'domestic' crime as distinct from 'ordinary' crime, the main reason being that 'victims' of so-called domestics almost always change their minds about going through with a prosecution, thus 'wasting' police time. But domestic crime can be just as serious as any crime, often moreso.

Take C. He and his wife had been at loggerheads for some time. In the end he ended up living in a flat in London. Out of sight, out of mind? Not a bit of it: he became obsessed at the thought of his wife with another man (if there was another man), so he decided to kill her. One day, as his wife parked outside her home, a stranger appeared and thrust a bottle containing hydrochloric acid into her mouth. Fortunately, her screams alerted passers-by, and the man dropped the bottle with its lethal contents, and escaped in a hired van.

I went to see her in hospital, where she lay on her bed wondering if the acid might be eating away at the lining of her stomach. Fortunately, she'd suffered minor burns around her mouth, nothing more. But there would be mental scars, too. Her assailant, as if you hadn't guessed, was her husband. He'd purchased the bottle and its lethal contents, disguised his appearance and turned up in a hire-van. We arrested him shortly afterwards. He showed no remorse.

'What gives you the right to try and kill someone?' I asked.

'She's my wife,' he declared.

That's it about domestics. If the guy had attacked a woman unknown to him, that's one thing; attack your wife and somehow it's different. To his wife, C had become a potential killer, to anyone else he was a perfectly reasonable chap. He had worked hard to provide a good home for his wife and family, and she had rewarded him by being unfaithful. She had broken the rules. His rules. Fortunately, the rules of England and Wales were different. He got eight years. Police officers who tut-tut domestics, please note.

*

I was now given the opportunity to 'act up' to detective inspector, a first step on the 'senior officer' ladder, with the responsibility of making wider operational decisions. It felt strange at first: after all, I was working with the same colleagues. Where before, detective sergeants and I shared a level playing field, now I was 'upstairs'. One of my first tasks as DI was being sent to a suspicious death, a man of thirty-odd found dead in his flat. Before, I'd have attended knowing someone else would have to decide what the police would do about it; now, as the senior detective, the decision was mine.

Every suspicious death, or apparent suicide, must in the first instance be treated as a possible murder, even though it might appear obvious it isn't. The man in the flat: he was young, his GP had known of no previous illness. Who's to say he hadn't been assaulted, or poisoned even? Only a post-mortem will discover the cause of death, and until that is known police must ensure all possible enquiries that can be done are done, and the scene thoroughly examined. It's no good not bothering and finding out he was murdered a day or so later, when vital clues have been destroyed or disappeared. The man in the flat had had a heart attack. No crime, no further police action required.

Being DI meant undertaking non-operational roles, too. Like reading every crime file, from uniform constables as well as detectives. This was a lot of files. I was expected to pick up any mistakes, even though the files had already been signed by a sergeant. Some were submitted by officers whose work, you knew, needed just a cursory glance before signing, whilst others required closer inspection. Happily, this outmoded practice became obsolete.

Throughout this period (1984) the miners' strike was in full swing, with uniformed officers packing their bags for such places as Nottinghamshire and South Yorkshire. They returned with faces grey from the strain of facing the pickets, and enduring the violence we saw on our television screens.

At the time, I went on a walking holiday in the Lake District, where I encountered a fellow who asked me what I did for a living. I made the mistake of telling him. He only turned out to be a coal miner from South Yorkshire. That was it. Every step on the climb to Esk Pike was accompanied by his opinions on police violence, how the police were Thatcher's puppets. I didn't argue.

Instead, I put forward the view, which I hold today, that despite my background I could not support the strike. I'd have felt different if there'd been a ballot, if to strike was the will of the majority. But it wasn't. The miners were led by a man whose cause was his own, not theirs. He came between the miners; he split communities. Watching the six o'clock news one evening, with my dad, I made some comment about the brutality of the pickets, jeering the miners – those who were still working – as they were being bussed into work. 'The police are just as bad,' he said. Maybe he was right; certainly his feelings were running high. To me it all went to prove the miners' leader wasn't only splitting communities; he was splitting families too.

I wondered how I would have reacted if I'd faced the miners. After all, my dad worked down the pit, and most of my school chums were miners' kids. I'm proud of my roots. I was brought up in a working-class community where people worked hard and were decent, kind and honest, where they scrubbed backyards to wash away grime and coal dust, and women, on their hands and knees, scrubbed the gutters by the side of the road. Years later, when the colliery closed, those houses were sold off as 'cottages'; I bet they don't scrub the gutters now. I was saddened to see those tv pictures. I didn't join the force to fight coal miners. Then again, helping their cause against anonymous men shouting 'scab' from the safety of a crowd wouldn't have caused me a problem. Without that ballot I would still have done all I could to allow those who wanted to work through the pickets.

One day, the chief constable sent for me. I was going to be promoted.

'Congratulations,' said the Chief.

'Thank you, sir,' said I, wondering where I'd be posted.

He flicked through the papers. It was so important he didn't know without looking.

'Ah,' he declared. 'Welwyn Garden City. That'll suit you, living at Redbourn. Pleased?'

'Yes, sir,' I lied. 'Only I live at Hemel Hempstead.'

He flicked again, saw the mistake.

'Oh, well,' he replied, his voice tailing off. It was *fait accompli*.

He stood up, shook my hand and wished me well. It only remained for me to collect my brown gloves and fancy hat.

*

'That lot should keep you occupied.'

She was pointing at one of those in-trays, the sort with papers yellowing with age the nearer you get to the bottom. There were two distinct bundles, each with a date marked on the front. They seemed to be well organised – whatever they were.

'Good luck.'

Then she was gone, leaving me to fulfil my role as her replacement, Group Two inspector at Welwyn Garden City.

I picked up the two bundles. One concerned a cycle race, to be held on a forthcoming Sunday; the other a marathon, to be held on another forthcoming Sunday. It would be my job to formulate an operation order for each event, to organise manpower, to ensure each went smoothly and safely. After all, both would take place on public roads.

The cycle race was a high-standard affair, thirty or so speedsters who'd cover a hundred miles or so over a series of circuits on a given route around the town. There were two main considerations: one, to keep the way clear so they could pedal like hell without having to worry about traffic; two, their safety. A copy of the operation order for the previous year was attached, a ready-made guide requiring only minor adjustments. The marathon was a free-for-all for anyone who wanted to run it, which lots did, mainly for charity. Again, road safety was paramount.

First, though, I had to meet my shift, men and women stationed in a part of the county I hardly knew. Not even through the Regional. Somehow, there'd never seemed much call for surveillance at Welwyn Garden City. Except once. It was on a guy who lived within spitting distance of police HQ. A burglar, we were told. We'd take him off, catch him on the job. Fair enough. We sat for hours, four or five cars, each with two detectives, all prepared for mobile and foot surveillance. Nothing. Same again the next day and the day after. On the fourth day (or was it the fifth?) an excited voice broke the radio silence.

'Target out on foot.'

Half-eaten bacon roles and copies of *The Sun* were hastily dispatched to the back seats.

'Target heading towards the town centre *on a bike*!'

Following someone on a bicycle in a 2-litre Granada or whatever is far from easy. It's just that no matter how hard you try, you're liable to catch up. And if you don't overtake or peel off somewhere, he's gonna get sussy. Anyway, he signed on for his benefit, then went home. As we took up our positions again we congratulated ourselves on not showing out. Don't ask me what happened in the end. I can't remember.

One of the pleasures of my new role was spending time on foot patrol. It was very relaxing, and reminded me of my days on the beat. One morning, as I took in the fresh air of Welwyn Garden town centre, I encountered a woman probationer, notebook in hand, pen poised. Allowing her time to recover at the sight of an inspector on foot, and ignoring her non-salute (she probably never knew you were supposed to) I asked her what she was doing. She explained that with the new seat belt laws being implemented, she was on the lookout for offenders. Even as she spoke, she brushed me aside, and stopped a car whose driver was seatbelt-less, and took his partics. There followed general conversation between us, punctuated by several more knock-offs, after which I resumed patrol, wondering if knocking off motorists for not wearing seat belts was how police officers should spend their time.

Then I remembered another young probationer, a 9½ stone bloke who, 20 years before, waited ages to knock off a motorist for parking on a bridge. Like me, she was striving to make an impression. Probably making a better job of it, as the fellow who parked on that bridge had me over. Somehow, I didn't feel the young woman I had just seen in action would be so easily deceived. Anyway, PC's had to do something to show results in Welwyn Garden. There were busy spots in town, but they were few. Most trouble occurred in Hatfield, in the other half of the sub-division. But, I reasoned, there was always nightshift. Then we'd have some action.

10.20 p.m., Friday evening. Memories of the Bigg Market and Neville Street: bottles crashing onto pavements, loud, drunken voices calling out across the street, noisy traffic roaring through the city, shattered glass as a window goes in somewhere. I looked along the Parkway. It was deserted, save for a couple of cars proceeding sedately past the fountain, and a black and white mongrel returning home after a night on the town.

I called up a young probationer, and together we visited the railway station. We were the only ones there, apart from a porter. I think he might have made us a cup of tea. Sadly, I can't recall. Finally, after checking a few doors I left the constable to his beat and returned to base. I could always add a few finishing touches to those operation orders.

*

If I drove the route once I drove it twenty times. Along the A414, back towards Panshanger and along Black Fan Road. By the time I'd finished I'd produced the most accurate, most comprehensive operation order since Robert Peel. The way was clear for the greatest cycle race ever.

Came the day. I briefed the troops. Hitherto, briefings for me had been about arresting criminals and searching premises. Now I found myself talking to a parade room full of regulars and specials, spelling out the hazards of this part of the circuit, stressing the need to ensure traffic shouldn't encroach on the cyclists at that junction. It hardly dawned on me that they had covered the race for years, had little need to hear their duties spelled out by the new bloke with the funny accent who probably didn't know where most of the locations were anyway. It wasn't until I'd dismissed the parade I remembered traffic cones were supposed to be put out first thing. But there was no problem: the sergeant had seen to it shortly after six. Just as he'd done for years.

Those cyclists can't half go! For hours they whizzed around the circuit until the grand finish, where they raced pell-mell for the line. There were no incidents. It was all over, job done. Next day I became aware of someone standing in my office doorway. I looked up to see the chief inspector.

'A word.'

This brief sentiment usually means something serious is afoot. But no...

'That cycle race yesterday,' he said. 'The organisers say it was very well organised.'

One cycle race and I was a hero.

'Fancy a crack at the milk race?'

The milk race. Isn't that where international cyclists race around Britain for weeks on end? It is, I was told, in such a way it was a privilege to be asked to prepare the operation order.

'I'll need subsistence for the weekend it passes through the Lake District.'

Alas, it was just for the leg that finished in Welwyn Garden City.

'You could be on tv,' he said, offering the proverbial carrot.

I'd been on tv before, on the perimeter of the pitch at St James's, and even running across it, not to mention the *Police* series on supergrasses. The novelty had worn off long since. Sorry, I said, but I was on holiday then. Another inspector would have to deal. Sad, but there it was.

Soon after, it was the turn of the marathon. This time I made sure about the cones. I didn't want anyone run over by Sunday drivers.

The trouble with a marathon is that the standard of athleticism among those competing varies from the super-fit to the bloody-hell-they'll-never-make-26-miles brigade. Consequently, the field spreads out, the former striding off at the front, geriatrics and people dressed as ostriches at the rear. Again, it all went without a hitch, with various charities benefiting from the commendable efforts of the participants.

Cycle races and marathons aside, there were, naturally, the usual suicides. Two of them shared one common factor: they were both lonely people. The first was the sad case of a young chap who, for reasons he explained in a 20-page letter, ended it all in front of the Edinburgh express. We knew the train had hit someone, as the driver had seen him walking along the centre of the tracks directly ahead. At circa 120 m.p.h. there was little he could do. Our suicide wasn't very considerate: he chose the entrance to the mile-long Welwyn North tunnel.

As usual, our torches had batteries barely able to produce a beam strong enough to reach the ground let alone find a corpse, but half a dozen of us picked our way in the darkness of the tunnel, seeking what we knew must be there. It was damned eerie, I can tell you. It seemed an age before we made the first discovery, one of the dead man's hands. It lay by the tracks, so white it looked like it had broken off a wax dummy. Further on, someone else found a mangled heap of flesh, all that was left of what had been a young bloke. Needless to say, he was unidentifiable. Fortunately, we found something else: his wallet. It contained a cashpoint slip, and the code number led us to his bank and his identity. But that still wasn't proof that the corpse and the name were one and the same. Ah, but we had the hand, and when we took its fingerprints they matched those found on the 20-page letter he'd left in his flat. It was addressed to his parents. I should honour its confidentiality. Suffice to say he was a very lonely young man.

At the inquest into his death the train driver had to give evidence. He said he'd seen the young man walking along the tracks at the entrance to the tunnel, had given a blast on the horn, had even felt the impact as the train hit him. But there was nothing he could do.

'Would it have been possible to stop the train?' said the coroner. He had to ask, I suppose.

The train driver pointed out the stopping distance is one mile, then he broke down in tears, apologising for killing the young man on the railway. As if he could be blamed. Wrapped up in their own grief, depression, whatever, I don't suppose suicides stop to think about the poor old train drivers.

One late turn I was called to Harpenden, where a man had suffocated himself by attaching a pipe to his car's exhaust. The engine had roared undetected from around eight in the morning until eight at night, even though it was just off the High Street. He turned out to be a chap who was fed up with living alone after the death of his wife. He'd obviously given careful consideration to his lonely predicament, as he'd written letters to all his family, which he carefully placed on a table, along with a copy of his will and other relevant documents – bank statements, insurance papers and so on. In other words, he'd put his affairs in order before setting off on that last, short journey. There was even a letter of apology to the police for the 'inconvenience caused'.

My 'links' with crime continued, except that where before offenders appeared before the courts, now they appeared before me in the police station, school children mainly, arrested for shoplifting and minor damage. Although aware of police cautions, I had never actually been present at one, nor received any instruction about how to carry one out. It seemed there were no guidelines other than common sense. Fine by me. They say you always remember your first of anything, and I remember my first caution. He was a boy of twelve or thirteen, arrested for a minor offence. Before wheeling him in, I decided to have a word with his parents. They were upset at their son coming to police notice, but supportive of the system.

'Make sure you give him a good telling off,' said dad, stressing I had his backing to give his son one almighty fright. He didn't want a repeat performance. Mum nodded her agreement. Fair enough. I wheeled the little blighter in and gave him the biggest bollocking since Squelchy caught Bunter at the biscuits. Unfortunately, it was too much for the boy – and his parents. They dragged him off, mother and son in tears, dad visibly shaken. Maybe I went too far. Then again, if it cured him, maybe not. From then on I took it a bit easier with the recalcitrant kids of Welwyn Garden City.

Another caution concerned a 70-year old man who'd stolen the *News of the World*. I felt that the decision to caution him for stealing a newspaper was made on account of his age, and no other reason. As though 70 made him incapable of being responsible for his actions. I disagreed with the decision, but it was my duty so I wheeled him in. If he'd expressed regret, or offered apology, it might have meant something. But he was smiling, meaning he'd had a good result – i.e. got away with it.

'I just forgot to pay, that's all,' he explained with a shrug.

'Did you steal it or not?' I asked.

The question was relevant: if he denied it I couldn't caution him. You can't caution someone who maintains innocence. Such people should face a court. I said as much. This gave him a problem. If he denied the theft, he might end up being prosecuted. But he didn't want to admit it either. Considering that he had secreted the newspaper underneath his jacket before leaving the shop, I knew where my beliefs lay. Yet I could hardly start going into the why's and wherefore's; this wasn't an interview to establish guilt or otherwise. In the end I put him out of his misery, gave him a bollocking and told him if he had to read the *News of the World* to pay for it next time.

As with most things, people adapt. I adapted at Welwyn Garden City. It was hardly the Bronx, but there was still much to do if you wanted to do it. First, I checked licensed premises, a practice, as far as I could see, which was all but defunct. But it is the job of the police to police, and that includes pubs. Not the nice, cosy, well-run ones, but those frequented by your local villains. I went regularly, always taking a probationer constable. Good experience for them, good experience for me. By and large, licensees seemed pleased at the unexpected presence of the law. Officers who check pubs (by going in, not just peeking through the window, no names mentioned) will know of the sarky comments from their patrons, whispered usually from the relative safety of a group. Okay, so I gave 'em back, usually to everyone's amusement. In fact, we got to know one another, even said hello when we passed on the street.

Then there were 'road checks'. Nightshift was the time, usually right outside force headquarters, where there happens to be a convenient lay-by. Remember Alf, the tattooed man, the guy who said criminals could travel safely at night these days? Not when Group Two were on nights, they couldn't. Sadly, we turned up no stolen safes or wanted murderers.

If one thing opened my eyes at Welwyn Garden, it was the attitude of youngsters to the police. Things seemed to have changed so much since I was last in uniform. That summer I spent a week in Benidorm where, lazing in the hot sun one afternoon (as you do), and ignoring the intrusive noise of rowdy Brits (as you also do), I suddenly became deafened by the sound of total silence. I looked up to see a lone cop, strolling along the sea front, truncheon (or whatever they call it over there) in hand, gun swinging lazily from his hip. He looked neither right nor left, just ambled along, shirt collar undone. You could have heard a pin drop. Then, when he was no more than a wee speck in the distance, the noisy Brits resumed their Mediterranean-style activities. (It was all harmless fun, actually)

Yet, at Welwyn Garden, the presence of a uniformed police officer in England had precisely the opposite effect. From a small group outside the Kentucky Fried Chicken one evening I was treated to a barrage of foul and abusive language. It was all there, everything from your F's and C's, along with the usual: 'Pig', 'Filth', 'Scum,' etc. This, in a *Garden City*, in Hertfordshire. Why? Might it just be down to the knowledge that, in Spain, abusing your local *el policía*, will lead to arrest and incarceration in a cockroach-infested cell, whereas here, your English bobby can't lay a finger? Or won't lay a finger if, as will probably be the case, there'll be a messy complaint to sort? Or is it, in part at least, because there are so few foot patrol officers on our streets these days, that when one is seen he or she is seen as fair game for abuse? For some reason, I no longer felt proud of my uniform that night.

Anyway, I was a senior officer and, like anywhere else, staff looked to their senior officers to make decisions. Like the morning someone knocked on my door. I looked up from the vital work I was doing to see the constable from the enquiry desk.

'Scuse me, guv. Just I can't seem to find the super or the chief inspector.'

It was important, obviously.

'What's the problem?'

'There a chap here with a Coca Cola machine.'

I waited.

'Is it okay for him to connect it up?'

Seemed a good idea. Okay, I said. Five minutes later, the same officer.

'Sorry to bother you again, sir.'

This time he was with a guy in a blue overall. The Coca Cola man, presumably.

'I'm not sure where he should put it.'

Resisting the temptation to tell him the obvious, I got up and found a convenient corner of the building. Half an hour later, one Coca Cola machine, loved by all for its cold drinks. It's probably still there.

I have made light, I know, of my time at Welwyn Garden, but I should point out that in no way do I deride any of its officers, past or present. Police officers get posted somewhere, be it a busy station or a quiet backwater, a city centre or a remote village. It's just I was used to working in busier places, and found great difference in the uniform and detective roles. I enjoyed working with Group Two at Welwyn Garden, and was pleased when they supported an idea of a sponsored hike in the Lake District. Our cause was a local cottage hospital. None of the group will forget it, especially Jenny, who earned a special award: *For Effort*. She deserved it.

*

After a year I was posted to Hatfield. This suited me. For one thing, the town had more *oomph* about it – more incidents, including crime and public disorder – and for another, it was supervised (or should I say managed) by just two inspectors, independent of the sub-divisional commander. We were in a position to run a fair-sized new town in whichever way we chose, a responsibility enhanced by the need to ensure the security of such luminaries as Barbara Cartland and Samantha Fox.

Hatfield was locally famous – or infamous – for problems at the Hilltop, and in the town centre. It all evolved around pubs, drugs and booze. Not long before, there had been serious disorder at the Hilltop. 'It's a no-go area for police', one PC told me, meaning the Hilltop pub, so just to prove it wasn't I went there one evening with Sergeant Stuart Gibson where we had coffee at the bar and made our presence – in uniform – made known to the locals. The reputation of the pubs in the town centre was accurate enough. One night a man was stabbed to death, and next morning over forty knives were found lying on the floor.

There were more juveniles to caution, of course. Only where, at Welwyn Garden, their faces bore the worried appearance of someone in trouble with authority, at Hatfield they usually bore the look of indifference, defiance even. To tell the truth, I never found it easy, going through the procedure whilst a young fellow, usually in for damage or theft, burglary even, shuffled from foot to foot, knowing the routine, that ultimately that he'd simply walk away. Some were cautioned two, even three times. I was never happy with that. How many chances do they need? Then again, you might wonder, what chance had life ever given them? Actually, one or two of the cautions at Hatfield were reduced to farce, thanks to the proximity of a toilet, sited on the other side of the door. You could hear every sound. Your best endeavours to extol the virtues of leading an industrious life suffer badly when dire warnings and promises of a bleak future are accompanied by a barrage of farts.

This was the era of the 'area inspector', whose role was the responsibility for a given area, rather than the supervision of a shift. For example, at Hatfield, I attended parish council meetings, where I listened to concerns about local crime, traffic hazards, problems in schools. I was then able to plan a strategy as well as putting the police point of view. All good stuff, except the shifts no longer had a 'leader', a senior officer who was in charge. This area inspector nonsense came to a head one Sunday, when I was covering division. Entering an out station, I found a constable – and *two* area inspectors. Three inspectors, one PC.

1st inspector: 'Is your pocket book up to date, officer?'

Constable: 'Er…'

2nd inspector: 'And have you checked the property register this morning?'

Constable, handing the first inspector his pocket book: 'Well, sir, I...'

3rd inspector, staring out the window at kids cycling on the footpath: 'I have an insatiable desire for a crispy bacon sandwich.' (Makes insatiable desire noises).

Used to spending weeks on end without seeing a soul, the constable is bewildered.

1st inspector: 'Your pocket book's not up to date.'

2nd inspector: 'Neither is the property register.'

3rd inspector: 'Got any brown sauce?'

To my mind, an inspector should be a senior officer who identifies with a shift of officers under his/her control, and who leads from the front. Not some vague, often unknown and unrecognised character who may turn up, sometimes more than one at a time, as happened that morning.

I mentioned the Hilltop. As well as taking an interest in checking licensed premises, I decided to put myself out a bit by walking Alfred Wainwright's 200-mile Coast to Coast walk across northern England, sponsoring myself on behalf of the Gateway Club for the Mentally Handicapped, based at the Hilltop. This proved to be an enjoyable venture, both in terms of the walk, across three national parks – the Lake District, Yorkshire Dales and North Yorks Moors – and the satisfaction of presenting a four-figure sum to the club.

Money rolled in from colleagues, friends and, not least, local business in Hatfield. It was all high-profile stuff, meriting such headlines as 'An Inspector Calls' when the local press covered the presentation of the cheque. The best bit was the visits to the club, where, along with two neighbourhood PC's, we were more than willing to lend our hats to some of the less-fortunate members of society, who, for a brief moment in their lives, paraded as police officers, proud of the uniform. Afterwards, in my inspector's role, I gave after-dinner speeches to the patrons and workforces of local organisations who had contributed to the cause. Incidentally, nothing of this venture mattered as far as my 'career' was concerned. In fact, I don't think anyone in the force knew anything about it.

*

The sergeant knew his job, and ran a tight ship. And the sergeant was angry. A young 'yobbo' had just been bailed by the magistrates 'to an address that doesn't exist'. It was my first experience with the newly-formed crown prosecution service. When I heard the circumstances, I was angry too. He'd pleaded not guilty, and applied for bail. The magistrates were favourable, provided he was of a fixed abode. He provided an address, which, his solicitor told the court, was correct. So they bailed him.

There was no such address. He'd made it up, but what made us angry was that the CPS solicitor had accepted the address as genuine without asking for the case to be stood down for a short period to enable it to be verified. That's what police had done in the past, and if the CPS had done it they'd have discovered the truth. So, in part to show support for the officers in the case, and in part to take steps to ensure it never happened again, I decided to speak to the CPS solicitor. I thought it would be simple: can you ask the magistrates to stand the case down next time? The response: 'Solicitors act to a strict code of conduct. If a defendant provides information to the magistrates through his solicitor, it is the duty of the court to deal with it.' In other words, the solicitor's word is gospel. Well, goodbye common sense, and welcome stupidity.

Another young bloke hit the nationals when the local neighbourhood watch, frustrated at their perception of police failure to curb local crime (an accurate perception), decided to take things into their own hands by naming him publicly in their crime publication. *Yob of the Month*, ran the headline, along with his name and address. A bit like *Wanted, Dead or Alive*. I spotted the story on the front page of the *Daily Mail* when on holiday on the Isle of Wight! All it did was enhance his notoriety, and urge his mates to earn their place as *Yob of the Month* afterwards. So much for the case for vigilantes.

I was at Hatfield when the problems of the Police and Criminal Evidence Act came home to roost. Sergeants were *Custody*

Officers now, compelled to maintain an impartial role in any investigation, and obliged to look after the welfare of prisoners. (And there was me thinking they had a part to play in helping the public – like getting stuck into villains! And supervision of officers on patrol, for that matter).

The custody sergeant must tell a prisoner that he or she is entitled to a solicitor. It's automatic: name, address and do you want a solicitor? Never mind the arresting officer might have to wait hours until the solicitor completes whatever other work he/she has on that day before turning up. Investigating officers used to rely on getting in a quick interview to get results. There was nothing dishonest. There are enough rules and regulations without preventing honest coppers have a crack at a suspect, face to face. Yet I'll never forget the words of a police inspector at a pre-PACE training session.

PACE had so many new rules and regulations the force decided to run a number of training courses. Good idea. When it came to the new requirement to compel custody sergeants to give prisoners the opportunity to have a solicitor present early on, the inspector held up his palms and shrugged. I thought he was going to say something like: 'Fair enough, we're stuck with it, it's the law.' Not a bit of it. Instead, he asked: 'Does it really matter?' Well, if he didn't know by the time he'd reached inspector, he never would. All I can say is that anyone arrested for a criminal offence who admits it without asking for a solicitor is either a basically honest person who has gone wrong, or a fool. Real villains keep schtum.

PACE affected inspectors, too. Where before (as a detective) I arrested criminals and interviewed them about their wicked ways, now (as an inspector) I was paying them welfare visits in the cells.

'Is everything alright?'

A look of mistrust falls over the prisoner's face.

'What d'you mean?'

'I have to enquire about your welfare.'

'Yeah? Well, I wanna be out of here pal.'

'That's two of us.'

The CPS and PACE were, I suppose, the two biggest changes that affected the police in thirty years (along with personal radios, pandas and force amalgamations, of course!). Neither seemed welcome at the time of their introduction. But, like it or not, they were here to stay. I suppose police men and women, like anyone else, dislike change from what they are used to: change is usually seen as interference with something which, in their opinion, worked perfectly well and didn't need changing. But police officers adapt, as they must. And young officers, who join the job *after* new rules come in, know only the new rules and regulations. But they, too, in time, will have to face change. Nothing is forever.

Anyway, when I wasn't checking prisoners' welfare and cautioning kids, I took an interest in other matters, like the day I was asked to give a talk to some 14-year olds at a school in Hatfield. The subject: The Rank Structure of Hertfordshire Constabulary. I decided the occasion could also be used as a forum to talk about crime and drugs, not least because a local schoolgirl had just died through sniffing glue, an associated pastime, in my view.

As I turned to the blackboard, it started: the tittering, the sniping. Each time I turned, innocent faces looked up at the board, as though fascinated by what I had written. Then, as I turned my back, someone flicked a piece of paper across the room. Again, the innocent faces. It was clear enough: what I had to say was interesting only to me. Without the skill or expertise – or authority – to capture their undivided attention, the entire exercise would be a waste of time.

How anyone can teach 14-year olds I do not know. I take my hat off to those who can, I really do. Truth to tell, my patience evaporated within minutes. And no, I'm not blaming 'today's kids'. I well recall my own schooldays when a young woman teacher with dark features and even darker hair whom we cruelly called Gypsy Rose Lee suffered the outrageous behaviour of a class of recalcitrant brats, with me a contender for Worst Offender. Running across the tops of the desks and shouting at the top of our voices, nothing serious. Many, especially of my generation, recommend corporal punishment, and I'm not against it in principle, but again I look back to my own schooldays.

Although the deterrent of physical pain may ensure the undivided attention of children, there is no way I could support corporal punishment in schools. Not after what I went through. I won't name them, but they were my maths and geography teachers. They thrashed us boys – and I mean thrashed – for no reasons other than their own gratification.

The former would give you six of the worst with a stout leather belt, a flogging witnessed by all classmates. His face crimson, his tongue pushed forward between his lips as maximum force was applied. And for what? Well, in one case, for walking downstairs with a hand on each stair-rail at the same time. And, okay, I admit I once drew a cow in my maths exercise book (I wasn't much good at maths. Nor drawing cows for that matter). Fortunately, this sadist was mad about chess, and I was able to avoid further punishment by enlisting in his chess club (it's how I learnt to play the game). The latter would mete out punishment either by bending you over and strapping your backside, or, just for a change, your outstretched hand. Not once, but half a dozen times. You'd be in agony afterwards; maximum effort on his part maximum pain on yours. Wholly unjustified behaviour.

Thrashing kids with such severity has nothing to do with discipline. They're bloody perverts as far as I'm concerned. Over the years I longed to meet these two again. If either of them reads this – they'll be over 80 if they do – all I can say is: thanks for teaching me how teaching *isn't* done.

Before leaving Hatfield, I had to deal with the sad case of the woman probationer who would not – could not – patrol alone. She was smart, intelligent, eager, polite, possessed common sense, had done well at training school and in after-course examinations. All the qualities you would look for in a young copper. But no way would she walk down the street on her own. Her appearance before me now was an acknowledgement that there was nothing more that could be done. I tried to persuade her it was just a matter of doing it once, to get her confidence. After that, it would come natural. 'Just walk down to the traffic lights,' I said, 'then come back and report to me.' It was a Sunday morning in Hatfield, Hertfordshire, not midnight, downtown Manhattan. Could she do it? 'Only if you come with me,' she said.

Alas, it was no good. She resigned, a waste of a career. I offer no criticism, just regret, and to remind older officers (of whatever rank) that even though someone has joined the police force, it's far from proof that he or she is necessarily mature enough for such a role.

9

"The only place where success comes before work
is in a dictionary"

Vidal Sassoon

First, they beat him to death. Then they threw red, blue and
yellow paint over his broken body. Then they tossed him down the
steps of a cold, dank cellar where, in an eerie atmosphere of the
torchlight's dancing shadows he might have passed for a clown,
the victim of a circus act gone tragically wrong. You can't help
wonder what reason there is for such wickedness. From cycle
races and cautioning kids, to murder. The change in responsibility
could hardly have been greater. Only the pay stayed the same.

We wouldn't need to look far to find who killed our tramp. It
was soon apparent his killer was one (or more) of a number of
dropouts who would have made their way in the world like anyone
except for booze, drugs and Evostik. One even happened along as
we stood at the scene, around 4 a.m. He was arrested for his
trouble, a decision seemingly vindicated when he did no more than
admit the crime, but when he gave his address as 'Planet Mars' we

smelled a rat. It wasn't his fault; years of wandering the streets in caring Britain had affected his brain.

Two factors were against us: the scene was in a non-residential area, so no-one would have seen or heard anything; and contamination – tell-tale particles on clothing – would lead us nowhere. The building was the haunt of every dosser in Watford. They'd all been there at some time or other. Many were known by a name that betrayed some feature of his character. Like Dublin John and Wibbly-Wobbly. We rounded them up, one by one, worked out who had been present when the deed was done. But as each gave his account of events, he would change it again the next day. They were confused, even the decent ones who tried to remember. They didn't know what day it was – and neither did we by the time we'd finished.

We charged one man with murder, another with assisting in the disposal of the body. Alas, the jury threw the murder charge out, convicting them both of disposing of the body instead. They got the maximum, two years, the police got their 'detection', and I was able to tell the coroner we weren't 'looking for anyone else'.

Murder enquiries aren't routine – yet. Routine for a detective inspector was, for me, a day where the first ports of call each morning were the custody suite and the CID general office to find out (a) how many prisoners had been arrested overnight for crime, and for what; and (b) what crimes had been committed over the past 24 hours. In addition, there were missing person enquiries to look into, and 'read up' of the occurrence book and messages from other divisions and forces.

One week in three I was 'on call', liable to be turned out from a cosy bed to investigate suspicious deaths, including the inevitable suicides, sexual offences, assaults and woundings, arsons and any other offences you can or can't think of. To ensure I couldn't hide they gave me a pager which went 'bleep' whenever someone thought calling me was justified, and just as often when it wasn't. It was go-go-go, but it was what I wanted. I was DI. I had arrived.

Two relatively new developments had taken place: police liaison with an organisation called Victim Support, and the Child Protection Unit.

Victim Support is a mainly voluntary organisation whose members visit victims of more serious offences, such as sexual assault, and burglary. The latter are often the elderly, conned by the bogus water board official or gas board inspector. It's a good idea to ensure the old and the vulnerable get sympathetic and tangible support, whilst the police concentrate on catching the offenders. This support extends to victims' court appearances where, as witnesses, they are liable to come face to face with the perpetrators of spiteful crimes, an admittedly rare occurrence – police catch few 'distraction' burglars.

'Child protection' includes liaison with other 'agencies' in cases where child and offender live under the same roof, or where child and offender come into mutual contact, e.g. at school. Information comes to one of the agencies, all parties meet to discuss it and decide on a course of action – from monitoring the situation to arresting an alleged offender. The bottom line is always the welfare of the child. As DI, I was part of the child protection team, along with representatives of the 'agencies', including social services. One hears, from time to time, of cases where, for one reason or another, the 'agencies', especially social services, are severely criticised for failure to respond in serious cases of abuse or neglect. All I can say is, the professionalism and judgement of all agencies in south-west Hertfordshire impressed me greatly: the caring approach of social workers, the input by probation officers, with added responsibility for supervising offenders, the skill of the medical profession and dedication of carers and, not least, the judgement of detectives dealing with child and offender, giving them far more responsibility than many officers of even the highest rank. Non-operational police officers – and there are plenty – are simply not in their league. Some said it was a 'waste of time' for a DI to be involved. I disagreed. If anyone can think of anything more serious than crimes perpetrated against kids, I'd like to hear what it is.

There used not to be a child protection team. This suggests there wasn't any 'child abuse' in the old days. No-one really believes that, I'm sure. It wasn't reported because there was no system in place to deal with it. I can recall just one case, from my early career, where a man raped his stepdaughter, and that only came to light because a firearm was involved. The gun, not the rape, was the reason it came to police notice.

Many sexual offences on children are disclosed years after they've been committed, when, as adults, they can no longer contain the pain. Such cases are difficult to prove. One concerned a woman in her twenties, who reported being sexually abused years before by her stepfather, who was a doctor (offences against children occur right across the social spectrum). When interviewed, he broke down and admitted everything. He got eight years. Sometimes prison sentences help victims come to terms with what happened, sometimes not.

A good rule of thumb is: the younger the child, the more likely an allegation will be true. Tiny tots are unlikely to lie. An older child, alleging rape a few hours before, may be corroborated by her demeanour, early complaint, a medical examination. It's more difficult when, as in one case, a woman of nineteen reported being sexually assault by her schoolteacher six years before.

She told police that on several occasions he had kept her behind after class and indecently assaulted her. It was a serious allegation, not least because he was still teaching. But was she reliable? She was bullied at home by a drunken father, whose wife had long since fled; was she seeking some form of retribution against a male, *any* male? There was nothing to corroborate her story, which was further weakened by the delay – six years – in reporting it. I had to consider whether arresting the alleged offender was merited at all. It's a serious business, depriving someone of his liberty on the say-so of another person. Yet I could not ignore her testimony. If her schoolteacher had abused her he would probably be abusing others. It would be understandable if, as an eleven-year old, she had been afraid to report events at the time. We arrested her former teacher, who denied everything. Without the proof, he was released, as he had to be. To this day, I could not say if I believe he did or did not abuse that girl.

This seems an appropriate point to return to the subject of rape. Things had improved dramatically since those early days I mentioned. 'Rape-trained' officers now focus on victims' welfare.

And there are 'rape suites', where victims are interviewed away from the environs of a police station. In the 'old days' they were liable to appear in full view of the curious glances of anyone not connected with the case, and medically examined in the cold ambience of the cell block, just a few feet away from prisoners, station staff and anyone else who happened to be passing at the time.

First contact is crucial: *all* operational officers – uniform and CID – need to know how to deal with a victim of a sexual offence. Yet this seemed neither apparent, nor important even, to the force training department. Courses were few and far between, and only then for a selected few (although the standard of training, by course tutors, was excellent). So, as well as fulfilling my operational duties, I found myself a willing participant in officers' 'rape training' at headquarters and on division: what to do when responding as first officer to a scene, or being the first officer to speak to the victim, and so on. As for the training, or lack of it, I hope things have improved, but here, for what it's worth, is a potted guide...

First, even though the victim will want to bathe after the offence, she should, if possible, be dissuaded from doing so. Bathing will wash away vital evidence: the offender's pubic hairs, for example (one hair can be used to match DNA), or fibres from his clothing – every contact leaves a trace. She may want a drink. Again, she should be dissuaded: the offender might have ejaculated semen into her mouth. Semen can provide a match for DNA. If she was placed into a police vehicle, the same vehicle should not be used for the arrest of the offender. If it is, defence counsel will argue (with almost certain success) that any cross contamination of fibres (from clothing) came about from their common use of the car, not his presence at the scene. The victim should always be treated sympathetically whilst seeking the truth, and convincing her she is believed (even if she isn't).

Her statement should include the hoary details of the offence. This may seem basic, but there is – or was – a tendency to miss them out. Most *untrained* officers, aware of the need for detail, include the time, the place, what she was wearing, what he was wearing, his description – but a minimum of detail about the actual event, usually because the victim or the officer was too embarrassed to discuss it. Specifics are needed, *exactly* what was said and done. It's no help to the victim if she has to wait until the trial for it to be dragged out by defence counsel – as it will be.

There is an unfounded belief about the *number* of rapes. How many in the county in a given year? I asked one group of officers. A hundred, said one. A thousand, said another. In fact, according to figures, there were nine in the year in question (and only one or two by a 'stranger'). Having said that, figures (as usual) are meaningless. They meant nine *recorded*, and then only those where the offender had been charged or not identified. They didn't included those where the victim had withdrawn her complaint, nor, significantly, women raped by husbands and partners – so-called 'domestics'. Nor, indeed, those not reported at all through shame, self-blame, embarrassment, fear of giving evidence at court, fear of the offender and more. The fact is, no-one knows how many, but the police should ensure that any victim of rape can seek justice, and be treated properly in the process. It's a serious offence, second only to murder. Some might say worse than murder.

One day, I read that a local 'women against rape' group were critical of the manner police dealt with victims, or 'survivors', as they call them. I invited them to the police station for a meeting, my purpose being to convince them that police dealt with victims properly, and to exchange points of view. Around twenty turned up, many victims – or survivors – themselves. We started talking at 8 p.m., and finished at one the next morning. A lot of emotion flowed that night, I can tell you. I told them the police encouraged women to come forward, that we were training more officers. That's more than I could have said a few short years before. I thought they'd understand. Not a bit of it. The main bones of contention were (a) the need for medical examination; and (b) the need for corroboration. They said neither was necessary.

The medical examination is an unfortunate but essential part of any rape investigation. A serious allegation has been made against someone who, if convicted, faces a life sentence. It is in the interest of the victim, if what she says is true; of the alleged offender, if he is innocent. It also provides damning evidence: DNA – genetic fingerprinting – proves intercourse and, crucially, may identify the offender if his identity is unknown. But, they said, a woman would not make up a false story; a man is guilty on her say-so, and corroboration, including the medical, is unnecessary. But the say-so of one person should never in itself be sufficient to prove anything against another.

Corroboration is not, strictly, a requirement of law. It is possible, though usually unlikely, to secure a conviction without it. The boxer, Mike Tyson, was charged with rape (in the United States) on the sole testimony of the woman. Intercourse took place: with consent, he said; without, she said. She couldn't prove he raped her, he couldn't prove he didn't. On her uncorroborated evidence, Tyson was convicted. Someone said 'You only have to look at him', meaning if you're black with fists like shovels you're guilty. But no person is guilty of anything because of his (or her) skin colour, or physical appearance.

At the time of writing, I read of a move to switch the burden of proof in rape cases to the defendant. In other words, on the issue of consent, it will be for the alleged offender to prove he had consent, not for the woman to prove he didn't. This is utterly wrong. The burden of proof should always be with the accuser, no matter what the crime.

Statistics (that word again) suggest that only one in ten men are convicted in cases where a woman can't prove she did not consent. Will society be happier, then, if nine out of ten are convicted where she did consent and now says she did not? Some allegations are false, as I have shown in these pages. Still another was the case of a 15-year old schoolgirl, who said she'd been raped in a copse after school by one of her schoolmates. It happened some months before, she said. In fact, she was pregnant, and had made the story up rather than admit responsibility to her parents for her own voluntary actions. Imagine the situation in these circumstances if they switch the onus of proof to the defendant; unable to prove there was consent, this 'offender', a schoolboy, would be convicted.

Rape is a serious crime, they say (rightly), and a 'one in ten' conviction rate is not enough. But you can't say 'one in ten isn't enough, so change the law to get a few more convictions'. We are talking about prison sentences for people who will have no defence if someone, for whatever reason, points an accusing finger. Prison sentences handed out in kangaroo courts, that's what it amounts to.

It may sound trite, but if they do change the law I suggest in future that a man should require a woman (including his wife) to sign a 'consent' form, in the presence of two independent witnesses, before sexual intercourse takes place. It makes sense. After all, we have to have weddings and wills and things witnessed, and you don't face a life sentence there if anything goes wonky. Witness forms could be available at post offices, or in dispensing machines in pubs and clubs, next to the fruity condoms. Better still, don't have sexual intercourse at all. Then maybe everyone will be happy.

Some have little sympathy with rape victims, saying they 'deserve it': the woman in the mini-skirt, the woman who ventures out alone. But no-one 'deserves it'. I had to say as much to some colleagues once.

A young woman visited a local nightspot, got drunk and ended up dancing on the table, stripping almost naked, much to the delight of the males present, one of whom escorted her home in a taxi. Once in her flat, he raped her. This was a 'deserved it' issue – even to policemen. She might have been a fool for getting drunk, irresponsible for allowing a stranger into her home, but no-one deserves to be assaulted, abused, penetrated against her wishes. You may as well say a man who gets drunk deserves to be robbed, or someone deserves to have their house burgled if they leave a window open. They may be irresponsible, too, but they don't deserve it.

Although 'stranger rape' is a rare phenomenon, the fact remains: the rapist can strike anywhere, anytime...

A woman in her fifties worked all hours cleaning at local schools. One day a young fellow was sent (by the Job Centre) to help her. He did no more than drag her into a classroom where he raped her. She went through with the case, and he got time. She seemed very calm about it all 'She's strong-willed,' said her husband. Perhaps, but rape trauma can hold a latent agenda. No-one can say she won't suffer the effects of the attack years from now, long after her assailant has been freed.

A young woman answered an ad in the 'personal' column of a newspaper. She made the mistake of inviting her unknown date to her home address, where he raped her. Date rape, as it's called. The advice must be to meet first in a public place, such as a busy pub, and get to know someone before inviting him home.

Another case is worth mentioning, if only to highlight public apathy.

It's a typical early evening on the M1, where a continuous line of slow-moving traffic heads out of London. For slow-moving read almost stationary, as many who have to suffer that stretch of motorway will testify. A lone woman sees a lorry's headlights flash in her mirror. Then the lorry driver appears at her door, says there's a problem with her lights. She steps out from her car, now illuminated in the bright glare of headlights of traffic. Without warning, he grabs her, and drags her up the grassy embankment by the side of the motorway. She screams, waves her arms, does everything possible to attract the attention – and help – of those motorists now surely witness to her ordeal. Not one gets out of his (or her) car. Mercifully, her assailant flees, drives off at a crawl in the slow-moving traffic, leaving her alone and shaken on the hard shoulder. For the record, he was arrested and convicted.

Yet another example raises the issue of 'consent', or would have done if the case had gone to trial. Although 'consent' was given, the woman was adamant that she did not give true consent; the man said she did. Imagine you were a member of a jury, and see who you would believe.

Carol was forty-odd, a loner, the daughter of respectable parents. She lived in a one-bedroomed squat above a parade of shops. Her room was filthy, what furniture she possessed amounting to no more than a load of junk covered in old newspapers and dust. She drank heavily, in her room, and slept the rest of the time in a single bed in the corner. Carol bothered nobody, sought the company of nobody and lived her life the way she chose.

One night, asleep in her bed, Carol woke to find someone standing next to her in the semi-darkness. The man, a stranger, had easily popped the insecure Yale lock on her door, and was now looking at her in such a way it was obvious he had just one thing on his mind. As he leaned over her prostrate form, she could smell alcohol on his breath. The man didn't say anything, offered no violence, and was not armed. Without offering the slightest resistance, not even a token 'no', Carol allowed the man to have intercourse with her on her bed. When he had finished, the man left without a word, and Carol remained where she was.

Carol did not report the incident to the police. The following morning, she did tell someone, then the police were informed.

When I visited Carol at her 'squat', I was appalled at the conditions. This, just a few minutes' walk from the busy shopping precinct of a large provincial town. It didn't take long to identify the stranger. He was a smart, professional young man, the last person you might have thought would even enter such a room, let alone to seek out the female occupant he'd heard lived inside. Nevertheless, he admitted after having a drink with some friends, he'd forced his way into Carol's room and having intercourse with her – just as she said. Except, of course, to add that she had allowed him to do so freely.

So, member of the jury, it's one against one. Imagine the scene: it's the middle of the night, and a woman alone in her bed wakes up to see the stranger. Was it rape? Or did Carol 'consent'? There was no weapon, no violence, no injury to the victim, no spoken threat, no refusal to have intercourse. She just lay there and succumbed.

I know what I believed: there was no consent, and it was rape. Earlier I mentioned there had to be something to support a woman's allegation on 'consent'. So what was there in these circumstances?

Common sense, that's what. Alone in her bed, a woman whose self-esteem was ready at rock bottom, had no option but to allow the stranger have his way. Imminent injury, death even, was the alternative. And what reasonable guy could expect to force entry into her room and expect its occupant to 'consent' to sex? It's when alleged rape is 'domestic', where they know each other, that's when consent becomes blurred, and at the risk of repetition, something more than an allegation alone is needed: in Carol's case, the circumstances spoke for themselves.

Carol, incidentally, would not support a prosecution. Instead, she did everything she could to force the incident from her mind. Well aware of the meaning of 'rape trauma', and taking into account Carol's wretched lifestyle and her undoubted lack of self-esteem, I became more focused on her well being than the criminal investigation. The 'rape trained' woman constable who worked with me on the case felt the same, and we called at Carol's squat almost daily, enquiring after her. In addition, I contacted Carol's GP, who called to see her but was refused admittance, and tried to persuade her to seek help, in confidence, through Rape Crisis, as well as suggesting she contact her parents, to ask them to visit her. The woman constable and I even took Carol out to lunch, when I found myself trying to persuade her to allow us to take her then and there to her parents' home in Wales, where she would be looked after by her family.

Carol would have none of it. She thanked us for our trouble, said she just wanted to be alone. In the end, I sent a report to the crown prosecution service, recommending no further action, first because without Carol's testimony, there would be no evidence to convict the man of anything, and second because to try and force her to do anything would only have made things worse. She was 'victim' enough without being made to face added pressures brought about by authority.

This incident also proved that it is so easy to become too involved in cases where, as a police officer, one should strive to remain detached. OK, we're all human, but if I'd just up and taken Carol to Wales that day, I guess my superintendent or DCI might have had something to say about it – like what about all the other pressing matters at a DI's door, and why was I running around the country with someone who didn't want the police to take any action anyway?

*

Burglary falls into two categories: residential and non-residential.

Residential burglary is rife. It was when I was DI anyway. It's committed during the day, mainly. It's simple enough: select a house and knock on the door. If someone answers, give a cock-and-bull story, like asking directions; if not, you're in. Good-class houses are likelier targets for the so-called professionals; terraced houses, often owned by young couples at work during the day, are sitting targets for younger burglars.

Burglars get away with nine out of every ten houses they break into. Very few are arrested committing the offence. Most 'detections' are the result of prison visits, where offenders, after sentence, admit their crimes, thus improving the 'detection rate' – the figures game again. In such cases there is little hope of recovering stolen property and offenders get no added punishment.

Non-residential properties are usually burgled at night. A morning would never pass without the inevitable phone calls from staff in offices, factories, shops, schools, reporting their premises broken into. Few of those responsible would languish in the cells. Few criminals are 'pulled', as my friend Alf pointed out years before. Yet 'nights' are tailor-made for pro-active policing. It's amazing what you can hear: the breaking of glass, the furtive footsteps, a car door closing. You don't hear it in a patrol car. Yet I could never ascribe the low arrest rate to a lack of willingness by patrol officers. On the contrary, if there is one shining light it's the men and women on patrol; they want to make arrests, and prove it whenever they respond to the call of 'intruders on', or a suspicious vehicle. But arresting criminals is about more than responding. It's about taking the initiative. I guess I was lucky: in my day, shift inspectors and sergeants taught young bobbies the ropes – like staking out premises, turning flashlights off, staying silent and waiting for the prowler.

Today, area inspectors play little or no part in supervision and leadership, whilst the divisional inspector has too much on his or her plate, is responsible for too large an area – if there's one on duty, that is. And many sergeants are confined to their statutory Custody role, which should be a civilian post.

One can be critical of a lack of foot observations where, if they tried, the police couldn't fail to catch offenders. Yet there are times when there are so few officers on duty it's no wonder they can't spare the manpower for obbos. I mentioned this to the operations chief inspector once, only to be told it was a uniform matter and I should concern myself with crime! Operations chief inspectors should get officers on the streets, and if they can't their divisional commanders should go and see their chief constables who should take them from non-operational roles and computer terminals and put 'em there, senior officers included.

Burglary is crime, so what about the CID?

In some forces, there is no such thing as 'nightshift CID'. There should be. Crime doesn't end at midnight or whenever. To my mind, the only reason for CID not operating at night is if there's no crime at night. I don't think we're quite there yet. When I argued the case for a nightshift CID, I was asked to give reasons. I did, and I'll give them again.

Detectives (at night) can interview prisoners (in the admittedly unlikely event of their not requiring a solicitor). Detectives (at night) can 'double up' with uniformed constables, possibly in an unmarked car, to patrol and keep observations on selected premises/car parks. Detectives (at night) can seize prisoners' clothing following an offence where later forensic examination will be required, perhaps showing inexperienced officers how to wrap exhibits. Detectives (at night) can attend serious crime scenes, including murder and suspicious deaths, and 'hand over' to a senior detective. Detectives (at night) can be available at the morning 'handover' to CID, ensuring continuity of the case.

One in three of all recorded crimes are thefts of or from motor vehicles – car crime – committed mainly by young blokes, often to finance drugs. Compared to the vast total, there are few arrests. Despite this, car crime boasts a fairly good detection rate. In the past, police relied on good old t.i.c.'s – offences taken into consideration. You made your arrest, the offender admitted it, then elected to have, say, twenty others t.i.c. Police got their detections, prisoners cleared their slate.

Later, with increased legal representation, offenders are liable to admit nothing, or at best only the offence for which arrested. T.i.c.'s are old hat now. So there's the prison visit (if he goes to prison) where the prisoner admits all his crimes in the knowledge that he won't be punished for them and can't be arrested later. Again, the play on figures. But then, who can blame DI's or indeed chief constables if, as is the case, the Home Office, the media, the system demands high detection rates as a measure of the force's efficiency? It doesn't do anything to help victims or recover stolen property, but officers can tick little boxes on computer screens, if that's what they want.

As DI, I gave car crime no more than a cursory glance. Against burglary, and the usual robberies, assaults and sexual offences, I regarded it as significant only in terms of volume. True, it's a serious business having your car stolen or vandalised. But CID resources stretch only so far; *serious* crime should be the focus of detectives. To clear car crime up would have made me the greatest DI ever. But it wasn't figures that counted, not to me anyway. What counted was people: the young couple who'd come home to find their house broken into; the elderly victim of the distraction burglary; the girl who'd been attacked on her way home from school.

Nowadays, many adult offenders are cautioned and released without charge, a decision usually made at the behest of the crown prosecution service. The CPS have certain 'criteria', which must be met: a 51% chance of conviction before they will proceed with a case; first-time offenders cautioned, sometimes irrespective of the circumstances; and, worst of all, 'plea bargaining', where they will accept a lesser charge at court in return for a 'guilty' plea, thus ensuring an offender faces a lesser sentence, usually inappropriate to the actual crime committed.

A constable once told me of her frustration when, after arresting a shoplifter at ten o'clock one morning, she had to wait until five o'clock for the prisoner's solicitor to turn up. When the prisoner finally admitted the offence, she was wheeled into the next office, cautioned by the duty inspector and released. Whilst the decision to prosecute or otherwise should not be based on how long a suspect's solicitor takes to appear – and they can take all day (after all, their client isn't going anywhere!) – is this the best way to spend taxpayers' money? Is it justice?

Nor is the cautioning procedure confined to minor offences. I once ran an operation to trap three brothers who were selling drugs from their flat. Our information was that they had scales and all the necessary equipment to make up those neat little bundles, or 'deals'. Unfortunately, apprehending them had to be done the hard way – by observations. It was expensive, in terms of payment of overtime and police resources – equipment, cars, taking uniformed and CID manpower from other divisional needs. Worth it, though, if it meant arresting the offenders. Some of their 'clients' were kids; word had got round about the drugs.

Unfortunately, we were never in a position to know at any given time whether there were any drugs in the premises. So, in the end we went in on a wing and a prayer. We found drugs, but not enough to prove supply; only personal use. Still, as any detective will admit, when the going gets tough, you take what you can. All three were charged with possession and bailed for court. Imagine how we felt when, prior to the court date, the crown prosecution service returned the papers, withdrawing the charges and recommending cautions instead. All that time and expense for – what? An inspector having 'em in for a bollocking. They must have laughed all the way to their next deal.

Sometimes, criminals who are 'at it' are serving a prison sentence, yet they are not in prison at all. One guy was doing time for burglary. Around half way through his sentence, as part of the rehabilitation process, he was given day-release to work as a garage mechanic, his employer issuing a certificate to 'prove' his attendance at work. In fact, they had a cosy arrangement where the employer would issue the certificate in return for a £50 backhander, whilst chummy was committing armed robberies and burglaries. If suspected of committing a criminal offence, he had a cast-iron alibi: the certificate 'proved' he was at work. When we searched his house we found a firearm. Robber, burglar and

225

serving prisoner, all at the same time. Don't blame the police when these guys are busy. The police did their job months before. So did the jury.

P was sentenced to several years' incarceration – yet was free to return to his victim's home just months later, even though he was 'doing time'. He and his girlfriend had been involved in 'domestics'. No matter how many times police arrested him, she would retract her complaint. Finally, when he threatened her with a loaded firearm, she saw the case through to trial and P went to prison. Now she could live in safety. Or so she thought, for not long afterwards, P turned up on her doorstep. By the grace of God she was at Sainsbury's! When she found out (through another member of the household), she reported the incident to the control room, blaming the police for something that could have had serious consequences.

'Impossible', I protested, 'he's in prison'. I telephoned the prison to prove it.

'Is P a prisoner in your establishment?' I asked. He was.

'Could he be out for any reason?'

'Well, he does attend hospital for psychiatric treatment.'

'Really? And how does he get to hospital?'

'On the bus.'

This was a man with previous for violence, serving time for a firearms offence, in a prison not ten miles from his victim's home. The time of the incident was after six.

'Can you verify he has reported back to the prison?' I asked.

I heard footsteps, and a door open and close as the officer went off, presumably looking for P. A short time later the footsteps again.

'He doesn't seem to be back yet,' I was told.

He turned up later that night. In his own good time, of course.

*

Armed robberies at banks and building societies were prevalent everywhere in the late 80's/early 90's. Sometimes the robbers had real guns, sometimes imitations, sometimes just words or secret notes passed to cashiers, implying they were armed. Whatever, counter staff would hand over around £2,000, sometimes more.

A call to a robbery invokes maximum response from eager young officers in their unit cars. Which is not to say it's always the *correct* response. You hear them screaming out the station yard, sirens wailing, most, if not all, heading for the one place the robbers won't be: the scene of the crime. Especially once they heard those sirens.

Not many were caught at the time, but sooner or later they would be captured somewhere, doing the same thing. For this reason, much-vaunted detection rates for armed robbery were surprisingly high. Then they installed surveillance cameras, and started keeping the money in another part of the premises, so a demand, even with a gun, became futile.

Surveillance cameras are commonplace nowadays, used by police, security companies and large organisations such as hospitals and schools. Police use is mainly twofold: crime prevention, or to entrap speeding motorists. Of the latter I have little to say, except if 'speed cameras' slow motorists down that's fine by me. But the problem with all surveillance cameras is their perceived encroachment on civil liberties – the 'Big Brother' element. Frankly, I have sympathy with this view: as you fill up with petrol, or park your car, or walk along the shopping malls and through busy supermarkets, you're on camera. That means someone is watching you, or your movements are recorded so someone can watch later. Big Brother? Damn right. There should be good reason for such intrusion. I think there is, as the following demonstrates.

Late one night, when a young fellow walked through a deserted shopping precinct, he was accosted by two men. They demanded he hand his rucksack over, and when this was refused they seized it, and gave him a kicking. Finally, having left him almost unconscious, they walked off with his property. Sadly, it didn't end there. One of the men turned, and taking a knife from his pocket calmly stood over his hapless victim and ripped his face open. There were no witnesses to the attack, and the man was able

227

to give only scant descriptions of his assailants. The events, however, were caught on camera.

Several cameras, actually. And the films taken from them showed full facials of the men and *exactly* what happened, most useful to the jury who, like the detectives working in the incident room, were sickened when they saw the what the victim's assailant did with his knife. A picture paints a thousand words, and without these pictures detection of a serious crime would have been unlikely. Cameras have many uses: at major events, such as football matches, to identify crowd problems or the inevitable hooligans. Big Brother it may be. But if this is the society of today, it seems it is a price we all have to pay.

Dealing with violence is routine to police. It's their job. I could list reams of violent crimes in these pages. Instead, I'll mention just three. Okay, maybe one or two in the next chapter. That's what the press wanted every morning when they asked what there was for them to report, locally and hopefully for the nationals. Never mind stolen bikes and cars, what about sex and grievous bodily harm?

A woman hears someone rapping on her door at five o' clock one morning. When she opens it she finds a young man, H, collapsed on her doorstep, blood oozing between his fingers as he clutches his throat. A police patrol car arrives, and the officers save the man's life by stemming the blood-flow and whisking him of to hospital where, later, he tells police he doesn't know the identity of his assailant. He was lying. Out of fear, of course. But we weren't prepared to accept his reluctance to co-operate about an incident which, but for the grace of God, would have been a murder.

The offender was D, a young fellow of twenty, of slight build and outwardly quiet disposition. Yet he was a ruthless criminal, perhaps the most dangerous man I ever met. He terrorised the locals around his manor in London. If there was a drugs deal going down, he ran it. If he fell out with someone he would exact revenge, usually in the form of a beating, with more to come if they went to the police. If he was bored, he'd walk into a pub and make deliberate eye-contact with somebody – anybody – who,

228

finding themselves being stared at by a nothing bloke of ten stones, would naturally have something to say about it. It was always a mistake. Sorry, Denys, but in D's case, a good little 'un always got the better of a even good big 'un.

The previous year, D, and his friend, H, had been arrested for stealing a car. D alone was convicted, and as a result spent his birthday in custody (where it wasn't unknown for him to attack his guards). Later, none too pleased at being grassed up by H – as he thought – D attacked him with a machete. But that's by-the-by. On D's next birthday, by coincidence, they met up again at a party. D decided it was a fitting occasion to exact revenge. In the small hours D told H to drive him out to the sticks, and when they'd reached a point which might suitably be described as the middle of nowhere he was told to kneel on the ground and say the Lord's Prayer. H, now in fear of imminent death, prayed for probably the first and last time in his life.

'The Lord is my shepherd, I shall not want...'

Whether the fateful cut took place because D was determined in any event to kill his friend, or because H got his prayers mixed up isn't known. Whatever, he cut his throat, and left him for dead on the fairway. H survived, and bit by bit gave us the lowdown on D: details of his violent history, why he had cut his throat. We learned more, from a woman D had imprisoned and raped, and Met officers, unable to secure the support of witnesses when investigating other violent crimes perpetrated by D.

D was arrested, and appeared at crown court, where he stared threateningly at witnesses, a tactic designed to instil fear. He succeeded, although it hardly would have helped his cause with the members of the jury. He was sentenced to life imprisonment. As everyone knows, 'life' doesn't mean you're actually locked up for life, although if D attacked his guards you'd think they might consider detaining him at least a little longer than the usual handful of years.

Another nearly-murder took place one New Year's eve. A group of men, drunk from New Year revelry, were making their way along a quiet street when one of them broke a window. Not surprisingly, the occupants of the damaged property spilled outside in angry mood. The problem was, they were members of your normal, law-abiding fraternity, whereas those outside were toerags. There was no contest, and it almost cost one of the good guys his life when in the ensuing fracas one of the drunks picked up a piece of wood and struck him across the neck. The incident ended there, the injured man's companions attending to him, the drunks making their way off, leaving foul language in their wake.

At first, the injury to the man's neck didn't seem too bad. But a day or so later, after he collapsed and was rushed to hospital, they found a carotid artery had been ruptured, and he relapsed to the point of death. To all intents and purposes, we were dealing with a murder enquiry. It took some sorting, although we were able to identify and arrest the bad guys. Fortunately, the man who had dealt the near-mortal blow survived. I suppose the lesson has to be: leave a gang of drunks be, even when your property has been attacked. Better to have the window repaired without fuss than put your life on the line.

Finally, there was the woman who was murdered as she slept in her bed in hospital. The constable who attended her room was informed it was a routine 'sudden death'. Elderly lady, gone to bed, died through the night. But the blood and brain tissue splattered up the wall above her bed suggested otherwise. Someone had beaten her so hard she no longer had a face. She was a patient in the psychiatric wing, occupied by both sexes. It was staffed throughout the night, during which time the entrance was kept locked. Nice and secure, you might think. Tragically, security didn't extend to *within* the building.

If it wasn't an outsider, who was it? Another patient, that's who. He'd gone walkabout, entered her room, knelt on her shoulders as she lay sleeping and punched her face in, literally. There was no logical reason, nothing premeditated or anything. He did it, he said, because he hated women, and because God said he must. He was locked up indefinitely.

Didn't the staff provide security? Well, no, they didn't, as events proved, because they were asleep. I recall the press asking for my comments. I kept them to myself. It's not the job of a detective inspector to become involved in hospital security matters, but the judge and the coroner might have had something to say. And so would you, I daresay, if any of your loved ones were confined to a hospital whose patients were psychiatric cases and whose staff slept through the night as other patients wandered at large.

Another enquiry concerned a missing 9-year old boy. I'll call him Sean. He wandered off one Sunday afternoon and disappeared, last seen in a local park. There was a major search, with police assisted by local residents, but despite this, and widespread publicity there was no sign of him. The case made the nationals, and appeared on *Crimewatch*.

You can never foresee the human element in any situation, as events proved. As well as thousands of well-meaning calls from the public, most of which reported 'sightings' of Sean at locations as far apart as Cornwall to Caithness, letters began arriving from so-called mediums, all purporting to have had a 'vision'. There'd be sketches of trees, a stream, an obscure house beside a river, or some other geographical feature. They all had one thing in common: it was the site where Sean was buried. 'Just look near a river,' the letters would say. They never actually specified which one. Could've been the Thames or the Mississippi. Nor was there any evidence that Sean was buried anywhere, or dead even. I gave no credence to these letters, confining them instead to the 'mediums tray', and ensured their contents played no part in the investigation. Even so, a police officer with an otherwise rational mind suggested maybe we should check the fields by a local river, 'just in case'.

One afternoon, I decided to check one of these mediums out, just to get the flavour. I selected one at random, a woman who lived in Jersey. The telephone was answered by a male voice. Sounded like an old boy.

'Is that Mrs so-and-so's address?' I enquired.

'It is indeed.'

'Would it be possible to speak to her?'

'I'm afraid she's out.'

I told him who I was, why I was ringing.

'She thinks the missing boy might be buried near a mill by a river,' I said. The man laughed out loud.

'Oh, I wouldn't take any notice of her,' he said. 'She's daft as a brush.'

So much for mediums. Anyway, if she was that good, why wasn't she in when I rang?

As for Sean, he turned up, alive and well, not half a mile from the place he was last sighted. There was some criticism of the police for not searching the house where he was secreted by his abductor. We didn't respond then, but I will now. The house *was* searched, early on in the enquiry, along with dozens of others. Sean wasn't there at that time; he was taken there afterwards. It's never easy. The police don't have the power to search repeatedly, willy-nilly, houses where they might, with no backup evidence, think someone is being kept. They aren't invested with the powers of the KGB, not yet anyway.

*

Another feature of my DI's role was missing persons. That is anyone who, for some reason – or maybe no reason – was missing from home. More often than not police response in the first instance to the report of a missing person fell short of the mark. Truth to tell, I don't think most officers realise the importance of it all.

One mistake on taking a report about a 'Misper' is failure by police to search the home address. First, to ensure the 'missing person' is missing. This may sound silly, but it isn't. Three little kids were reported missing from home once. Police began a massive search operation, scouring fields and woodland – then their parents found the little blighters hiding in the airing cupboard because they'd been up to some prank or other. Such waste of resources isn't the fault of the missing person or worried parents, it's the fault of the police for not doing their job properly. And second, to ensure the Misper hasn't been murdered and buried under the patio. You must always consider the possibility of foul play – like the time that little boy was buried on the Northumbrian moors. Searching the homes of Mispers means searching *thoroughly*. It doesn't mean popping round just to show the flag, or take a few particulars. It means looking everywhere, including the loft and the shed.

One case concerned a woman reported missing by her husband. She'd just taken the car and disappeared, he said. Yet their marriage had been sound enough. She had a good job, was in good health. She *was* into the occult. But there seemed no reason for her to disappear. Naturally, I became suspicious…

I didn't actually accuse him of topping her, but short of a satisfactory explanation it seemed to me that he might have. I decided she might be buried in the house. There was nothing for it but to look. He was very co-operative. Even helped me lift the floorboards. As I peered into dark recesses and groped into dark corners among the cobwebs, he stood and watched. It occurred to me that if I discovered her body he might do me in too, but the problem didn't arise. She'd put a hosepipe on her car exhaust, and ended it all at a meaningful location – to her: Wookey Hole, in Somerset.

Another Misper who turned up dead was an old boy who'd wandered off from an old people's home and simply disappeared. It was a sad case. Police searched everywhere: the gardens of nearby houses, surrounding streets, the canal, wasteland. Details were circulated nationally, publicity went out in newspapers and on television. Alas, there was no sign of the poor man, until he was found, months later, lying among shrubbery in a supermarket car park.

Well, bits of him were found. A thighbone, a few ribs, attached to which were the remnants of his pullover, the sole means of identification. His skull was discovered twenty feet away, probably having been dragged there by a passing fox or something. I attended the post mortem, which bordered on the farcical, and in more than one respect. Taking into account that he might have been murdered, we employed the services of a Home Office pathologist. This is routine. Home Office pathologists have great expertise in examining possible murder victims. They know what to look for, and through their acquired experience they make sound witnesses at court in any trial. Sadly, this one rather undid that premise.

Found among the bits and pieces lying on the slab in the mortuary were a number of small bones. 'How odd,' said the pathologist, studying them one by one as we awaited his learned proclamation. 'It appears,' he declared at last, 'that a small dog, or a cat perhaps, must have already been dead and the deceased expired on top of it.' He nodded slowly, the way experts do when they've cracked it. Or think they have. And there was me thinking they were the dead man's fingers.

He picked up the skull. Peered at it intently. Alas, poor Yorick!

'You know,' he said, looking longingly at the skull, 'this is a most valuable item for the purposes of research. Could I have it?'

After a brief, awkward silence, Gerry, the coroner's officer, spoke up.

'We should really have the consent of the next of kin…'

The pathologist stared at the skull. Like a kid who picks up a toy, he *so* wanted it. Awkward silence time again. That's *really* awkward in a mortuary. Finally, Gerry's voice broke the silence.

'Oh, go on then.'

With that our Misper's skull parted company forever from the little of what was left of the rest of him. Obviously, the pathologist couldn't possibly give a cause of death. So, whilst we didn't know how our Misper had died, we couldn't say he'd been murdered either. I chanced a remark, *sotto voce*, to Julie, the scenes of crime officer.

'I could have sworn those bones were his fingers,' I said, marvelling at the skill of the scientist.

'They *are* his fingers,' she replied, in obvious disgust. 'I'll have a word with the mortician in the morning.'

I made a written note of the pathologist's name, and pinned it to the notice board in my office. After that performance, I made sure he was never called to do an autopsy again.

Sometimes things weren't done right, like when I was called to a house where the occupant had slashed his wrists in the bathroom. Blood everywhere – or there would have been if the sergeant who attended hadn't cleaned it up. 'Didn't want the family upset,' he explained. Nice of him, but of no use to me if it was a murder and he'd washed away the evidence. Then again, when a woman telephoned police to report she'd found her husband hanging in the garage, the well-meaning operator in the control room, applying the 'disturb nothing' principle, got it wrong. Slightly. 'Touch nothing till the police arrive,' she told the caller.' Trouble was, the poor man hanging from the ceiling *wasn't dead*. So, what chance there might have been to save him was lost. It goes without saying that saving life always takes priority.

At the risk of repetition, the reason a senior detective is called to the discovery of a body is that, in the first instance, foul play must always be suspected. Crime scenes should be protected, remain undisturbed if possible – you can hardly expect to discover vital clues if Uncle Tom Cobbleigh and all have trampled everywhere. In all cases the names of anyone present, including police officers, should be taken down. Training and supervision again.

I was called time and again to suicides on the railway, where the 'foul play' principle often bordered on the farcical.

Mangled remains on the line.

Everyone is waiting – the duty inspector and other officers, along with railway personnel. Hopefully, someone's had the presence of mind to have the trains stopped, otherwise a whole lot of others will have to be scraped up. Anyway, the inspector, the sergeant, the constables and a man who was walking his dog along the embankment at the time and saw the man deliberately stand in front of the train, all believe it's a suicide. Yet they call the DI. Crime scene? You wonder what happens to common sense sometimes.

The doctor's called, too. Not to try and put the remains together. Only God could do that and He never did at a suicide I attended. The doctor's the only one who can certify death, never mind the remains of wotsisname are barely recognisable as human, and his head's stuck on the front of the train, now pulling into Birmingham New Street. OK, all suicides are tragic. Sometimes people can no longer handle the stresses and strains of life, sometimes they've done something they shouldn't and for them there's only one answer, sometimes they've just lost their marbles. I always used to think that if I could have had ten minutes with the victim – and they are victims – I could have prevented many of them. Most people could, if you think about it.

*

The superintendent stirs his tea, carefully places the teaspoon into the saucer and picks up his bacon roll. Eyes watch as he takes a huge bite before looking up at his subordinates. As he comes to grips with the food now occupying the hole in his face, his eyes turn to me and he nods imperceptibly.

It's morning prayers.

As DI, I have to apprise the divisional commander and uniformed senior officers of crime over the past 24 hours. I scan the computer print-out, another rain forest sacrificed especially for the occasion, and look around the table at my peers who, like the super, are tucking into their bacon butties. Alas, it's a luxury I cannot share. I did try it once, only to find myself choking in the attempt to deliver the message.

'Six residential burglaries in the division, and a robbery at a building society.'

The super's ahead of the game. 'Wasn't one a distraction?'

All eyes are on me, all gobs are munching away.

'It happened around three o'clock,' I tell the eager throng. 'A man knocked on an old lady's door, said he was from the water board. He said he had to check her stop-cock.'

'And she let him in?'

'Yes. She went into the kitchen with him…'

'And someone sneaked in and stole her handbag,' says a knowing voice.

'No. Her purse. It was in the sideboard drawer.'

Gasps all round.

'The bastards.'

'They don't come much lower.'

'They should be locked up. I say, pass the sugar, Barry.'

The super has some important questions.

'Descriptions?'

'Vague. She *was* ninety-four.'

'I meant, did any of the neighbours see anything? We did house to house, I take it.'

'Yes. No suspects were seen.'

'Was there a vehicle?'

'None seen, sir.'

He chews awhile, deep in thought. Gulps down a mouthful.

'Victim support been informed?'

'Yes, sir.'

Someone is burning to side-track me. The question comes from an area inspector, possibly to impress the super, possibly because he wants to know the answer for some reason. Washing down the last remains of his butty, he picks up his copy of an incident log and asks about the suicide on the railway. Already the super is raising his eyebrows, meaning was I called out and did I attend the scene? I was and I did.

Some bloke had left a note saying how fed up he was, then went and stood in front of a train. 'No suspicious circumstances,' I say, not bothering to add that the nightshift inspector could have come to the same conclusion. Concern clouds the super's face. For a moment I think it's because I've been up half the night.

'You seem awfully sure.'

I was mistaken, obviously.

'British Transport Police have taken it anyway,' I announce. That's OK then.

More questions follow. How's the murder enquiry progressing? What about the rape trial? Are the witnesses still getting grief from the offender? How the hell did he ever get bail? What about those racist attacks? And that missing girl, wotsername, has anyone been round to see her parents? I deal with it all. Yes, sir. No, sir. Three bags jam-packed full, sir. Finally, when the gathering have pushed their now-empty plates forward, and mouths have been suitably wiped and teeth meticulously picked, it's the turn of my peers.

The car parking arrangements are in place for the annual fete. The new telephones will be connected up within the week, and the delay was the fault of the phone company not me, sir. The new system of issuing personal radios is in place as of this morning (after one had gone missing and been traced to a DC who ran out to a report of an armed robbery without signing for it). The super is looking at me again. A did-you-speak-to-him look. Yes, sir. I certainly did.

We're still going round the table. Policing arrangements for Watford's match against Scunthorpe or somebody are in place. The job description for the new post of property officer has been formulated and adverts will appear in the press this week. The cleaner has been off six months and will someone be paying a welfare visit?

It's the super's turn. He sits back, waits a moment until he's certain he has the undivided attention of his audience, then lets us have it, right from the top.

'The painters are starting upstairs in a fortnight,' he says, 'and we still haven't decided on the colour.'

This is serious. Only last week he specifically asked for suggestions, and here we are again, and still no decision.

There's a full minute's silence, as everyone strives to think of the colour that will make him a hero.

'I think a light colour's best. Makes the place look bigger.'

'Not magnolia, surely.'

'Wife likes it.'

Magnolia goes down like a lead weight.

'What about cream?'

'Bit bland, if you ask me.'

'Pink's nice.'

'Or green…'

There's a pause, as the division's leaders strive to come up with the answer.

'What about two-tone blue?'

We cover the spectrum, everything except indigo. I throw in my two penn'orth.

'What about indigo?'

For some reason, the super's gaze suddenly falls on a piece of paper, which has lain on the desk in front of him, unnoticed and forgotten. It seems my voice reminded him of it.

'There's been a complaint,' he says, clearly unimpressed with indigo, 'from a bloke who says the scenes of crime officer who attended a burglary at his premises wasn't very civil.' He pushes the complaint form in my direction.

'See what his problem is, will you?'

The image of indigo-coloured walls fades quickly as I look at the form, which was completed by an area inspector. He's here, at the meeting. I say so. The super shrugs. In other words, sort it. The area inspector's got to sort those telephones.

Finally, chairs scrape as the super and my peers depart. My briefing on crime will be forgotten before they reach the door, and in any case will have no relevance in whatever they will be doing for the rest of the day. I gather up the paper-mountain, and emerge from the room to find a detective sergeant patiently waiting to tell me about a man he's arrested for rape. There's a problem with finding facilities to interview the victim, and he needs his DI to help sort it. He's had to wait until I've told people with no operational responsibilities about crime, until they've told me about non-operational matters I didn't need to know about. It's all part of the culture: patrol officers left to their own devices outside, senior officers a-busy inside the nick, each caught up in his own world of misplaced priorities. And until they scrap the term management and replace it with supervision, 'inside' is where you are going to find your inspectors, and never mind what's going on in the real world. The world where Mr and Mrs Joe Public live, work and play.

After holding the rank of inspector for three years they sent me, belatedly, you might think, for a spot of training to Chelmsford. After another meaningful project, we went on a day trip to Access, where we saw scores of women sitting at computers, then to a huge oil refinery on the Thames estuary, where we saw no-one at all, and to the BBC, where I found myself in the *Top of the Pops* studio, next to Hank Marvin. I was going to tell him I'd met Cliff that time, but somehow I didn't think he'd be interested.

239

The course was about management, mainly. I can't recall anything about supervision being mentioned, anyway, although to complicate things at the end of the course I was awarded a 'Diploma in Supervisory Management' by the National Examinations Board for Supervisory Studies – Dip. NEBSS for short. I was told I could include the letters after my name, a really priceless asset for a detective inspector.

We also visited a police training centre on the course (I won't say which one). By now my opinion on officers' training was at an all-time low due to probationers arriving from their 'initials' unaware of the basics of the law. They wouldn't know what a burglary was, or what's meant by taking a conveyance. Or even what a conveyance is. Some couldn't define 'arrestable offence'. How, therefore, could they be let loose in the real world and consider arresting anyone?

One young probationer crimed up a burglary as a robbery. A house had been broken into, and property stolen. How did he consider this a robbery, I asked?

'They broke in and robbed the place,' he replied.

That's the sort of thing an untrained person would have said. But then, that's what he was. According to that 1965 booklet, *Your Career, Life in the Police*: "The aim of training centres is to give a thorough grounding in the things an efficient police officer needs to know". It was out of date, obviously.

By chance, a sergeant was taking a class of recruits for drill. Memories of Sergeant Hall came flooding back. What contrast there was to the class of '65. The sergeant was walking – supposedly marching – with twenty or so recruits. None was in step. They muddled along, laughing, passing silly remarks. Then the sergeant turned heel and headed off for his coffee break. 'Carry on till I get back,' he called out to the 'parade'. And they did. Some went left, some right. Two women officers peeled off from the main group, skipping and holding hands, ending up in a fit of giggles. Like my own course twenty years before, they were starting a rabble. But, unlike my course, they would finish a rabble. There are many first-rate young men and women joining the force. I saw some of them that day in their classroom, their eager faces staring at the visiting inspector. They were smart, polite, keen to learn, it was obvious. But I don't think they do learn much in today's world of political correctness, grievance procedures and 'awareness', whatever that is. As for the shambles I witnessed on the parade ground: it wasn't their fault; it was their trainer's fault. I believe the police force should be a disciplinary body of men and women who are trained in law and procedure, qualities far removed from what I witnessed that day.

*

I'd now been in Hertfordshire twenty years, during which my parents had continued to live in Newcastle. My mother had suffered from a long, progressive illness for some time, but I knew she had dad to lean on and to look after her. Then, suddenly, in 1988, dad himself took ill, and just two months later he was dead.

Mum had no other family living close, which meant she now lived alone, her policeman son having long since moved nearly 300 miles away. As she became weaker, I tentatively suggested a home for the elderly, but her response merely confirmed what I already knew, that it would take the army to remove her from the house she had shared so long with dad. The weaker she became, the more my feelings of betrayal increased. The pained look on her face each time I had to leave and drive back to Hertfordshire would linger in my mind for days afterwards.

Finally, on one of my visits, she was so weak I arranged to have her taken to hospital. At least she would be cared for there, I thought, as I drove back down the A1, only to discover she'd been released straight away. As the doctor explained: 'There is nothing more that can be done for her'. As good a reason as any to send her home, I suppose. This happened on several occasions, even when a neighbour found her lying helpless on the floor. By now I was riddled with guilt, at not being there for her when I was needed, and especially when called upon, as a policeman, to help other people – help them, but not my own mother. The job and its demands had still to be met. I was still the DI.

Finally, my mother went into hospital for the last time, and in September, 1989, I was at her bedside when she died. I recount events, partly to highlight the price anyone who moves away from their family home might have to pay when elderly parents are ill, and also to admit to the toll these events took on me as a person. Guilt. Failure. Betrayal. They were all there. They still are.

10

"The truth is never simple"

Oscar Wilde

Watford were playing Port Vale. Looking across the sea of faces that Saturday lunchtime, I doubted if anyone had the faintest idea where Port Vale was.

'Port Vale play in the Potteries,' I announced to the gathered throng. There followed a pause, before a whispered voice sought out the answer everyone was dying to know.

'Where's the Potteries?'

Where the Potteries were mattered not one iota, of course. What did matter was that the assembled officers were briefed before the game. Just like those cycle races, they were being briefed on something they knew all about by someone who'd never done it before. Still, as temporary Chief Inspector (Operations), I enjoyed the departure from crime investigation, and the calls on my new-fangled mobile and the phone by my bed. One thing that went with the uniform was a good night's sleep.

It also extended to other roles. Like when the Tactical Firearms Unit (TFU) were in town. Things had changed since my time as police marksman. In place of the Smith and Wesson revolvers, they were carrying automatic rifles and pump-action shotguns.

I went on some operations with the Unit. One was on a local housing estate, after information was received about an armed gang that was going to rob the post office. Armed officers were deployed, and we awaited developments. It was my job to give the go-ahead for them to use their guns if the baddies turned up. I had no formal training. (Lots of training in 'management skills', none in making an operational decision like giving the go-ahead to shoot someone).

First, though, I had to tell the armed officers that any decision to use their firearms was theirs, individually, and that 'reasonable force', always the rule when arresting or dealing with criminals, still applied. As we waited, I realised I would be loth to give the 'authority' to use guns, even if the robbers appeared, what with young mums with toddlers in pushchairs at the shops, and old folk calling at the post office to collect their pensions. Anyway, the robbers didn't show up, and just as well, although I needn't have worried. If ever I saw a professional bunch of individuals it was Hertfordshire TFU.

In fact, lots had changed in the time I'd spent with CID and squads. Another example was the introduction of search teams. An army band was scheduled to play at a local venue. Such events were potential targets for the IRA, who had already stamped their mark in the county when two of their number blew themselves to pieces in the process of planting a bomb. Prior to the concert, the hall was searched by a search team and, once 'cleared' it was the job of the Divisional Support Unit (DSU), under my command, to 'protect' it throughout the concert. This is a hell of a responsibility when you think about it. Imagine if we failed and a bomb went off inside the hall. It brings home to you just what this bombing business is about. Anyway, all went well: no-one was killed or injured and I wasn't blamed for it if they had been.

I was caught short one day when I had to see a young probationer constable about her progress, or lack of it. In fact, she hadn't measured up, and her visit to the chief inspector was, for her, the end of the line. I ushered her into my office, sat her down – and made an absolute pig's ear of it. As she burst into tears. I realised what I'd done. Used to dealing with experienced detectives, I had failed to take into account the obvious: that here was a young lass who, knowing her career was on the line, now found herself in front of an apparently unsympathetic chief inspector. I apologised, admitted my clumsy mistake and told her to go and compose herself, and return in thirty minutes. When she did, I spoke much more sympathetically, took her step by step through the sad comments of her supervisors – whereupon she broke down in tears again, inconsolable at her failure.

Earlier, I had become disillusioned with a process known as the *Force Review*. I'd nothing against a review in principle, although there seemed to be a universal belief that it was held for no other reason than to further the ambition of the then chief constable. In my opinion, it did nothing for the force or the people of Hertfordshire.

We sat in endless meetings, police and civilian staff yapping away for weeks on end about which room should house which department, whether traffic and division should amalgamate, and should the heading of the job description of so-and-so be in bold type or underlined? Officers on the review team prowled corridors, peering into offices. You'd never have dreamt there was crime on the streets. The result was some divisions were split up, one ending up so small you could see the divisional boundary from the top floor of the nick, whilst others remained huge, with disproportionate responsibilities for its officers. That, and the partial breaking up of the traffic division and dog section, is the only thing I can recall of this waste of time and resources. It's good for the executive to listen to its troops, but why can't they canvas their views directly and get on with what they are paid fortunes for: making decisions?

Then along came *Total Quality*.

My first experience with TQ took place when I was called into the office of a superintendent. The strange-looking, squiggly lines on his chart were common knowledge throughout the division, although no-one seemed to know what they meant.

'Tell me what you see,' he said.

I carefully examined the mysterious pattern. It looked like a big roundabout with lots of little roundabouts, and roads leading off in different directions.

'Looks like a map of Hemel Hempstead,' I ventured.

He stroked his chin thoughtfully.

'Hmm,' he said at last, 'an interesting analogy, but...'

He explained how the chart indicated how total quality provided by the police could help the public. There didn't seem to be anything about crime or operational matters (unless I missed something). For nearly an hour I sat until, mercifully, someone paged me to tell me about a suspicious death or something equally irrelevant. I left him staring at his chart. He never asked me what the incident was, then or later. (What happened to *his* total quality?).

In due course, total quality was thrust upon the entire force, and police and civilians of all ranks and status were dispatched for suitable indoctrination. So, total quality meant – what? It took days to preach the message, but in a nutshell: to listen, and try to help one another and the public. And there was me thinking I'd been helping the public for years.

Soon afterwards, I was in Cornwall, when I happened across a monument, dedicated to the evangelist, John Wesley, who died in 1791. The inscription read:

> Do all the good you can
> By all the means you can
> In all the ways you can
> In all the places you can
> At all the times you can
> To all the people you can
> As long as ever you can.

That's total quality. They should print it and issue it on laminated cards. It would have saved all that time and expense.

*

Reverting to my DI's duties, I was called to the murder of a young woman called Irene. She was a single mother who lived with her daughter in a flat on a council estate. To the best of my knowledge, and everyone else's I met during the course of the enquiry, she was a good mum who never did anyone any harm.

One evening two young male friends popped in for coffee, then they and Irene were joined by a fellow named Smith, a local dropout. As they chatted, Irene whispered to her two friends that she wished Smith would go. They lingered, hoping he would. When they had to leave (they said later), they did so uneasily, knowing she would be left alone with Smith. Even outside, in the street, they were loth to depart, and considered going back, making up some story about forgetting something. Sadly, they did not, and Smith, for whatever reason, stabbed Irene to death and fled, leaving her daughter crying beside the lifeless form of her mum all night long.

Smith had form for violence and had been seen recently carrying knives, so there was concern about what he might do before police could arrest him. What if he lost his marbles and stabbed someone else? What if we got into a hostage situation? In fact, he was arrested in a nearby park the following day, still carrying the murder weapon. He never gave any reason for killing Irene, although his actions might have been premeditated, as he went to her flat with the knife in his possession. He got life. It was a routine murder, someone said. Routine wasn't the word I used for it later when, with a colleague, I attended Irene's funeral.

Investigating officers attend funerals of murder victims as a gesture of courtesy and respect. Half-way through the service, the minister read out a poem, which had been written by Irene. Everyone at the service was greatly touched. I think she'd been a lonely young woman, and she'd certainly been a good mother. But a poet? Who'd have thought that she, living in that obscure little flat with her daughter, had such talent? A routine murder? Never.

Things could have got nasty at that service. After his touching address to the gathered throng, mainly relatives, friends and neighbours of Irene, the minister's final words were to ask God *"to have mercy upon and forgive the person who had so tragically ended Irene's life"*. Well, a man of the cloth would say that, but it didn't go down well with congregation. He walked out of the room then, and it's as well he did. The gathering in that chapel weren't too enamoured by those words, I can tell you. Aggrieved people feel anger, not forgiveness, when a loved one has been murdered.

The suicides continued, of course. (I wonder if people have any idea how many there are). I'll mention just two, if only because they were 'different'.

In fact, the first was a 'double' suicide, a retired gent and his wife, found dead in their car in the garage of their bungalow. It transpired she had terminal cancer and her husband, probably unable to endure his wife's suffering, and possibly at her behest, helped her take her life – and took his own.

He was, by all accounts, a meticulous man. He certainly made sure the suicide pact didn't fail. He attached a tube to the car exhaust, a common method to be sure, but in making absolutely certain nothing would go wrong he carefully cut to size and shape a piece of wood which fitted the open car window exactly, then cut a hole with a circumference exactly the size of the tube, ensuring that no air could enter into or fumes escape from the interior of the car, a most carefully planned and premeditated venture. They must have talked it through, made a joint decision. I wonder, though, if they considered for a moment the feelings of their family. Or did they believe the right to take their lives was theirs alone? I suppose they must.

Then there was Shaida, who took a fatal overdose in a bedroom at her home. I categorise this as 'different' because of all the suicides I attended over the years, Shaida was the only person I knew. We'd met months before when she reported her husband had left her and gone to Pakistan, taking their kids with him. Then, fearful that Shaida would sue for custody, he and the children disappeared. Despite all her best efforts, Shaida was unable to trace her family. So Shaida informed the police, who circulated the children's particulars through Interpol. Sadly, they drew a blank. So Shaida, in desperation, asked if we could go to Pakistan to find her children. Of course, we could not. Where would we have started, even if we could?

Shaida understood. Thanked us anyway. Told us she was working at Tescos to finance a scheme to hire a couple of heavies to fly to Karachi, trace the kids, seize them, get them out of the country somehow. Who could blame her? By now her children had been gone over a year, she was desperate. She was the sort of person who, given just one half-chance, would surely have taken it. But the months passed, and Shaida, increasingly distraught, got nowhere.

When I attended her house that dark night, I didn't recognise it as Shaida's. It was only when I found myself staring into her tormented face I realised who she was. Instead of the usual sadness, or perhaps even indifference at yet another suicide, this time feelings of guilt, of somehow being responsible, flooded through my veins. If we – the police – had been able to help, Shaida wouldn't be lying before me now, her young life ended after months of what to her had been a pointless existence. I wanted to say sorry. Instead, my duty now was to determine whether there were any signs of foul play, and not allow personal feelings to encroach upon my judgement: I noted the pills spilled across her bedsheets, found her note, written in a desperate hand. Its contents should remain confidential; they belong to her family. Suffice to say, if she couldn't have her kids she didn't want to go on living. I gathered the evidence for the coroner, then left, taking my feelings with me. It's grand when you can help someone: from the victim of crime to just helping an old person cross the road. But it's an awful feeling when you can't. Especially when the consequences end in tragedy, like Shaida's.

Around this time the Home Office announced it was reviewing the ranks of chief inspector and chief superintendent, both seen as unnecessary and costly. I agreed with this assessment. There were so many chiefs around, it was difficult to know where to put them. So, qualified candidates like me were put on hold. I consoled myself with the thought that I would not be alone, that there would be hundreds up and down the country in my position. At least I had my 22 years 'good conduct' medal, presented to me with great pomp and ceremony by someone of such high personage that I haven't a clue who he was.

Actually, isn't awarded for good conduct at all. It's for 'exemplary police service'. That's what it says on it, anyway. But why 22 years? Why not 25 or 30? In my case, I went on to complete eight years as detective inspector, when my conduct was just as 'exemplary' – honest! I wasn't given a medal for that. Perhaps I should have been, if only for surviving the pitfalls of instant decisions, explaining this and that to crown court judges and so on. Maybe there'd be too many words to fit on a medal.

Anyway, thus cheered, I was able to help the man who thought someone was trying to kill him.

He'd been badgering us with persistent calls about his perceived imminent demise. As it had gone on for months, during which time he had somehow succeeded in surviving, I batted it away until, at last, I was persuaded to see him. He turned out to be a middle-aged, self-employed, respectable gent. The sort who paid his taxes and had a right to have his concerns heard.

'Why do you think someone intends to kill you?' I asked.

His reply was damming: 'I just have this feeling.'

Nothing would persuade this tormented soul that if anyone had indeed intended to kill him they could have done so a dozen times over. Just as I was about to tell him there was no evidence to merit any police action, he threw in his ace.

'I'm sure I was followed home last night.'

In triumph, he handed me a note bearing the registered number of a car. It came down to a man who'd run a local pub for about twenty years and who, to the best of my knowledge, had never murdered anyone. I told him I thought it unlikely he intended to kill him. Doubt clouded the poor man's face. Did he think I was lying? He looked at me long and hard before the warped logic of his sad mind came up with a blinder.

'How do I know you're not in cahoots with this man?'

As *Your Career, Life in the Police*, said: 'You will have a varied, interesting and exciting life.'

*

Things have gone wrong in the job.

Not because of a low standard of recruitment. Far from it. I found young officers eager to learn, to seek out the right way to do things, to serve their public. In fact, what you might expect of youngsters seeking to get stuck in to their new vocation. We must look elsewhere for the causes.

The culture of accepting people with degrees and offering rapid promotion on that basis only is a good starting point. Why, pray, does a person with a degree, almost certainly in a subject unconnected with their role as a police officer, merit rapid promotion? Or promotion at all? Are they better officers than those without degrees? I think not. You see them, in division (for the 'experience') or at headquarters (where most end up sooner or later). All those operational officers out there know what I'm talking about. Damn right they do.

Is it the same in HM Forces, I wonder?

Trouble in the Gulf. On board HMS *Invincible*, Midshipman Cranberry-Ffanshawe emerges from a strategy meeting. They've been talking about planes and missiles and things, and he feels a bit lost. And no wonder; his rank was won by virtue of his degree and not on merit. In fact, he doesn't know much about the navy at all, and never ceases to wonder how those Harrier things can take off from such a short runway.

As he tries yet again to remember what VSTOL means, Sub-Lieutenant Smith appears. He's one rank above Cranberry-Ffanshawe, has about forty years in, been everywhere, seen everything, done everything (including tell Cranberry-Ffanshawe six times that VSTOL means Vertical Short Take-Off and Landing).

Sub-Lieutenant Smith is busy-busy.

'Where you off to?' asks Cranberry-Ffanshawe.

'The poop deck,' says Smith. 'You comin'?'

'Er, I went before breakfast, actually,' says Cranberry-Ffanshawe.

It's OK. Smith's used to it, knows it's just a matter of time before he'll have to say 'sir' to him.

Meanwhile, there are problems in the engine room. The chief engineer's worried. 'Never mind,' someone says. 'Cranberry-Ffanshawe's on duty.'

'Cranberry-Ffanshawe?'

'Aye-aye, sir. That bloke with the degree.'

'A degree in what?'

'Er... Psychology, I think. Or is it philosophy?'

Oh, well. Whatever. As long as *Invincible* keeps going, everyone's happy. And if it doesn't it'll probably be Sub-Lieutenant Smith's fault anyway. He should have known better, a man with his experience.

I'm not knocking people who have degrees. I'm knocking the system that gives them unfair advantage over those who do not. Many 'academics' are good coppers. There are men and women who work hard at their job as well as seeking professional qualifications in other fields. They are a credit to themselves and their force. But others never achieve anything except the promotion they seek and which is their solitary objective. And not only academics. Too many are on the career ladder and they don't want to fall off it by getting involved with such things as complaints and crown court appearances.

Some, a few, infiltrate the crime department, senior 'detectives' who aren't detectives at all: never have been, never will be. 'Detective Chief Inspector so-and-so'. Sounds grand, except in many cases they have less operational experience than their subordinates. They are managers, or figureheads; they are not investigators. Some will freely say so.

At a murder scene, they won't have a clue. I say 'won't have' because it's unlikely they'll be called to a murder, or many other incidents. If they are, what relief he – or she – must feel when a *real* detective turns up, of whatever rank. That's how they survive, because someone else sorts it. I used to urge detective constables and sergeants to pass the promotion examinations. Many declined on the basis that promotion meant reverting to uniform duties. I disagreed with this philosophy. It was a good thing, I'd say, both for themselves (in broadening their experience) and for younger, uniformed officers (who would benefit from their experience). Now I'm not so sure. Their skills are needed at that murder. It's no use if the senior detective turns out to be someone whose only experience of murder was the time he worked out it was Colonel Mustard with the dagger.

There are plenty of good inspectors who've won promotion fair and square. But confined to 'area inspector' and other non-operational roles, many of which could – and should – be done by civilian staff, they are wasted. If someone is promoted on merit, what's the point of putting him or her in charge of organising the new telephone system, or managing so-called 'areas'? Their knowledge and expertise should be put to real use, like supervising – and managing – a shift, and being its accepted leader.

Another about-turn I made was over the promotion examinations. I didn't think anyone deserved promotion if they couldn't pass the exam. Yet if they do scrap it, the higher ranks could be filled with experienced officers. Better to have someone who knows what they're doing than someone who focuses on nothing but his or her own career. And the public think those at the top are the ones with the talent.

One day I happened to bump into a woman acquaintance whom I'd known but not seen for over ten years or so (but we won't go into that). I should mention she was a successful career-person, a high-flier, who, years before had expressed a belief that I would be the same.

'Hello,' I said.

'Hello,' she said.

Then, after a slightly awkward pause (it's difficult to know what to say sometimes, isn't it?) came the inevitable question.

'What rank are you now?'

'Inspector,' I said.

'Oh,' she replied, clearly impressed.

'Detective inspector, actually,' I said.

She hesitated, her mind striving to come to grips with the rank structure of the police.

'Is that, um, *higher*, then?'

I told her that, strictly, it wasn't, although it did involve lots of responsibility, and I was on call a lot. 'I've dealt with lots of murders and things,' I said, showing her my pager. Alas, that meant nothing to her. Rank and status, not what I actually did, were what mattered. She went off to catch a train, probably ruing the day we ever lost touch

So, what happened to my promotion? The word came through: they would retain chief inspector, phase out chief superintendent. Those, like me, who'd passed the promotion board to chief inspector were in line for the coveted third pip. But they moved the goalposts – candidates would have to go to headquarters first, for 'assessment'. It was a big fix, designed to eliminate officers long in service, and clear the way for their younger peers.

It certainly eliminated me. First, candidates were put into groups and told to discuss a given subject, whilst individual 'assessors' made secret notes. As we rabbitted on about sweet FA, I wondered if *experience* might play a part: like patrolling the beat in the days before radios and back-up; CID and crime squads; arrests, informants, crown court battles; dealing with murder, child abuse and rape – victims *and* offenders; organising cycle races. I'd worked successfully as 'acting' chief inspector, uniform and detective, and passed the promotion board. Sadly, experience wasn't on the agenda. If it had been there would have been no need for 'assessment'.

The rank of chief superintendent, incidentally, was re-introduced by the Home Office in 1999. To quote the Superintendents' Association National Secretary: "The chief superintendent rank is particularly useful where there is a number of superintendents in a basic command unit, and where it is required for one of them to take charge." (Somebody has to).

Anyway, we then went to a classroom where Chief Superintendent Thomas supervised a series of written tests. He paraded up and down the room, hands clenched behind his back like a schoolmaster, placed the question papers face down on the desks, made threatening noises about the consequences of taking a peek before he gave the word. Terrifying, really. At least I remembered not to draw any silly pictures. I didn't want another thrashing.

I think the public should be aware of the nature of those tests. It's only right they should know the system used to select some of the chief inspectors in their police force.

1. A ferry leaves Dieppe at two o'clock, another leaves Calais an hour later. If their respective routes are such-and-such, and the respective distances are so-and-so, which one will reach Dover first?

2. If the price of a hundred barrels of oil produced by Mobil is such-and-such, and by Esso so-and-so, how many barrels will one need to sell to match the profits of the other?

3. If a train with an average speed of 70 m.p.h. leaves Glasgow at noon, and another with an average speed of 80 m.p.h. leaves London at one o'clock, which train will be closest to London when they meet? (When they meet they'll be the same distance from anywhere. Okay, I made this one up).

The 'assessors', presumably, mustn't have rated me. Maybe I was too forthright for their liking. It's best to take the middle ground, keeping one's opinions to oneself. I should have known. As to the written tests, my knowledge, or lack of it, of cross-channel ferries and the price of oil, let me down. (If only they'd asked me something about Australia).

It must sound as though I was utterly disillusioned, but I wasn't. I was still the DI. With much to do, like the call to the house of a young Danish woman, Marie, whose husband reported finding her body on the floor in the spare room. It was a case that proved things aren't always what they seem to be (and which, fortunately, didn't require knowledge of ferry timetables or the price of oil). Marie was young, attractive, as the framed photograph proved. I'll never forget the sight of her lifeless form as I stood in a silence broken only by the muffled sound of trains as they rattled by at the bottom of the garden.

She had multiple stab wounds to her chest, and her wrists had been cut. There was blood everywhere: in the shed, on the pathway to the house, on the stairs and all about where she now lay. To all intents and purposes, this was a murder scene.

There was no sign of any forced entry into the house. As you might guess, I didn't consider I'd have to look far for her killer. Nor, indeed, the weapon, a bloodstained knife, which lay on the carpet close to Marie's body, along with an empty bottle of white spirit. Arresting Marie's husband without further ado seemed a formality, especially as his hands and clothing were soaked in blood. Yet he was inconsolable, his grief seemingly genuine. But then, murderers can act out anything to bat away blame or suspicion. I could have arrested him, there was ample 'reasonable suspicion' that he had murdered his wife. Yet I held off, listened to what he had to say.

Marie had become very depressed, had started drinking heavily. Only the previous evening he had had taken her to hospital to get help, which she refused, demanding to be taken home again. They had slept in separate rooms that night, a not uncommon occurrence, and he had found her dead on the floor that morning. The post mortem revealed that Marie had been stabbed repeatedly in the chest, that her wrists had been cut – and that she had been stoned on the white spirit; and that this was, in fact, a suicide.

She probably had had a go at her wrists first, in the shed. Then, unable to make a deep incision, she had turned the knife to her chest, as she ran along the garden path. The incisions were not deep, but the angle of thrust was consistent with self-infliction, and the end she staggered upstairs, drunk on the white spirit, and bled to death on the floor of her bedroom. All this as her husband slept in an adjoining room. The blood on his clothing was explained by the fact that he held his wife's body when he discovered her on the floor.

Why did she do it? No-one will ever know. We were able to ascertain she was unhappy, and that she wanted children. But to take her life in such a brutal way, she must have been desperate over something. It all goes to prove that even someone with so much going for her – a husband, a job – Marie was a nurse, and by all accounts enjoyed her work – happiness is by no means assured.

*

People asked me if I ever got 'stressed up' through being a DI. What they meant was through dealing with so many tragedies like Irene's murder, or suicides like Shaida's. But tragedy is all part of a police officer's work, and not just a detective inspector's; there was no reason for me to more 'stressed up' than anyone. My work I never found stressful at all. Stress came from another direction.

The demands of my role as DI brought stress, mainly due to unnecessary and time consuming matters, like the farce of morning prayers, which ate into a busy day, and an imbalance in responsibilities between myself and another seven or eight inspectors: the constant tannoy and pager messages; the knock at my office door, not by detectives whose legitimate queries naturally concerned crime investigation, but by uniformed officers, whose equally legitimate queries should have been directed to their sergeant or shift inspector (if they had one); being telephoned at home with itty-bitty problems that could – and should – have been directed at the duty inspector (if there was one), or any inspector. There were plenty kicking about.

Stress is a so-called 'modern disease', although in reality it has been around for years. It's just that people have coped and got on with their work and their lives. Yet stress is the cause of much apparent sickness in today's society, particularly, it seems, among police officers. They have welfare departments now, especially to help them cope. I wonder, though, if their presence just encourages them to go sick. Recognised officially, they're halfway to having a good reason. Certainly, police officers are liable to attend gruesome incidents, and it is reasonable to believe some cope better than others. But to *invite* stress counselling? This happened to me after I attended a fire where two people died.

It was an awful sight, blackened walls all that was left of a detached house, now no more than a pile of rubble occupying what had been the ground floor. Police who had attended through the night and early morning had no idea if anyone might be lying buried, as the house was rented by two Australians, business

257

partners who may or may not have been at home. The neighbours thought it unlikely, as their car, normally parked in the drive, was missing. They had gone off the previous evening, and parked at an Underground station before going into town. Later, after lots to drink – from the accounts of their friends – they took a taxi to their ill-fated, rented home. The taxi driver remembered the fare. They'd gone to their beds not knowing it would be for the last time.

It was probably due to a cigarette, no-one knows for sure. But what seems certain is that toxic smoke, possibly from a sofa or bedding, permeated throughout the house in the small hours as they slept. Death came by asphyxiation before, inevitably, the house went up. The first floor and the roof collapsed, and when they dragged all the rubble away their charred remains were discovered, still lying on the now burnt-out spring mattresses, blackened faces betraying nothing of the terrible deaths they had suffered. They'd been oblivious to the smoke, a creeping death, their bodies, literally, barbecued: roasted on the outside, 'uncooked' on the inside, still so hot the pathologist had difficulty carrying out the post mortem. She was able, nevertheless, to determine cause of death by asphyxiation: their lungs were filled with smoke. It was a gruesome episode. But, as any police officer (or fireman) would tell you, it's all part of the job. Yet, next day, I received a message from force welfare department. Acknowledging my attendance at the fire, counselling was available if I wanted it. I was amazed. They'd never said so before. Why this time? And why only my name on the message? 'Yours is the only name we have,' I was told.

But there were night-duty and early-turn officers, not to mention detectives and scenes of crime officers and press liaison. I was asked to forward all names for this and future incidents. So, as well as investigating an incident which may or not be a crime, perhaps arresting the offender, sorting out house-to-house and other enquiries, arranging the post mortem, ensuring relatives were informed and so on, I was to find time to provide a list of all personnel who qualified for stress counselling. I never did. Instead, I got on with my job.

I wonder about this new culture. The public needs strong characters in the police force, men and women they can rely on when *they* need help. If police officers can't do that, they should do something else. The Occupational Health Unit (as it now is) maintains counselling helps staff to avoid sickness. Maybe it does, but you can't help feeling it's also useful in today's compensation culture for batting off any possible litigation. There's plenty.

Soon after the fire, I was turned out to an attempted murder. It was a typical Sunday morning: a quiet close in a village on the outskirts of town, modern-day houses surrounded by manicured lawns, Vauxhall Astras on the driveways. The sort of place where nothing ever happens – until two lovers fall out. Why they quarrelled was never clear. But the offender, a fellow I'll call X, took a knife from the kitchen and plunged it into the stomach of his victim, a fellow I'll call Y. Then, leaving him apparently dying, he fled, the screams of his car's tyres alerting neighbours over their cornflakes and Sunday newspapers.

The tell-tale drips of blood on the pavement showed the route taken by Y who, in desperation, staggered onto the road where a neighbour came to his rescue, stemming the flow of blood with towels. He was rushed to hospital where he would face a fight for life. Typically, the identity of the offender was obvious; it was just a matter of catching him. We circulated particulars of offender and car, and took statements. I was still at the address as scenes of crime officers were examining what might turn out to be a murder scene when the telephone rang. When I picked it up, I heard the sort of silence you hear when you know there's someone there.

It was X on his mobile. I told him his lover wasn't dead, that it would be better all round if he gave himself up. The silence prevailed. He wanted to know more, obviously. But what more was there? Just one thing. Somehow, I felt that if he thought his boyfriend was dead we'd have a suicide on our hands. So it was vital to convince him he wasn't dead. I did my best before he hung up.

There was nothing more to be done other than concentrate on the examination of the scene and await developments at the hospital. The arrest – or suicide – of X would follow in time.

Rather quicker time than anticipated, as it happened, for X made another call, this time to his mother. He told her what he had done, and they arranged to meet at a roadside diner in Bedfordshire, at a specified time. The call was overheard by chance by a 'radio ham' who, no doubt scarcely able to believe his ears, telephoned police. He insisted on anonymity, but his information was invaluable, for without being able to make an early arrest who knows what X might have done? In any event, when he turned up at the given time and place the police were waiting.

Y survived, and X was charged with attempted murder. That, it seemed, was that. But love is a many splendoured thing, and when we learned that Y was paying prison visits to X we realised – as in so many 'domestics' – we might find ourselves with a retraction of the complaint. Sure enough, Y indicated a desire to have the whole thing dropped. He said he would refuse to testify. Abandoning a prosecution in a minor assault is one thing, but in an attempted murder it's not on. Neither police nor the crown prosecution service felt it appropriate to withdraw proceedings, even when Y made it clear he would refuse to give evidence. Tell that to the judge was the only advice we could give, and he did.

At crown court, X clearly hoped Y's refusal to testify would mean acquittal, notwithstanding the overwhelming amount of evidence against him. The judge took a dim view, told Y he was in contempt of court, and ordered him to 'reconsider'. But Y insisted that he would not give evidence. He was left in no doubt that if he refused to testify he would find himself locked up until he changed his mind. Powerful people, judges! In the end, X pleaded 'guilty', possibly to save his lover being sent to prison for contempt, possibly because he knew there was no way out, no matter what.

*

I've criticised what I regard as unfair laws and practices in the criminal justice system: the PACE time clock, too-ready access to solicitors (delaying interviews and wasting officers' time), the crown prosecution service (although I acknowledge their high workload, and things did improve). But there have been improvements, too, making things fairer for police and suspects alike. This includes the scientific progress made with DNA – genetic fingerprinting, as it's known.

Just as no two persons' fingerprints are identical, neither is their DNA (except identical twins). So, to establish proof or otherwise by DNA, a sample of blood or saliva, say, may be compared with a sample of blood or semen taken from a victim. No reasonable person could possibly object to this practice, especially when applied to cases such as murder and serious sexual offences. Blood and semen are so often the agents that provide damming evidence. Equally, they provide evidence that a suspect *isn't* the offender. The civil liberties lobby lost all cred when they criticised the new power to take samples routinely from prisoners for DNA testing. Their standpoint works against the interests of the innocent. We have the technology to help establish guilt or innocence – let's use it.

Nevertheless, holding suspects against the clock, and a suspect's right to silence means investigating officers operate under a strict handicap. Take the ill-fated case of the murdered black teenager, Stephen Lawrence. Of that incident and subsequent police investigation, I know no more than anyone with access to newspapers and television. Yet the findings of the Macpherson report into the police investigation had far-reaching implications. Quoting Macpherson:

"The investigation was marred by a combination of professional incompetence, institutional racism and a failure of leadership by senior officers."

Professional incompetence? Criticism of the Met for not making early arrests may not be justified. (I'm talking about the time following the incident). Without any independent or corroborative evidence, what would have been the point? All that would have happened would have been interviews without replies, conducted against the clock, followed by release of the suspects, as 'custody time' was used up. It's better to find evidence first, *then* make arrests. Maybe that's what the Met were trying to do.

Time was, early arrests, quick interviews without waiting around for solicitors to tell prisoners to say nothing, would yield results: admissions, coupled with the possibly of leading police to the murder weapon, bloodstained clothing or stolen property. To those who make the laws I say: you cannot have it both ways. You either trust your police officers to pit their wits – honestly – against criminals; or you tie their hands, in which case don't expect miracles.

Institutional racism? Whether or not officers in the Lawrence case were racist, it cannot mean officers unconnected are. Ordinary people aren't going to say 'Oh, it's only in London'. How can police officers *anywhere* now feel confident when dealing with ethnic minorities? Will they feel comfortable about giving a black or Asian suspect a 'pull' if their actions are justified solely on the outcome of a search of the car he is driving? In other words, if you find stolen property or drugs that's OK; if he's clean you're racist. Or will they first ensure the driver of that suspicious car is white before they turn on the blue light? Would I have stopped Milton – the guy with the Beano up his jumper – if I risked being branded racist by a judge? Macpherson branded everyone. That's what he meant by 'institutional'.

Here is a message from an ex-DI of 30 years' service, all of it as an operational policeman, to Lord Macpherson, who lives in a castle in Scotland, who has never been operational: the police force is not institutionally racist. Period.

Failure of leadership? Macpherson was not alone in this regard. To quote the chief constable of Kent (whose force investigated the Met's investigation):

"The men and women in the front line take the brunt of criticism."

It was Aristotle who famously said: "That which no-one owns, no-one will care for". (I didn't actually hear him say it myself). In other words, where there's a bollocking going, patrol officers are the ones who take it.

For failure of leadership, read lack of supervision. Supervision on the street, that is. That's where patrol officers should be. On the street. Walking, standing still, it doesn't matter. Not whizzing past at 40 m.p.h. on the way to nowhere. I'm not suggesting the police should go back to 'the good old days' of the sixties. I am saying they should use unit cars properly – to respond to incidents, to back up foot patrols. 'The policeman is your friend', parents tell their kids. So he – or she – is. Not much of a friend, though, if you can't talk to him, if he drives past without ever talking to you. Some will argue foot patrol is outdated. It isn't. It's driving around in circles that's outdated.

You read about police 'initiatives', designed to tackle burglary, car crime, disorder. No expense is spared in reaching out to the public: force newspapers and circulars with fancy logos, telling everyone what the police do and asking what they think; neighbourhood watch schemes; crime prevention panels. All good stuff, but it should complement foot patrol, not replace it. Mr and Mrs Joe Public would say so if they were asked.

Officers nowadays seem to regard foot patrol as naff, something to be endured, until the day they can get mobile. They don't *want* to walk. You can see it in their faces as, with eyes fixed to the front, they stride purposefully to the nick. They've flown the flag for twenty minutes and that's that. Maybe they'll get to ride in a unit car or something instead. But it isn't just about walking, it's about talking. Talking to the public, mixing with the public, being accessible to the public, helping the public. The culture has changed, and it needs changing back. Get police officers on to the High Street and keep them there, I say. And just as important, get them to *want* to be there. Foot patrol should be the best days of a copper's service.

Sometimes officers don't patrol, on foot, at 'closing time' at weekends – times of expected public disorder. Instead, you see them behind the wheels of patrol cars, or peering through misty windows of personnel carriers, while young drunks kick litter bins and shout obscenities. Whilst exercising common sense, they should be *among* the crowd, not scared of it. Sergeants should be on the street, too. Three stripes shouldn't be an excuse to hang about in the police station. They should be freed from admin and custody duties, and be what they joined the job to be: police officers.

Chief constables and the hierarchy should forget about roles with fancy titles, the endless meetings about policing plans and other cosy little numbers for so-called 'team leaders'. You don't need policing plans if the job's done properly. They should ensure that senior officers have operational responsibility, that senior detectives are real detectives, and get rid of those chief superintendents – all of them – along with a busload of other 'senior officers', and use the fortune saved in salaries to pay for the recruitment of operational police men and women, patrolling on foot under the supervision of sergeants and the overall leadership of their shift inspectors. Then there wouldn't be failure of leadership.

*

I mentioned stress. Ultimately, stress was the reason for my retirement. True, I'd completed over 30 years' service, but I was young enough and fit enough to go on. Experience, surely, is too valuable a commodity to cast aside just because of a mathematical figure. But stress sent a clear signal to me, providing an ultimatum: stop or drop dead! I countered stress in two ways: walking in the Chiltern Hills, and climbing the fells of the Lake District and the mountains of Scotland; and when I wasn't able to do that there was always the White Lion.

Booze and good company! I was always pleased to drink with detectives. Real detectives, that is. We were all on the same plane, we all needed to wind down, come back to earth after whatever the day had brought, to enjoy the crack: the job, football, women (usually in reverse order). But then, one day in Langdale, in the Lake District, I looked up at Side Pike, and wondered if I could get to the top. There was nothing wrong with my legs; they were fine, after years of hillwalking and fetching the discus for Arthur. It was the pains in my chest.

I'd been to my G.P. Was I going to have a heart attack?

'Any history of heart problems in your family?' he asked.

'None.'

'Do you smoke?'

'Never tried'.

'Do you exercise?'

'I go hillwalking, cycling, swimming...'

He listened with his stethoscope. 'There's nothing wrong with your heart,' he declared, and off I went, reassured. But the pains continued, and now, looking up at a moderate hill, it occurred to me this might be the time my heart might pack in. As good a place as any, I supposed. Well, I made the summit, and a few others besides, but the pain went with me. I went back to my G.P. He shrugged. 'It's probably stress.' Most people are reluctant to accept they might have stress, including me. He sent me for a checkup anyway, 'just for your peace of mind.'

An old boy hooked me up to lots of wires. I looked like the six-million dollar man. Electric impulses, generated by my heartbeat, sent the instruments dancing. 'There's nothing wrong with your heart,' he declared at great financial cost. 'It's stress.'

The stress, or what stress was doing, moved up to my head, a persistent droning from the moment I awoke, and lasting all day. There was a Lancaster bomber in there; it was flying around and around, and it couldn't get out. It was hell. I went back to the doc. He examined my head, gave me some pills. They did no good. I told him there must be something seriously wrong.

More pills. I was turning into a junkie. I said I thought I might have a brain tumour. He said I didn't have a brain tumour. I asked him how he could know without taking my head apart. I must have sounded like that bloke who insisted someone was trying to kill him. It was time for another checkup.

The consultant hit my feet with a hammer, shone a light into my eyes, prodded me with a blunt instrument.

'You've got stress,' he declared, mentioning his fee to make sure.

What could I do about it? I asked. Stop whatever's causing it, he replied. It was change the system or retire. The first wasn't an option, the second was. I had completed 30 years. But I had much still to give and I wanted to give it. 'His drive and determination have not waned,' the super had written on my assessment. But if I had to stop being DI, what could I be?

Shift inspector? In one division they had opted out of working nights; why have inspectors at all? Area inspector? I wanted to be operational, not one of the gaggle at coffee every morning, outnumbering the two or three patrol officers in for grub. There were lots of inspectors at headquarters: I'd seen them at the photocopy machines and on their computers. They worked in obscure departments, such as process improvement, corporate planning, management and policy support, and focused on vital issues like policing plans, long term strategies, impact statements, networking and benchmarking, and organisational understanding. Nothing there for an operational bloke with over thirty years in. Such a shame.

So, retirement imminent, I was asked: Would I miss the job? No, I said. (For the record, I haven't). Would I miss the people? No, I said. (For the record, I haven't).

Like hell I haven't! Not working with detectives? Not those nights in the White Lion? If my career started at a time when camaraderie was second nature between coppers, it finished when camaraderie was second nature between detectives. Would I join again? Bloody right I would!

One morning, I overheard a wistful remark in the canteen. It came from a policewoman of long service.

'The fun's gone out of the job now,' she said, sipping her tea.

It was a sad thing to hear, but she was right. Her institutionally racist peers, in a medium-sized provincial police station, were on early turn wearing stab-proof vests, carrying side-handled batons, quick-cuffs, and two-way wirelesses. Once they'd have had a whistle and a piece of yellow chalk for marking the road at the scene of an accident. But, fair enough: today's world demands today's officers are suitably equipped.

I thought back to my own days on the beat: the ringing in, the camaraderie; the leadership and supervision of shift sergeants – on the street; the support you got from senior officers, the courts, the public. You could focus on the job then: catching the burglar, the car thief. Now officers must focus on themselves if, collectively, they are institutionally racist, if they are liable to be investigated if there's a complaint, however spurious, if they alone take the brunt of criticism. That's what the policewoman was talking about. Today's police officers spend their time tip-toeing through shards of broken glass instead of catching criminals. Watch your back, mate. Think before you act. Is it worth the aggro?

*

Having been detective inspector for eight years, I suppose I should proffer some advice to anyone else aspiring to the role. I'll start with the down-side...

First, despite the weight of extra responsibility, you won't be paid a nickel more than your uniformed peers, including those with no responsibility. There was a time when twelve-hour shifts and call-outs at nights and weekends merited overtime payment. Not now. A 'buy-out' negotiated a few years back awarded *all* inspectors an allowance on top of basic salary for such occasions, even those with non-operational roles. This was fine by me, except those who never have the need to work extra hours and are never called out don't earn it. In fact, in one division, the need for inspectors to work overtime miraculously disappeared at exactly the same time this new allowance came into force.

Second, as DI, you will find yourself accountable to the chief constable, the deputy chief constable, the assistant chief constable, and your divisional commander, along with officers more senior in rank than you, operational or otherwise, capable or otherwise. Those with operational experience will want to know the answers to searching questions, and will be able to offer advice and support if needed; those with no operational experience won't want to know anything and won't be able to offer you anything

Among others liable to be on your back, or with whom you will otherwise be involved, are: complaints and discipline, press liaison, the media, force welfare, force training, traffic section, dog section, career planning, family planning, FOR, DOR, the DSU, TFU, OSU and CPU, the FAO, SAO, LIO, FIO and EIO, the Home Office, judges, barristers, magistrates, solicitors, the crown prosecution service, race relations, close relations, sexual relations (if you're lucky), the coroner, the coroner's officer, typists, clerks, cleaners, civilian drivers, canteen staff, and uniformed officers, constables, sergeants and inspectors, who will seek your advice or should be given advice. You will, naturally, be responsible for your own staff.

And remember: the department you run, hopefully success-fully, the murder you sorted, the detection rate you got up, the high risk strategy in handling informants, the case of rape or child abuse you dealt with, the staff appraisals you somehow managed to fit into your busy schedule, the welfare advice you gave to the many who seek it, whether your responsibility or not, will count not one iota towards promotion. In fact, these are liable to impede promotion if, as is bound to happen at times, things go wrong with an investigation and it's your fault. Or is seen as your fault. Wallowing in the cacky never did anybody's promotion chances any good. But, if you're happy with all that, well and good. For the record, I was. There are always the White Lions of the world if things get on top and, as a (real) detective chief superintendent told me once: 'At the end of the day, whatever happens, they can't make you pregnant.' He was right, although it might sometimes feel like somebody's trying to.

The good side is damn good. The DI's job is important, front line policing. You will deal with serious crimes and nasty criminals, and those under your command will do the same. You will need to be a good leader, a good judge of people and situations, a strong supervisor, as well as a good listener and counsellor. Don't seek to be popular. A DI I rated told me popularity is a bonus, and he was right. If you're a good DI you'll be respected and popularity will follow anyway. Ultimately, you will glean heaps of job satisfaction, you will have served the community well and you'll have a bloody good time.

Focus on the vulnerable, especially children. For those suffering abuse, the police may be their last hope, their only hope. As DI, you have the power to help them: yours is the decision that removes offenders from helpless victims. Be fair to people, colleagues and public alike – and offenders, too. Remember, many criminals never had a chance from the start, had no-one to keep them on the proverbial straight and narrow when they were kids. That's where most criminal records start, when people are kids. Treating people fairly never did any harm. Even really wicked bastards merit fair treatment, for professional reasons if nothing else.

Be smart; lead by example. That way you can expect others to follow. Pray for a good divisional detective chief inspector and a bunch of good detective sergeants and constables, scenes of crime officers and civilian staff. I was lucky, on all counts. As DI, I served under four DCI's, all operational coppers, all supportive and, above all, all first-rate detectives. Some of those of higher peerage were the same; others were on the career ladder I mentioned. The former took the weight of serious crime investigation, the latter occupied themselves by attending meetings and other vital work. There were good DS's and DC's, working as investigators and team leaders. In most cases they hadn't passed the promotion examination; they were not qualified to move up the ladder. More is the pity. The job needs them up there. High-fliers on the career ladder can't hold a candle to detectives, of whatever rank.

Finally, buy a pair of wellies. So many of those murders, suspicious deaths, suicides and sexual offences occur in muddy fields, woods and byways. If you are going to be a senior detective, you will have to visit the scene. Not much point going back to the office in your Saville Row suit looking as if you've spent the morning mucking out a cowshed. You'll visit suspicious fires, too, where the fire brigade has a habit of pouring thousands of gallons of water into buildings now no more than blackened shells. Wellies, not brogues, are for wading. Keep them in your car boot at all times.

*

'You can go in now.'

I stood up, glided silently and with reverence across the carpet, knocked politely. As you do.

He set me at ease, ushered me to a chair.

This was it, my interview with the chief constable on the eve of retirement. I almost didn't bother turning up. Couldn't see the point. But the man held kudos. He'd come to the force talking about making crime a priority, served as detective, been out to see the troops, even bought a round in the White Lion. So I decided I'd have my two penn'orth.

He talked about his days in Sussex, drew a parallel with his time in Brighton and mine in Newcastle: foot patrol and street supervision, the CID. It had been the same for us: same routines, same rituals, same experiences, including force amalgamations. He'd known the Johns and Sids and Arthurs, suffered frustration over the criminal justice system, felt the satisfaction you get when you get a result at crown court. Things had changed over the years, we agreed. It's harder than ever on today's police officers to deal with criminals, cope with ever-tightening rules. He wanted crime to be at the forefront of everyone's mind. Not itty-bitty, politically correct clap-trap. Crime. If he could have said it in capitals, he would have. Over thirty years in the job, and it was the first time I'd met a chief who was a copper. We were the same kind of animal, except he'd gone on to be leader of the pack. If only all leaders were like him. He made me wish I wasn't leaving.

I retired 1st December, went home and slept till Christmas.

***

"It is better to wear out than to rust out"

Bishop Richard Cumberland

The fun's gone, the policewoman said. Maybe. But you didn't join for fun; you joined to be a police officer. To help and protect the public, whatever the rules and the pitfalls. The old lady still needs a helping hand to cross the road; the rape victim, the child who suffers at the hands of a wicked tormentor, the victim of robbery, burglary, the person whose car has been stolen – they need someone to help them, to deal with offenders.

Forget those who fashion their own glittering careers. Instead, focus on what *you* can do. Strive for promotion if you will. If you work hard, you will succeed. Police work is important, no doubt about that. I retired stressed up, as they say. Still enjoying the job, though, and that's important. Try and avoid ticking off the days on the calendar, as many do. *Better to wear out than rust out*, the man said. He was right. If you wear out, you end up like a vintage car: out of date, but respected for what you were. Rust out and you're only fit for scrap.

Be lucky. I was. Not all my colleagues made the finishing line. Good coppers, too many to name, passed on before their time. I salute them. I learned a lot from them. Their cause was my cause.

The early days were best. So it is, probably, for everyone. When you join, there are wide horizons, with clear, blue skies. But things change; the weather closes in. There are different perceptions, different procedures, driven in the main by those you never see. You will not like change, but change there will be. There's nothing to be done but to get on with the job, to do your duty, until it is time to go.

We all have that time.